FAM

FAM

ROLLING IN A
LONDON GIRL GANG

Chyna

CORONET

First published in Great Britain in 2011 by Coronet
An imprint of Hodder & Stoughton
An Hachette UK company

1

Chyna's story is real.
There are hundreds of Chynas in the UK. This Chyna's story
combines elements from the life of more than one Chyna.
Names and other identifying features have been changed,
but everything described in this story really happened.

A CIP catalogue record for this title is available from the British Library

ISBN 978 1 444 71430 2

Typeset in Futura Book by Hewer Text UK Ltd, Edinburgh

Printed and bound by Clays Ltd, St Ives plc

Hodder & Stoughton policy is to use papers that are natural, renewable
and recyclable products and made from wood grown in sustainable
forests. The logging and manufacturing processes are expected to
conform to the environmental regulations of the country of origin.

Hodder & Stoughton Ltd
338 Euston Road
London NW1 3BH

www.hodder.co.uk

PART ONE
TIEFING

'What you got for me?'

– Chyna

ONE

Everything's gonna be OK

'I'm gonna kill him,' my uncle Finley says.

A Rottweiler throttles itself on a lead wrapped tight round Finley's knuckles.

I hate dogs. Been scared of them ever since I was a little girl and a friend's Rottweiler-Staffordshire cross bit into my leg. When they bark, I freeze up like ice. I'm not scared of guns or blades. Seen bare of them in my life. But a dog puts me on edge.

The dog's mad angry and so is Finley. A sword hangs from his other hand. He's looking at my mum, at her swollen eyes, busted nose and bloodied lips. She's mashed up something chronic, and the man who did this to her is my dad.

'I'm gonna kill him,' Finley says again. 'Just watch. I swear to God, I'm gonna fucking do him.' He turns to me. I'm seven years old. 'Let's take you upstairs. This ain't for a young lady's eyes.'

My uncle was wrong. I'd already seen a lot of bad tings. The beating my mum had taken didn't even shock me. I'd spent the early days of my life in a waste estate in South, in a crammed flat with a busted lift so far out in the boondocks it seemed as if London city wanted to wash its hands of us. The only escape I had was the toys my relatives bought for me: Barbie dolls, dollhouses and a big Little Princess tent set up in the middle of my room.

They had boxing matches daily, my parents. I'd stand in the doorway of the living room while my dad fucked up my mum. He weren't the tallest, but he was tonked from where he used to do weights. My mum was like me: five feet nothing and slim as a lollipop stick, and when Dad raised his fists, Mum didn't have no chance.

Usually the beatings was over nothing. My mum would be washing the dishes or cleaning the table or whatnot and my dad would come rushing into the room, pumped and aggressive, shouting and waving his fists. He'd drag my mum out of the kitchen and into the living room, slamming the door behind him.

To protect the eyes of his little princess, I guess. But he couldn't prevent me from pressing my little princess ear close to the door and listening through the hollow wood to the thumps and bangs and screams. A few minutes later, my dad opened the door and stormed out of the flat, leaving my mum crying on the sofa, bare bruises on her arms and face. Hours passed. He'd come back. Say sorry to my mum. She always took him back in.

When I was little, the fights seemed scary. I'd cry and cry some more. As I grew older, they became normal, like playing in the roads and the sound of the ice-cream van. I just figured other families were the same, and mums getting beat on was a way of life.

I was a proper daddy's girl, and I loved him. He never once hit me, didn't even shout at me. Could be the most kindest and caring dad in the world.

My mum's friend Yolanda, who lived up the road from us at the time, always used to be lecturing her, 'You should leave that man, you know. He's no good.' But no matter how much my dad and mum fought, she'd always let him come back. Back then I didn't understand. Nowadays I see it ain't such an easy choice. Kicking out a man means raising kids as a single parent and struggling to make ends meet. My mum knew the score – she seen the love my dad had for me.

When my mum announced we was moving to a new home, I was like happy, happy, happy. I was eight years old and I'd be moving to another place in South. New endz and a new start for our family.

Just before we left, my mum went to visit Yolanda. She'd dropped her fourth baby from her belly a couple of weeks earlier. Given birth to a little boy. Later my mum came back from Yolanda's looking all teared up.

'How was the baby?' I said.

'There'll be no more talk of Yolanda in this family,' she said, staring at me with bloodshot eyes.

'What? When am I gonna see the baby?'

'You won't,' my mum said.

End of.

I discovered that my dad was cheating on my mum with Yolanda, and her baby boy was my half-brother.

Our new flat had peeling paintwork, threadbare carpets and the kitchen was infested with mice and ants. The ancient heating system sometimes worked and sometimes choked, meaning we'd wake up in the winter numb from the cold. But I thought maybe moving home would calm my dad down and put a stop to the arguments.

They got worse.

So you see, by the time my dad properly messed up my mum in a real vicious fight, I knew all about what was and wasn't for my eyes.

I let Uncle Finley cart me up to my nan's bedroom. My mum had gone to my nan, hoping to get some help. That's when my uncles had rolled up, seen my mum and decided that they weren't gonna let my dad box up their sister like that.

My uncle shuts me in the bedroom, but I have to see what's going down out in the street. Peering out the window, I clock Finley and my other uncle, his brother, Taylor, backed up by a bunch of mandem. My dad's approaching them. They throw heated words at each other. The Rottweiler growls. Finley heckles. I'm terrified my dad's gonna get bitten to pieces.

But my dad's armed himself. He grips something with his left hand: a samurai sword. His favourite hobby was collecting swords. He had a skill for doing them up and selling them on for a good profit. The one he's holding in his hand is a black blade twenty-five inches long.

Someone is gonna get hurt. Someone I love. My belly curls up into a ball.

Uncles Finley and Taylor, they've been like dads to me too. I used to say to people that I had three dads – my father and my two uncles. They treated me right, spoiled me with bare creps and the latest toys. I loved them off.

I can't look no more. I run downstairs, race past my mum and my nan and into the street, screaming for every-one to stop fighting. Running up to my dad, I hold on to his tree-trunk leg and beg with my uncles to put their weapons down.

'Don't kill him!'

'I told you to stay upstairs.' Uncle Finley's voice is flat.

'Don't hurt my dad.'

'Go back inside,' my dad tells me. But I don't. I cling tighter and tighter.

'Your family don't need you,' Finley says to my dad as he and Taylor back off, tugging at the Rottweiler. Everyone's cooling off except for that dog. 'Stay away from them. I'm warning you.'

As long as I hold on to my dad, I think, no one's going to hurt him.

A big crowd gathers at my nan's house on my dad's side. Me and my mum have gone there to meet up with my dad's mum, my granddad, my dad's sisters. Bare relatives listen to my mum's story about the drama with my uncles. She's almost done when a banging on the door makes us all jump. The thumping hand belongs to my dad. He's piss-drunk and wants to come inside. Barricaded in the front living room, my mum threatens to call the boydem – the police. The standoff confuses me, twisting my insides this way and that. I just want to see my dad and I want my mum to be OK with that. I want everything to be OK.

Finally my nan lets my dad into the house. My mum is barricaded into a separate room to protect her. Nan lets me into the kitchen. I find my dad at the table, almost sliding off the chair. His eyes are varnished.

'Come here,' he slurs.

I sit on his lap. His hands are unsteady, and when he talks, I catch the smell of Hennessy on his breath, sickly and sweet. His eyes are dimming as he tells me that he loves me, and when I cry, his giant hands brush my tears away.

'Can't you and Mum stop fighting?' I ask.

'Just . . .' He waves his hands in the air. Drops them. 'Everything's gonna be OK.'

We sit like this until the cops show. They take my dad away on something called a drunk-and-disorderly charge. My mum shouts at him as the boydem lead him away. I stay seated at the table. My dad shows no emotion. The liquor has worn off and he's too tired to be angry. He gives me one last look and a half-smile before he's marched off to the waiting car.

All night long that kitchen smells of Hennessy. I can taste it on my lips. No one in the family says a word.

I won't see my dad for years.

From that day on I never really had a family no more. It was me and the world. And I had to learn how to survive in it.

TWO

Fresh endz

Me and my mum had to be moved for our own protection. Staying at the same flat was out of the question, because my dad knew where to come look for us. The council woman said it would be for the best if we stayed somewhere else until a new, permanent home could be found.

'Don't worry, we'll put you in a safehouse,' she said.

I think she must have meant 'nastyhouse'. Built in the outskirts of South, the so-called safehouse was a bed-and-breakfast joint that made its profit out of people's misery. We had to sleep together in a horrid little room, with a filthy bed infested with ticks and a sink with brown stuff congealed in the basin. The room smelled like a hospital ward. Pissy, stale, musty. All the stuff from our flat had to be moved into a room smaller than my Princess tent.

In the room next door to me and mum lived this Russian woman called Natasha. She had nine kids and had fled to the safehouse for the same reason as my mum. I soon stopped asking why the other women wound up there. The answer was always the same: men. The safehouses sheltered every pimped-out, beated-on, raped woman in London endz.

We had no private washroom. All the families shared an

old bathroom. We also shared the bathroom with the most fattest cockroaches, types that had wings. The sickest part was, the shower base was built from wooden slats rather than solid tiles and in the gaps between each slat I'd wash myself in the morning and see bare roaches flapping about in the drainage area below.

We found the cockroaches and the bad smell and the general hygiene hard to put up with. Mum prided herself on having honest values, and while she didn't have much money, being clean, tidy and disciplined were important tings to her. She had standards, and living in squalor really got her down. She retreated into her shell and avoided talking to the other women, only speaking with some white English lady by the name of Julia, who was hiding from her boyfriend after he tried to pimp her out.

Julia's story was typical of the women in the safehouse. A lot of the men in the world, it seemed to me, thought the best way to make quick p's was to get their women to fuck other men for cash money. Julia was a strong woman, confident and determined to do her own ting in life, not be whored out by no man. She helped keep my mum's spirits up while we lived there, and took care of me in the daytimes while mum worked.

Time went slow at the safehouse. In the early mornings my mum set off to work, and I'd watch the Nickelodeon and CBBC in the lounge with Natasha's Russian kids. If I got really bored, I'd wander around the streets, looking for kids to play with, returning home in the evenings just in time for my mum. She'd lie on that mattress, conked out from the stress. I'd stare out at the littered street below, wondering how long we had to suffer in this place.

Two months passed in the safehouse before the council found us a new flat, a two-bedroom gig in a maze of flats called Wood Hall. To be honest, I didn't really care what our new home looked like, or where it was located. I was just so happy to leave that grot house behind.

From a distance, in daylight, Wood Hall looks like a decent place to live. The council had recently built the estate and the blocks were light brown, modern-furnished and spacious. Four main roads fed into the estate, with twelve alleyways criss-crossing between the blocks. The estate was huge. It'd take you half an hour to walk from one side of it to the other. There was a big blossom tree in front of our block and in the spring it'd turn fluffy pink and shower the roads in blossom snow. We had a church at the end of our road and on Sunday mornings people would be singing hymns top-loud. A park stood to the side of our block with a great big field at the back.

Our flat was fresh-painted and clean. No cockroaches or mice or ants. We were on the top floor and had a brand-new kitchen, carpets, all the fittings and trims. First ting I did was rush into my bedroom and set up my Little Princess tent on the floor. I heard kids laughing outside. Went over to the window looking over the park and saw bare children playing games. I knew I'd have some fun days down there.

But Wood Hall weren't all it were cracked up to be. The swings in the playground had no benches, just a couple of sad chains dangling from the metal poles. The slide was always streaked with piss and shit. Children didn't play in the park. Teenagers chilled, smoking weed and graffiting the walls. Glass was sprinkled on the ground. Fights happened daily, and the yutes set alight the bins of a night. After seven o'clock in the evening, kids were locked inside their homes as the shotters, the gangs and the cats came out to play.

I met some new friends in the park, like a few of the girls who'd later times join the gang. As for my mum, she got a good job and started going college at nights. I enrolled at primary school – while I stayed in the safehouse, I didn't go school – and my mum dated some new man. Soon she was pregnant with my little brother. Devan was born when I was nine years old.

When Devan popped out of my mum's belly, his dad visited daily. He'd sometimes live with us for weeks on end, even though he had his own place, and seeing how happy he was with Devan and how much attention he gave him, I started realizing how much I missed my own dad. Devan had his dad around to be with him and I just thought, Rah, it should be the same for me too. But asking about having my dad around caused problems with my mum. Obviously she didn't want to be around no man who beat her up, and anyway, she had Devan's dad in the boyfriend role.

'Your dad's off doing his ting,' she said to me, when I asked about him coming back to live with us. 'We're better off without him. We're happier now.'

We *was* happy, but I felt we was incomplete. Devan's dad did try his best to be nice to me and that used to piss me off. I'd come out with stuff countless of times like 'You're not my fucking dad.'

I tried to tear up the relationship between my mum and Devan's dad. If he said I had to be in at a certain time, I'd ignore him and only come in when my mum said so. It weren't his fault, but I felt like him being around was just throwing in my face the fact that my dad wasn't in my life.

Around these times, about the age of nine or ten, I started getting bad.

I'd fight at school. Boys and girls, older, younger. I'd fight whoever I wanted and I didn't need a reason neither. Any excuse to start throwing fists and I'd be in there. Bashing kids was a part of my routine. The only ting that mattered to me was giving some boy or girl a proper licking. I'd slap boys around the face so hard they'd turn red as a rose. Pull girls' hair until they screamed for mercy. Box on someone for trying to trip me up on the way back from assembly. I was mad angry inside and ready to fight the world. Kids were terrified of me. I got a rep as a brawler girl.

I met Felicia at primary school. She was a mixed-race girl

and me and her proper clicked from the get-go. On the first day she came into school, we ended up going home best friends. She was rude like me, running her mouth and not afraid to talk back to the teachers. I felt like I'd met my twin. I was happy because I didn't really get on with the other boys and girls, and thought, Rah, we can play together every day now.

We'd meet up after school, at nights and weekends. We weren't interested in girl tings like make-up. Our behaviour was more tomboyish – going to the park, climbing trees, getting up to mischief.

I also became friends with another girl who lived down my road. Her name was Shontal. She was two years older than me, had a big physique on her and I felt safe when we hung out together. She had addictions to certain words. Like, she couldn't say a sentence without adding 'for real' on the end.

Three years after the boydem took him away, my dad came back into my life.

Sort of and sort of not. Because my mum didn't want my dad knowing where we lived, I only saw him at weekends. We'd go shopping in town, or go to his flat and watch the Spice Girls movie. But having my dad around didn't help my attitude at school. I got more ruder, showed more face, was kicked out of classes time after time for behaviour problems and moved from class to class. None of the teachers wanted to deal with me. After I'd boxed and bad-mouthed my way through every other class, the school threw me into the same set as Felicia. More time to piss about and cause trouble.

When I left primary school, I scored Level 5s in all my subjects except maths and science. The grading system was from Level 1 to 6, with 6 being the bigs and 1 meaning you was basically a hopeless wasteman. Even though I'd never worked hard in classes, I came out with good levels. My mum was pleased but not surprised. I've always had a good brain, and my common sense and street instincts helped save my life on the streets. I hope people understand that when they see kids in gangs, they're not automatically stupid. Some of them boys and girls are over clever. It's just they sometimes don't get the chances that other kids get.

I enrolled at Burnell Secondary School. For me, Year 7 is when everything started going downhill.

Me and my mum became distant. We clashed, and with our stubborn personalities neither of us was willing to back down. I believed she was against me. She had my little brother, Devan, her man, her family and I felt, Rah, I'm on the outside looking in here. I started getting cocky, answering her back and running my mouth. Before, in Years 4 or 5, I properly feared my mum; she had total control of me. She was a strong-willed, strict lady with old-skool values. And she could see this hyper attitude growing in me. By Year 7, I turned into a loud, aggressive teenage girl.

I wanted to live my life according to my rules, not

whatever my mum said. And if I have my mind set on some-thing, no one can persuade me otherwise.

By the time I reached Year 8, Shontal had completed the transformation into a made-up bad girl, filling out her figure and taking on a distinctive look: she had the short hair and the tracksuits, never, ever wore skirts or dresses or girlish shoes. Her best friend was a boy; no girl would fight Shontal due to her size. As she had a year or so on us, Shontal got to experience new tings like tiefing and street robbery. I thought, Rah, there's a whole other world out there.

These days I met my good friend Roxy.

THREE

On our ting

Roxy was born to an Asian family and originally lived in East, so I didn't know her until we both started at Burnell. She had a rap sheet by the time she was ten, having broken into her primary school and vandalized the place, nicking shit, trashing equipment and scrawling threatening messages that put the frighteners on the teachers. Instant respect. We clicked. Like me, she had it rough growing up, being moved around big council flats. She also had a relative deep in the gang lifestyle: Roxy's cousin, Sonita, was one of the most feared girl gangstas in our roads. She had status. People respected her. She'd formed her own gang, mixed girls and boys. Like me, Roxy was intrigued about having a fam of her own.

I had a good laugh cotching with Roxy. She weren't the type of girl who worried about the consequences of her actions or got intimidated by boydem. If she wanted to do something, she'd just do it. She grew up in a household full of girls, with her sisters and her mum for company, while her dad worked late at restaurants, getting home around three o'clock in the morning. In our roads, no man means no rules. Sometimes I'd crash at Roxy's and we'd be out till past two, causing mischief.

I'd go to Roxy's road of an evening and affiliate with

people in a big cul-de-sac at the back of where she lived. Past seven o'clock, the endz took on a new shape. Bare young people chilled in that cul-de-sac, majority boys. We clocked drugs being openly sold, people smoking weed and drinking liquor, fights breaking out.

The mischief started off as innocent fun. Stuff like calling the boydem and getting them to chase us. One of us dialled 999 from a BT phone box and said there was a big fight breaking out in the endz. A few minutes later, we looked down the road and seen boydem cars tearing up, sirens bleeping. As the cars approached, someone shouted, 'Everybody run!' We breezed out. The boydem knew they'd been set up and chased after us to find out who put in the call. I was the fastest sprinter at school and the boydem never catched me.

Other days we'd play with abandoned cars. There were plenty of them around Roxy's roads, old motors that people had dumped. Then we'd cause unnecessary aggro, cussing people as they walked by. These times Roxy got me smoking on the regs. That girl was a born smoker from the age of zero. Took up the habit when she was nine years old and in primary school, bumming the butts from her dad's ashtray. Cigarettes, roll-ups, weed – if it contained nicotine, Roxy smoked it. I reckon she popped out of her mum's belly with a cigarette between her lips.

And I got my first proper look at the gang lifestyle. Roxy's cousin Sonita hung on the same endz as us and told us not to follow her when she rolled with her fam. We'd tail her anyways. In our eyes, Sonita was glamorous. She had this way about her. People looked up to her and that made us want to have the same level of rep. Sonita never encouraged us to be in a girl gang, but just by watching her we started getting ideas about how we could affiliate and embrace the gang lifestyle ourselves.

In Year 7, I began smoking weed. I'd bing up a spliff in my room, not bothering to open the window, and my mum would smell the skunk and come rushing in, rifling through my wastebasket. She'd pick out the paper end of the reefer and accuse me of pulling on a draw. 'Skonk', she'd call it, couldn't say the name right. And I'd be like, 'Nah, that ain't me, that's Marlon – he just literally been and gone.' This poor boy from school got accused of smoking bare weed at my mum's. My friends all binged up outside in the fields, but I preferred to be in my comfort zone, surrounded by my TV and tunes.

From day one me and Roxy didn't care about secondary school. Roxy and me already had status, because we had people in the older years looking out for us – Roxy's cousin Sonita and my cousin. Roxy got sent home most days from school for wearing grimy creps. She had bare creps, a different pair every day of the year. Creps was her ting, all about the trainers with that girl. Soon as the teacher clocked a pair of bright-pink Nikes on her, she'd be told to leave the class. Boom. Head home early. Bing a spliff.

Smoking weed brought us together. In the mornings, we'd pick up a draw, meet in the bus station, get smoking. At school, we'd go into the fields and light up a spliff at the back of the bicycle shed, where I affiliated with the other girls who'd later become my fam. But before we formed the gang, we was good friends with each other, had a tightness and a love between us.

Shontal had accumulated experience in tiefings and such. She took on the name No Angel, or Nang for short. Because she was in the year above us, she became like a mother figure to us, passing on her knowledge, teaching us the right way to tief tings. Nang was the pro of street robbery. She taught us the four most important lessons about licking it: spot the victim, grab it, keep it moving. And whatever you do, don't get catched. That sounds obvious, but when you're thirteen, fourteen years old and doing it, you sometimes find yourself doing stupid acts.

Outside the fam, I counted Tantrum as my close girl. Inside the gang, me, Roxy, Felicia and Nang was hardcore, and girls like Tantrum a little bit more on the edge of the main activities. She robbed occasionally, and didn't much go in for fights. She busted a girlish style, dressed dainty and always had her hair done neat, like. She never went in for the tomboy style. Bubbly and loud, Tantrum was the less ghetto version of me.

Split weren't so serious about the gang neither. She would more make up the numbers and sometimes got boyed – victimized by other boys and girls. Split got her tag on account of her reactions: first sign of trouble, that girl panicked and was scarce. She had nerves like a first-time gambler, but a good heart.

We gave Felicia the tag of Styles because she had the looks. Growing into her teens, every other girl hated on Styles. She was pretty, what we call peng, and wore them tight jeans and tops to show off her model figure. Her mum came from Spain and her dad from Ghana and she had tanned skin, like she'd coated herself in St Tropez body tan. Had Mediterranean olive-green eyes and hair that reached down to her lower back. From an early age she got bare attention from the mandem.

Smiles had herself an older brother, a known shotter on the endz who dealt in big bits of food. She had the connect, so Smiles quickly became our main weed supply. Her brother consigned over heavy packages of food. Smiles would tief from his supply and he'd never realize he was down on weight.

Bigs was a Yardie girl and the big momma of the gang, fists the size of bricks. She comforted the group when one of us was upset or pissed off. She was loyal and without a doubt she had my back in a heated fight. If we had a box-up and she wasn't there, she'd be calling me after-wards on my Nokia: 'Why didn't you ask me to come down?'

We all loved Bigs. Although we didn't have no gang

leader as such, Bigs and Nang was the ones who helped keep us together when times got tough.

Trubbs was short short, four foot tiny. This didn't stop her being able to fuck up any girl who wanted it. Brawling was her ting, and that's what got her into the fam. First day at school, we saw her box up a girl who stood at six foot three. Everyone stood in the playground waiting to see Trubbs get the shit kicked out of her. Instead she knocked the tall girl out, clean on her arse. Me and Roxy nodded at her and we was like, 'Yeah, cuz, you're with us.' In a gang, everyone's got to bring something to the table. A skill. You need lickers who can make money, shotters who can source you food, and brawlers who can check you in a beef.

These were my girls.

Tings was sweet until I got excluded from school over the dumbest waste. A boy flicked pencils at me in class. I told him to quit. He didn't take my advice seriously. I retaliated, accidentally stabbing the boy in his head. The teacher threw me out of the class and told me to wait for Miss Fredericks to deal with me.

Miss Fredericks was the headmistress at Burnell, and she didn't fuck about. A few minutes later, I heard Miss Fredericks before I seen her. That *click-clock, click-clock* of her heels. I tried to look like I didn't give a toss, chewing gum and humming a riddim. Miss Fredericks towered over me, her jaw working with rage.

'Get. Out. Of. My. School.'

In the space of me quitting the school and arriving home, she'd done called my mum, done sent a letter to my house. Verdict? Excluded for three weeks.

I cared less now, if that's even possible. Smoked bare weed. Two joints before getting dressed and figuring out what to do with my free time. I had a couple of friends at the PRU across the road – what's called a Pupil Referral Unit. Basically, once you've been kicked out of school, the government washes its hands of you and dumps you in a PRU. It's a centre for all the kids that the schools in the area have expelled. You go there and do a half-day, say nine till eleven, and you don't do no GCSEs or nothing. The kids at the PRUs ain't fooled. They know people given up on them, so they give up on people.

I knew a girl called Anne and a boy called Kwame from the roads. Both of them were sent to this PRU, so we spent time chilling. In the mornings, I'd meet them at the PRU and we'd breeze over to my house and smoke weed. Head to the park. Smoke more weed. With them two I started binging it extra heavy, up to an eighth a day.

Exclusion ended, but my attitude firmed.

I pulled weed on the way to school. In the fields during break and lunchtime. Every lesson I was high. Giggled and munched my way through classes. Teachers taught maths, I was high. English, I was high.

I went into business selling weed to kids during lunchtimes. My cousin would consign me a half; I'd sell it in £5,

£10 and £20 draws, keep my share of the profit, about £40, and hand the rest back to my cousin. In the mornings, I operated a different service. The kids from different schools met at the same bus-station terminal where all the school buses departed from. They'd ring me up in advance and put in orders for readymade spliffs. Some boy would say, 'Hook me up with three draws,' and the next morning I'd hand him the readymade spliffs at the bus station for £5. That's how I'd do. In a week I'd make £250 pure profit. Not bad p's for a thirteen-year-old girl.

Everyone in school knew me as Weed Girl. If you needed draw, I was your girl. When my cousin ran out of supplies, I started getting it off shotters, who would consign me in the same way my cousin did, giving me the draw up front and me paying them the money at the end of the week. If you didn't have the p's, you were gonna get hurt, but that's the way of the roads. Word spread quickly. Soon the teachers had their suspicions. Not to mention the fact that I was buzzin' in class. Every time they saw me, my eyes were like, *Ching*. Munching Doritos and Snickers whilst they banged on about stuff. It got really bait. I started doing crazy tings, grafing my name on school buildings, tiefing mobiles from boys and girls during PE, that kind of stupidness.

We was on our own ting, with a mind to cause havoc wherever we went.

FOUR

A little bit bad

To most people, a retail park is a place to go and buy brand-new sofas from DFS, or a nice big hi-def TV in the Currys sale. For me, Styles and Roxy, Goldstone Shopping Centre was the money farm.

We learned that tings were there for the tiefing as long as we played our cards right. Goldstone had all the brand-name shops, JD Sports and Topshop, Outfit and Next, as well as a big arcade where all the young kids went after school and at the weekends. Our usual ting was to go into JD Sports, pick out a tracksuit we liked and dash into the changing rooms. We'd take the tracksuit and pop the electronic tags, put the garmz in another shopping bag. To begin with, I was scared, but the adrenaline rush was like a natural high and the nerves electrified my body. I'd try to control myself because if you panicked, the security guard would instantly clock you and ask to look in your bags.

Keeping it real, I'd make for the exit. It was hard to try and act relaxed and innocent while every part of me wanted to sprint for the door and get out of there.

Then I'd barge out through the doors and into the street, no one chasing me, no alarms going mental. No boydem officers. The fear and adrenaline would drain down to the soles of my feet, and I'd feel happy that I'd gotten away with it. I never worried about being caught once I breezed out the store. Once I'm gone, I'm gone.

Electronic shop tags used to be easy to pop. Well easy. When you taken a plastic tag there's a little bit that connected to the rings through a tiny hole in the garmz. When the tag popped cleanly, the pieces fell apart in your hands. Later days they put ink in the tags, making it impossible to pop as the security guards would clock straight away that you were tiefing garmz.

The first few times we tried to pop tags, me and Styles ended up tearing holes the size of 10-pence pieces in the garmz. But once we got the hang of it, popping tags was second nature. I could rip tags in my sleep. Five, ten seconds in the changing room and I'd be good to go. We got so good at it that we'd be down Goldstone every weekend tiefing stuff. I never bought no garmz. Everything I owned I tiefed. Trainers too; I'd get the left foot from JD and the right foot from JJB.

Me and Roxy upgraded our skills and became experts thanks to a friend of hers called Ashleigh.

Ashleigh was the biggest tief ever. Kind of girl who could walk out of a shop with a fucking forty-inch plasma TV and not get arrested for it. Her special ting was knowing what shops to go into, what tings to tief, then getting the cash back on the stolen goods. First, Roxy or Ashleigh would enter a shop and tief something. Breeze out. The other girl went into the same store a few hours later and demanded a refund for the same item.

They went for clothes, mainly, because they could damage a garm and claim that it was faulty when they took it back. Stuff with zips were always easy to bust, but the best items was ladies' bras. Ashleigh would tief the most expensivest bra from Marks & Spencer, costing like £30 to £40, dump it in her bag and take it outside. Roxy ripped off one of the clips and strolled back into the store.

'Rah, my mum bought me this,' she'd say, handing over the tiefed bra. 'And it's broken.'

'Got a receipt?'

'My mum bought it as a present.'

The girl at the counter usually parted to Roxy instant cash refund. This was the times when pin cards and whatnot weren't the ting, so returns policies in the stores had their weak points. I don't reckon you could get away with this today. Roxy would split the profits with Ashleigh; they'd buy a ben, a £10 bag of weed, and do it all over again. Sometimes bare times in a day.

Roxy and I learned the ropes from Ashleigh. Between us, we became brilliant tiefs. You quickly discover that being good at it isn't just about technique and luck. It's also about the type of stores you go into. One of our favourite places to tief from was Alders, because they never used to tag anything. They probably thought they saved money on the tags, but I reckon they lost a big load of p's on nicked garmz. Other stores were good because they had bare entrances and exits, which increased the chances of escaping if someone did catch you, or ones that was over busy where the staff couldn't keep an eye on every person in the shop.

After a while I started tiefing stuff and selling it on to girls in my year at school. They'd come round to my mum's house and be like, 'If you can get me a pair of Icebergs, I'll give you twenty quid for 'em,' and I'd be like, 'Cools.' I had to keep tings secretive when it came to my mum. If she discovered her daughter licking garmz daily, I'd be in deep shit.

Sometimes I went licking stuff with a girl's mum. This woman was a crackhead, and she had a special method of tiefing stuff, more snakish than a bit of crude tag-popping. She'd get a thick plastic shopping bag, like one of them ones they give you in House of Fraser, and line the inside with baking foil. The foil stopped the alarms from kicking off, so we'd put stuff into the House of Fraser bag and calmly stroll out.

I did a good trade in tiefing and shifting gear. Got to the stage where word reached the girls' mums and dads. They put in requests: Nike tracksuit bottoms, Topshop jeans, House of Fraser dresses, River Island tops. A few times I tiefed stuff from Peppermint, a name brand for young kids, when the baby mothers needed some new clothes and were short on p's.

On account of my nonstop tiefing, I had a massive wardrobe filled with designer garmz. I'd open the doors and clothes spilled out, I had that much stuff. I rolled to school in £500 Prada shoes and stylish Avirex jackets, my self-esteem through the roof as boys and girls gave me bare compliments on my ability to drop a ting.

The boys from school tiefed too. Boys being boys, they licked PlayStations and Xboxes instead of garmz. There was a small alleyway next to Goldstone with a big HMV store next to it. One day, the boys worked out that the delivery vans to the HMV store drove down this dark alleyway. So they'd lie in wait for the van to arrive and tief all the gear from the back of the van. After a while, the HMV van needed a boydem escort to make deliveries. Times later, the HMV shut down.

We weren't interested in tiefing electrical gear, but ambushing deliveries? We could see potential in that.

A friend of a friend of ours worked at Ikea and knew all the delivery dates and times. This friend called us up and said, 'Rah, there's a van delivering stuff Saturday morning, nine o'clock sharp.' At five minutes to nine on the Saturday morning, a group of us girls made our way to the back of the store and watched this massive lorry pull into the parking space. Soon as the driver opened his door, we jumped him and forced him to open the back of the lorry. Bare table lamps, kitchen knives, sofa cushions inside. We quickly gave up tiefing from Ikea after we realized that most of the valuable stuff was over heavy, impossible to run away with unless we had access to rims – and you actually had to build it all as well.

A new girl joined our group in Year 9. Her name was Fierce and she was a light-skinned girl who lived with her nan. Her mum had a lot of kids and couldn't support none of them. Result? Nobody wanted Fierce. There are bare kids like Fierce in our endz. Street rats, we call them. They have alcoholic mums, crackhead dads and whatnot. If it hadn't been for us, Fierce would've been on the streets. She was an attention-seeker. Needed much love daily from her girls.

When we didn't tief, we licked. That meant a bit of travelling for us to find the choicest licking spots. Obviously, if we went tiefing in the middle of big West or big Central, there was bare CCTV cameras and boydem stations around, but if you go to housing estates in the boondocks, ain't hardly no cameras there to trouble you. Zero boydem, the estates being far from the city. The other benefit to going to those housing estates is that the people who lives on them is mostly white. So everyone's proper shook when they clock someone with a different skin colour beating on their trail.

People on them estates took one look at me and thought, Ghetto. The way I looked, with my hoodie popped tight and the sovereign gold on my fingers, the harsh tone of my voice, I knew if I robbed one of these people, I could say, 'Boo!' and they'd jump out of their skins.

Here's how you go street tiefing. First, you got to select the right target. Ideally you're scouting for white girls bustin' the latest creps and fashions. You know this type of girl; they got a mummy and daddy, nice house, the latest mobile. Age and size don't matter. Could be twelve or twenty. If they're tiny, we'd rob them, but if it's a big woman, your best bet is to run and snatch. Big girls are usually too fat to catch you anyhow.

Street robberies need to be done in groups. It can't be just you by yourself, or with a friend, because if the person you're robbing puts up a fight, you need your friends to come and sort it out. These days, me, Styles, Tantrum, Fierce and Roxy went out licking it as a team and this is how our gang first started to take shape. By working street robberies together, we became loyal to each other and bonded.

The first time we licked it, I was out with Roxy, walking down the street and whatever-not. These two girls happened to walk in our direction. They were white, looked about our age and build. The one on the left busted in a black Two Angle hoodie while she texted away on a mobile. The phone caught my eye; I was hot on the latest models and clocked that she had a brand-new Samsung. But I didn't think nothing of it, until the girls were a couple of metres away and Roxy paused right in front of the girl's face, me as stunned as the girl.

'Rah,' she said, 'gimme your phone.'

The girl's smile was wiped so far off her face it was on the road. I curled my hands up into hard fists, ready for a fight. I reckoned that if some girl told me to hand them my Nokia, I'd box them up.

The girl handed her flash Samsung to Roxy. Not a word. Not one.

I acted quickly. The second girl, one opposite me, was about to piss herself.

'Rah, gimme yours too,' I said.

This girl quickly passed me her Samsung like it was a bomb. We both had brand-new phones, confidence and a rush from the robbery.

'Now fuck off,' we told the girls, booting them in the opposite direction, and sent them packing.

'That was shower,' I said to Roxy. 'But the next time, we should plan it out.'

I was a smart robber, planning my plays and sizing up the opportunities. I had to make sure tings was in my favour. My most successful tactic was to scout such-and-such a street for a little bit. Pick a target and watch her do her ting. Making notes in my head: is she distracted by her mobile? Does she have an iPod in her ears? How many people is she with? Is she relaxed and settled, or tense and edgy? Once I made a target, I'd tell my girls about my plan.

'Rah, I'm gonna rob this girl, you know.'

'All right,' my girls would say. 'Heads up.'

I'd walk up to the target.

'What you got for me?'

The girl blinked, wondering if she recognized me from somewhere. School, maybe.

I'd ask them again. 'What you got for me?'

All the time you make sure you're in their faces. Staring them down. A stare's good. It's intimidating. Makes the other person feel scared. They're afraid to look back at you. The girl now realized I weren't no familiar face and planned to rob her.

'Lemme see your phone.'

She didn't want to give me the phone, but she'd be frightened of holding on to it too. Afraid of the threatening way about me: my voice, my eyes, my fists. I plucked it out of her hand. Off I went.

Sometimes lickings didn't go that smooth.

I'd get the occasional girl who thought she was a little bit bad. Here's how it would go.

'Rah, give me your phone.'

'Fuck off.'

The girl's expecting a fight, but I'd fool her. Give it a shrug and look all relaxed and whatnot.

'All right, you ain't got nothing for me. Cools.'

This made the girl relax, or at least worked her up into a confusion. Then I'd attack. Wrap her in a headlock, pulling my arms tight, tensing my muscles. In a headlock it's all about technique. Get the grip right and after a few seconds the girl would give up and I'd be free to rummage through her pockets. The secret to street robbery is confidence. If you look sure of yourself, the other person gets worried. They start to think that you're ready to do some damage to their face. And, of course, they weren't expecting you to lick them. They was just on their way to the shop.

I always made sure that when it came to girls who thought they were bad, I violated them a little bit more than the others, because they'd tried to give it some front. A normal girl, I'd take her phone and her p's and leave her be. With the bad girls, I'd tief their bus pass too. Drop their house keys down the drain. They'd have no way of getting home, have to use a phone box, make a reverse-charge call to their parents, get picked up. Made them feel weak and proper humiliated. My whole attitude was, Fuck with me, I fuck with you twice.

Styles's game plan was . . . Well, she never bothered with no plan. Styles just went for it. She'd see a girl waiting at the bus-stop, our bus would come, and she'd rush the girl, snatch the phone or the purse and jump off the bus. Rest of us running after her and wondering what the fuck was going on.

'You gotta give us a heads-up next time,' I'd say to her.

'KMT,' she'd reply. That was her favourite saying. KMT this, KMT that . . . It stands for 'Kiss my teeth', which is another way of saying you're annoyed with something someone has said. Styles had her own way of doing tings and that basically involved not giving us the heads-up. This could be a real problem, especially when she snatched phones on the bus and breezed off at the next stop, leaving us girls on the bus with the girl she's tiefed the phone!

We never got caught robbing people, but we definitely rode our luck. Once, with five of us on the bus, Styles spotted a woman with a Motorola Razr V3, totally new to the market. Like me, Styles loved her phones. She didn't say nothing to us, but I could see in Styles's eyes she was gonna tief it. I just *knew*.

The bus stopped. Soon as the doors opened, Styles snatched the phone out of this woman's hand and scattered. But the woman she'd robbed was young and fit and unafraid: a bad mix. She chased Styles off the bus and round the block twice. Now, Styles's a big girl, tall and strong, but she's not the quickest. After five minutes, she was wiped and the woman finally caught up with her. Turned out she was a fitness instructor.

'I want my phone,' the woman said.

'All right, fine' – Styles panting big-time. 'I'm gonna leave your phone round the corner. Stay there for ten seconds. Then you'll get it back.'

Styles had to go round the street corner and dump the woman's phone, angry that she'd lost her opportunity of owning a Razr but thankful that the woman just wanted her phone back and nothing else. Built like a bodybuilder, she could easily have licked Styles if she decided to. A robber can't afford to be careless like that. That's why we scoped out our victims and gave each other the heads-up. Don't plan your robberies carefully, you run the risk of getting caught.

Phones was the main ting we robbed. Back in the day, phones didn't have no blocks and we'd sell them on to

Indian shops in South, dodgy backstreet shops where they didn't ask no questions. But sometimes the backstreet shops got cold feet and we'd have to sell them on the street.

The problem with selling stuff on the street is that the value goes down instantly. Street sales are all about quick cash, and there's bare stuff being sold on the street and more product means lower prices. We'd phone up a couple of people we knew, shotters and the like. Say we got a phone, a Nokia 8310, shop value £150. We'd be lucky to get £60 on the street. The person you're selling it to, they know you tiefed it, and stolen goods is always worth less.

We licked money as well, but not on the regs. A middle-aged woman's handbag is full of useless bank cards and lipstick and you'd be lucky to find £25 in cash money. For big amounts of p's, we'd rob girls on their way to Goldstone, thirteen- and fourteen-year-olds who were too young to have bank cards. If a teenage girl was going to Goldstone, she intended to buy shoes or a jumper, hit the cinema, maybe grab a bite to eat. Them girls would be carrying £60 or more on them.

These times another girl started rolling with us. Her name was Pasha. Tall and elegant, skin the colour of the sunset and with round, wide eyes, Pasha had a timid way about her that fooled people into thinking she was weak. Really and truly, Pasha was tough as they came.

I'd known of Pasha for longs, but her family had her on lockdown and stopped her cotching with me and the girl-dem. The moment Pasha rolled with us, she got stuck in with robberies and licking it, over hungry to do tings. Maybe all them times Pasha weren't permitted to roll, she stored it up inside her and became extra attracted to life on the roads. Or maybe, like me and Roxy, when you've got relatives in the gang lifestyle, you're fated to follow in their footsteps.

One day, me and Pasha hit Goldstone and noticed something had changed. We couldn't put our finger on it at first. Just a difference in the air. Then we clocked it: boydem patrols. CCTV cameras posted on every corner, down the alleyway and in the arcade. Bare yellow signs warning people to keep their phones, cameras and iPods hidden away.

'Shit, bruv,' Pasha said. 'Looks like the free-for-all days are over.'

'Yeah, but it was good while it lasted.'

'Time to move on to bigger and better tings, cuz.'

Boys our age had these times progressed to more blatant robberies. One boy I knew was walking from his house to visit his nan of a night and spotted the Costcutter across the road closing up, two Indian men outside sharing a cigarette. Damn, he thought, and why not? He crossed the street, beated up the two men before they could fight back, dragged them to the back of the store, ordered them to open the safe and emptied it of cash. A few grand in £20 notes. He stuffed it into his pockets and continued on to his nan's.

Us girls lacked the strength to go do this type of tiefery. We stuck to tried-and-trusted licks. Did I think I'd get shiffed one day? Honestly, no. I reckoned that most robbers get away with their crimes and only the careless ones ever got arrested. Even then, my experience was that most charges resulted in no further action by the boydem. I thought as long as I kept sharp and didn't make no mistakes, I'd never be sentenced.

When p's was tight and we were desperate for a draw, any type of robbing seemed like a good idea, no matter how risky the target. Summers was tough, as we had bare time on our hands. This one day I found myself stuck at home, sweating in the heat and badly in need of some p's. The flat next to ours belonged to a shotter who had a jezzy sister. 'Jezzy' means 'slag'. The mandem all used to go round there and get head off her, the sister blowing the man line by line while her brother shotted downstairs in the stairwell.

I wasn't sure about robbing this boy. He was friends with a boy by the name of Sweetz. I knew Sweetz – I'll talk more about him later. Sweetz was a good friend, and if I stole from the shotter, it might complicate tings between him and Sweetz. At the same time, I craved some weed. I had to have p's to buy weed.

My habit won out.

In the sweltering afternoon, I slinked across the corridor and knocked on the jezzy's door. No answer. I let myself in: they had an open house; that door never been locked. I called out for the sister. Still nothing. Heard noises coming from the bedroom. The jezzy doing what she did best. Thinking my luck might be in, I made my way to the living room, where my eyes fixed on a band of sterling lying on the coffee table, two £50 notes and a couple of £20s. I snatched the money, left £20 for the slag and went straight down to Smiles's flat, the other side of the estate. On the trip over I bought an eighth and chilled at Smiles's with her and Styles. An hour tick-tocked. My friend Sweetz phoned.

'Rah, Chyna,' he said. 'My bredrin's been on to me. He knows you robbed him and he's fucking mental.' Sweetz sounded like he was in a hype too, speaking mad fast. 'You got to give the money back.'

'I ain't handing anything over.'

Even if I wanted to, I couldn't. I'd already blown some of the p's on draw.

Very next minute, who rang my mobile but Miss Jezzy herself, running up her mouth, saying she was gonna do this, that and the other to me. I weren't intimidated by this girl. The day I'm scared of a slag is a sad one, but I'm yet to see it. Beating on jezzies was like a hobby for me. The girl wanted it. I was happy to give it.

'Hold on one minute,' I said, cutting her short. I killed the call, grabbed my gear and headed back to my flat, Styles and Smiles tagging along. On the way, I worked through my options for the fight. The brother couldn't touch me because I was a girl. And if he laid a finger on me, bare mandem would be on his case, including Sweetz. I only had Miss Jezzy to contend with. With Smiles and Styles along for the ride, that wasn't no worry at all.

I arrived at the flat. Found Miss Jezzy fuming at me, one foot inside her flat.

'What is it?' I said, fronting. 'You got something to say, tell it to my face.'

She said fuck all to my face, as it happens. That's the ting about jezzies. They're never up for a fight. I never had much time for jezzies and seeing how quickly the sister bailed out of a box-up, I had zero respect for slags and never wanted to be associated with them. Jezzies were the opposite of my fam girls: not loyal to no one, no principles and no tough-ness. Instead she retreated inside her flat and locked the door. Clearly, I weren't welcome in Miss Jezzy's house ever again.

Other times we'd lick the Chinese man selling pirate DVDs. You could find the Chinaman in the local pub or around the shops, bustin' a phat collection of all the latest counterfeit movies: *Finding Nemo, Transformers, Alien Versus Predator*. Our standard ting was to approach this old man and pretend we wanted to buy some films.

'Me give you five dee-vee-dee. Ten pound.'

'Yeah, comes then.'

Explaining that we didn't want to make the sale in a busy street, we'd lure him round the corner, where bare of us girls properly punched the man up, stole his money and DVD collection. Then we'd sell the films on for profit. Robbing the DVD man was safer than the pizza man because he was doing illegal tings anyway, couldn't speak no English and he's probably an illegal under the pay of the Snakehead gangs, so he's not in a position to go reporting us to the boydem.

When there was nobody to tief from, we'd chill listening to music. Tinchy Stryder and Dizzee Rascal was our favourite artists. Now they're over famous, but the music they did these times sounds nothing like the stuff they come out with today. Back in them days, Dizzee and Tinchy used to spit with songs like 'Tings in Boots' and 'I Luv U'. Then there was Wiley from Bow, part of the Roll Deep Crew, plus Pay As You Go, Heartless Crew, So Solid. As well, we listened to a bit of mandem MCing. Sometimes we MCed ourselves, spitting at the afterschool club.

I got hold of a portable magnet, same one the staff use in shops to detag the clothes. Some boy who worked in Next nicked one and sold it me for £10. With the magnet, tiefing became a lot less complicated. I'd walk into House of Fraser or Selfridges or wherever and pick up a bunch of clothes. Making sure I hid, say, a pair of jeans inside of a dress on the same hanger, so the changing-room girl didn't know how many items I took in with me, I'd use the magnet and stash the threads in my bag.

There's another reason I tiefed daily. I was over good at it. Started thinking, Rah, I'm unstoppable. Can't be touched.

Pasha pulled me aside one day and said, 'You should cut back on the tiefing, bruv. You're addicted.'

I frowned.

'I'm serious,' she went on. 'You can't even walk into a shop these days without stealing something. Keep it like this and you're gonna get caught, mate.'

'I'm not that bad,' I said.

'Tell me this, then. How many days have you *not* tiefed in the last year?'

I tried to think of one. I couldn't.

Every robber's comedown is when they think they'll never get caught. You reckon you've got sick skills and take risks, get a bit too big for your boots. Next ting you know, you're cornered.

I'd been to the JD Sports at Goldstone twice in two days. On the second visit, for some reason I decided to throw on the garmz I'd nicked the *day before*. It was a deliberate ting. Probably I thought it'd be funny, taking the piss out of the store staff. As me, Styles, Roxy and Fierce strolled in, this young girl working the counter clocked me. And I clocked her. She'd been working there the day before and seen me leave without buying nothing. And yet here I am, bustin' this brand-new white Nike tracktop hoodie that I'd tiefed in her face.

Me and Styles selected a couple of tracksuits and disappeared into the changing rooms. We had rooms next to each other and there was a two-inch gap between the top of the dresser and the ceiling, so we were able to chat as we changed.

'You know what, something's not right today,' Styles said.

'I feel you.'

'Should we leave it today?'

'Allow it. I'm not getting nothing,' I said. I put the threads I'd planned on tiefing back on their hangers. Styles agreed to do the same.

'Fuck,' Styles said.

'What is it?'

'I've already popped a tag.'

A popped tag meant damaged garmz. And damaged garmz meant trouble. If the store manager found the holes in the clothes, they'd know we was trying to tief and could do us on destruction of property. Styles decided to slip on the bottoms she'd popped and leave it at that.

'Just the one little ting won't hurt,' she said.

'Whatever. Let's just go.'

We quit the changing rooms, Roxy and Fierce entering straight after, carrying hordes of stuff. Tracksuits, jackets, jumpers, bottoms. Enough threads to clothe a family. I was anxious. This voice kept telling me, Leave here before tings turns bad. But no way could I abandon my girls. So me and Styles stuck it out in the store. Roxy and Fierce took flipping for ever.

Fifteen, twenty minutes inside the changing rooms and this security guard figures something ain't right. The woman who spotted me earlier had a word in the guard's ear. I was confident she couldn't pin nothing on me, because she saw me come out from the changing room with the exact same garmz I walked in with, put everything back on the racks. I'd tiefed nothing. As for the Nike hoodie, she had no way of proving I'd tiefed it from her store. But with my girls, it's a different story. A few years older than us, skinny with big chops – earrings – the checkout girl rushed towards me. Passed me by and shouted into the changing rooms, 'Can you two come out, please!'

'I'm getting changed,' Roxy said. 'Be, like, ten minutes.'

The girl was hopping mad. She crossed her arms, tapped her foot. 'You'll come out right now or I'll come in there and fetch you myself. We've got suspicions that you're stealing.'

A minute later and Roxy and Fierce came out, clothes they'd planned on tiefing on their persons. The woman inspected them and noticed that the tags were popped and there were little holes in all of the garmz. She held up one item after another, finding hole after hole. When she'd finished her little examination, she said, 'Right, I'm calling the police. You're gonna get done. All of you.'

We glanced at each other. Screw this. Our mentality was, we ain't gonna get in the shit over this. We knew what to do. The four of us girls literally mashed up JD Sports. We went nuts. Smashed down the mannequins at the front of the store, chucked garmz everywhere, kicked over displays. The guards had hit the alarm and the doors slammed closed. Them doors at JD Sports were magnetic, impossible to force open. The guards weren't able to get at us because they had their hands full with mad other customers demanding to be let out.

Meanwhile I looked to settle my beef with the girl who snitched us up. While Styles, Fierce and Roxy attacked the door, kicking it in, beating on the security guard, I stepped to the girl.

'I'm gonna fuck you up,' I said.

'You lot tiefed. I saw it!' She was running off her mouth a little bit. I wanted to box this girl up badly.

I was in her face.

'Next time I see you,' I said, 'you're gonna get a true licking.'

The customers demanded the guards open the doors. They allowed them to leave and in the confusion Styles slipped through the net. That pissed me off. I was like, Rah, Styles's meant to be my girl, and first chance that comes her way, she's quit on us. That wasn't right.

I didn't have time to be mad at Styles. The boydem came and saw that the store was a bombed-out mess. The store didn't want to kick up a fuss about the trashed displays and chucked clothes. End of the day, pressing charges is more hassle than it's worth for a lot of people. But the tiefing – they weren't prepared to let that slide. The boydem found the garmz with the holes in them, and the popped tags. Roxy and Fierce got shiffed. As they were dumped in the boydem car to go to the station, I walked outside to Styles.

'You abandoned me back there, bruv.'

'It weren't like that,' she said. 'I didn't know what was going down.'

I was right behind you, I went to say. Suddenly I felt someone right behind *me*. I u-turned and seen a boydem officer shadowing me.

'Show me your pockets,' he said.

I emptied my pockets. Keys, bus pass, money.

'What's this?' he asked, holding something else in his hand.

'What's it look like?'

'I can see it's a knife. What I want to know is, what's it doing in your pocket?'

That ain't an easy question to answer. See, most people when they read about gangs carrying knives or whatnot assume that the person with the knife is looking to cut people. The truth is, a lot of kids carry knives for protection. Someone's got some beef with them, they know if they're cornered in an alley or something, they need to be able to defend themselves against an attack. I had a knife on me because I had some beef with girls from another school. The beef, really and truly, was what drove me and my girls to form the gang.

PART TWO
BEEF

'We got nothing to lose'

– Styles

FIVE

Certified

The Abbott School for Girls was two minutes up the road from the Wood Hall Estate. They had a gang of girls who went by the name of the Hard-Bodied Chix. They started a beef with us, and that's how we made our fam official – and became a paid-in-full gang.

Me and my girls were tomboyish, but as we turned thirteen, boys began hanging out with us. Boyish or not, we had a rep on our endz as being peng girls. This bait boy attention made some people outside our girldem over jealous, and the Hard-Bodied Chix most of all, as the boys interested in our tings were from two local gangs who were both in with the Chix, the olders in the TK – Thuggish Kings – and their youngers, the TP – Thuggish Princes.

The youngers were the same age as us, thirteen, and both sets of mandem were keen on us in sexual ways. Once we got to know them, they made their moves. Ting is, we didn't return the interest. Really and truly, we had no time for man at that age and none of us had a true boyfriend until a year or two later. Compared to some of the other girls on our endz, we lost our virginities late.

Me and my girls repped the same endz as the Hard-Bodied Chix. We kind of knew them; they sort of knew us.

Not like friends or anything, not even 'Hi' and 'Bye'. We didn't never talk to them, and if a Chix girl was on one side of the road, we'd cross over. That's how it was between us. We had a truce ting going on.

One day, the peace was broken.

I sort of knew a couple of the girls in the Chix: Malene and her older sister, Trinique. We used to go dance class together, where we'd practise the moves to hip-hop and street-dance tracks from Missy Elliott, Ashanti and Janet Jackson. Malene was black and she had a man's type of build. Long legs, shoulders so wide it looked like she wore pads, all spiky elbows and bony knees. She also dressed like a hardcore chav. White creps, tight trousers, big boy's blazer with a rucksack on her shoulders, hair cut short and slicked down on one side.

Malene's boyfriend was a boy by the name of Joker. He was best friends with the boyfriend of another girl in the gang. The boy's name was Raver. He dated a girl called Sadie. Malene, however, had it in her head that Raver liked her.

But what kicked it off was that one girl hated on Styles. Her name was Erin. To this day, no one is quite sure what caused Erin to pick on Styles. Maybe even Erin herself would have a hard time working that one out. We just knew that this Erin girl was setting on Styles in one-on-one situations on the street. And from there tings snowballed.

Erin reached to her girldem in the Chix, asking for their

help in beefing with Styles. And the other Chix were only too happy to help out . . . especially Malene.

See, Raver affiliated with Thuggish Kings. As we cotched with the TK, we moved in the same circles as Raver. He hung out with us, and a rumour circulated that he over fancied Styles. Styles claimed she was unaware of Raver's interest, and I reckon she would've fobbed him off anyway. We had no time for boyfriends. We had laughs with the mandem, but that was as far as it went. Dating them seemed wrong, like going out with your cousin.

I don't know if Malene heard about these rumours. She definitely had her ear close to the street and was doubly vexed. Not only did she want to step to Styles to back up her fam, Erin, but she exhibited mad jealousy, hated the thought of Raver having eyes for Styles. The Chix targeted Styles, and a beating was on the cards whenever they seen her in town. First time, fifteen girls moved to Styles. She put up a good fight, but with them odds, you ain't walking away as the winner.

The boxings took place countless of times. On the way home from school, at weekends, in the evenings, Styles got rushed. Any time the Hard-Bodied girls set eyes on Styles, they stepped to her. She'd get on the bus, the girls would chase her on to the bus and fight with her. Sometimes me and the girls happened to be with Styles, and we'd engage the Chix together.

'Shit, bruv,' Roxy said one day behind the fields after

Styles showed for school with bruises up and down her face. 'Them Chix victimizing Styles.'

'For real, we need to certify,' Nang said.

'What you talking about?'

'You mean creating a gang?' Pasha said.

'Yeah,' Nang replied. 'Let them Abbott girls know we're clicked. Tell them if they want a war, it's fucking on,' she said, smacking a fist into the palm of her hand. 'For real.'

We decided that we wasn't representing no boys in our gang. Our fam had to be about who we was, and what we stood for. We came up with bare names during class at school, in between drawing pictures of our street names and practising our dubz styles.

We settled on the name N2L. Nothing 2 Lose.

Nothing to lose. All of us girls liked it. We didn't have no leader in our gang, so it wasn't like any one girl had the final say on our name, but it summed us up perfectly. We really did have nothing to lose, except each other.

Our gang name sorted, now we had to personalize and get the word out on the roads that Nothing 2 Lose girldem was rolling and ready for a drama with anyone who wanted beef. We were certified.

Our fam was all about loyalty and closeness. The other girls were my sisters, my bredrin, my fam. If one of us had issues at home or boy trouble, someone else in our gang would have gone through the same ting before and would be there to help and listen. People talk about kids dying on the roads because they came from a broken family. Ain't true. They got a fam all right, just not one made up of a mummy and daddy.

We rolled tight. Every day we'd link in the mornings. Bing up a spliff straight out of the door, smoke it. Pin up a second joint and smoke it at the bus station. Once or twice we'd break out a bottle of Smirnoff vodka and neck big shots on the bus. We chose vodka because you can't smell it on someone's breath. We'd rock up at school legless, bubblin' and chatting our way through classes. Sometimes the teachers would realize we were out of our heads and tell us to go home. Safe. Out of school, we hanged on the endz. Smoke more weed, jamming. Go tiefing. Drive with the mandem around the endz in old bangers that they owned, like ten of us in a single car, or riding on the back of peds.

To make sure people knew we were N2L, we each bought a black Eskimo jacket and took it to the football-numbering counter at the high-street sports shop, asking if they could do printing on normal garmz as well as football shirts.

'Yeah, no problem,' the man said, wondering why ten teenage girls were giving him each a black hoodie and asking for street names on the back. 'The price is eighty-five pence a letter.'

'Cool. What about them coats?' I asked.

'Sure, we can do them too.'

'Can you print "N2L" on the back of ten coats?'

''Course' – the man, smiling. 'You young ladies on the same netball team?'

'Yeah, something like that.'

The Hard-Bodied Chix were famous as mean, dirty fighters. They fought with tings instead of fists: knives, bottles, bats, bricks. They fought like men. As they operated close to Wood Hall, I took to carrying a knife to protect myself on the ways to and from school. I knew it was only a matter of time before tings kicked off between N2L and the Chix.

On a Saturday night, we had our first major fight with the Chix. A shubz took place in the hall on our estate. A 'shubz' is what we used to call an under-eighteens party. People rented out big halls and clubs for club nights, and although liquor was officially banned, all the kids used to sneak in bottles of drink to get pissed on: Lambrini, a drink called Alizé, which comes in different fruit flavours and rappers name-dropped in their spits, and MD 20/20, a £5 bottle of liquor that was much better than cider for getting you quickly fucked. I enjoyed going to the shubz and spending time with my girls, though I was wary of the boys at these hang-outs. They'd try and dance with you from behind, grinding up against you, and that didn't impress me. I weren't shy, just not attracted to the immature mandem at our school.

Our fam wasn't invited to the shubz, as it was a Chix gig, but we gatecrashed it anyway, busied ourselves with drinking and having a good time. The Chix kept to themselves. Normally we'd be fighting straight up, but it's a shubz, there were boys, bare tunes playing, everyone blowing up and wearing their most freshest garmz. We weren't looking for trouble.

Suddenly Malene moved to Styles.

'You robbed my girl,' she said.

'Fuck off.' Styles folded her arms and stepped back.

Malene had two Chix backing her up. One was a redhead, freckled, pale and with her hair styled into plaits. The other girl had so much fat on her body that her arse nearly touched the ground, but she was the fat-all-over type, big hands, thick arms and neck. Not the kind of girl I could duppy in a single blow. Me and the girls seen what Malene's game is. We stopped partying and closed ranks around Styles.

'That's my girl's chain, clown,' Malene said, pointing to Styles's ice, a neat-looking chain.

For us girls, garmz was a major part of our rep. We wore the latest gear. Phat Adidas and Nike creps, tracksuits, name-brand jeans like Moschino with flower patterns all the way up and down the legs, Iceberg ones with the ice motif splashed down the sides, Avirex jackets. We had a style of wearing them. Hoodies drawn low to intimidate people when we was out on the rob. Zip fully up to hide our school uniform.

With me, it was all about the chops. That was my ting. I used to be covered in ice. Sovereign gold rings on every finger, big bracelets and huge chops round my ankles. I also wore a gold chain round my neck that had a teddy bear on it that cost £550. Put it like this: people knew me as Gold Queen.

Styles also digged her jewellery, and somehow Malene suspected that she'd robbed one of her girls of this chain.

Fact is, Styles's chain was a present from her mum, and a gift that had special meaning for her. She never stole it. I reckon, deep down, Malene knew that, but she was itching to kick up a storm with Styles. As she backed away, Malene snatched at the chain – and popped it. Tore it clean off. I thought, Rah, Styles's gonna box Malene any second now, and I'm ready to bring it to the girl to Malene's right.

Instead of swinging a punch, Styles simply turned round and exited the shubz. I raced after Styles, worried about her. It was out of character for her to shirk away from a conflict. What's that girl up to? I thought.

She was nowhere to be seen. Unsure what to do, I headed straight to my cousin Zara's place. Zara had been in a gang in her day, and I had a sense the drama wasn't over for the night, that we needed some help before tings got out of hand. Zara happened to be at home. She came down to the shubz with me, telling me not to worry, that she'd sort it out and get Styles's chain back. By the time we arrived at the hall, Styles had returned to the scene. She stood at the edge of the hall, coldly scanning for Malene.

Massive big knife in her hand.

Zara tried to defuse tings. She grabbed the knife from

Styles and, being older and with status, forced Malene to hand back the chain. Styles took one look at her chain, seen it was broken and lost it.

She punched Malene square in the face.

That first punch was like a red light. A signal for everyone else to start brawling.

There were two types of fight that could kick off between us and the bad girls. One-on-ones, where you have people standing around and cheering on their bredrin, and the rules are that rounds are over as soon as someone falls to the ground, and ain't nobody can stop the fight until one of the girls is conked out for Britain.

Then there's brawls. All-out mash-ups, free-for-alls with girls lamping each other left, right and centre. In the brawl, there ain't but one rule: the girls standing at the end are the winners. And this here, in the shubz, this was a fucking street brawl.

Malene stumbled, recovered, moved for Styles's face. She swung erratically, missed, but managed to connect with her neck, sending Styles to the ground. Bigs and Nang were set on by the extra-fat girl and a big friend of hers, tackling them from behind, catching them by surprise. Bigs was hustled over and grappled with her rival, jabbing her in the chest with the point of her elbow. Nang went to help, but the extra-heavy girl headlocked her, rolled her on to her back and pinned her down, her knees pressed against her upper arms and her feet across Nang's legs.

I had to help out my fam. Rushing forward, I kicked the heavy girl in the back. Hardly no effect. I booted her again, this time in the small of her spine, and now the girl toppled sideways, loosening her hold on Nang. That's my girl, I thought. You don't mess with my girls.

A second or two after I'd kicked out, I felt a stinging pain in my shoulder. I went to turn, and suddenly I was off-balance, and the redhead was up against me, punching the side of my chest, below my armpit. My body howled. I scrambled to stand upright, but the blows had dizzied me. Reached out for something to support. A pillar. I looked around and saw the redhead smashing a bottle of MD 20/20 against the decks the DJ had abandoned not five minutes ago, liquid pooling on to the floor like glittery phlegm, the glass teeth of the broken bottle all shiny and sharp.

The redhead bombed towards me with her makeshift shank.

I had no time to react. She's gonna fucking stab me, I realized too late.

The bottle was inches from my face.

I blinked, and when I opened my eyes, the redhead's grip on the bottle had slackened and the bottle flung sideways, crashing a few metres away, breaking up. Nang had launched herself at the redhead like a torpedo, banging her up with a storm of punches. The redhead tried to fight back, but Nang caught her true on the chin and the fight was drained out of her.

Now Styles had Malene cornered, ready to dish out vicious bang, when another girl, with the world's biggest chops, set on her from behind. Malene escaped and made for Bigs, darting left and right, scouting for a tool. She settled on a Lambrini bottle. These are huge bottles. If Malene strikes Bigs full-on, she might put her in a coma, I feared.

I went for Malene, kicking her in the back of her thigh. Gave her enough time to turn round, see who'd done the booting and bang! In the face. Malene had a bit of height and build on me, but my punch had caught her off-guard. Bigs moved in for the finish, head-butting Malene smack in the forehead. I heard the *clack* as their heads collided, Bigs shouting, 'Fucking use a bottle, do you? Do you?'

My cousin Zara recruited a bunch of her friends and broke up the fight before we did more damage to each other, and the shubz.

'That's enough,' she said. 'Allow it.'

Zara was backed up by bare of her people. They were older than us, some of them fully grown men, and if anyone tried to swing another punch, they were ready to move in and block it. Their presence jammed the fight.

I caught my breath. We'd been rampaging for a half-hour. The Chix blew out of the hall. We were psyched, Tantrum so on it I thought she was about ready to jump through the roof.

'That was sick, b,' she said. Tantrum called everyone 'b'. No one knew exactly what it stood for. Maybe 'babe' or 'beautiful' or 'bruv'. We never asked her. 'I thought we weren't going to get out of there alive.'

'Long as we're together, they won't win,' I replied.

'Yeah, but they're brawlers, b.'

We marched back to Styles's, drank some vodka, smoked weed and went over the fight in detail. I was pumped and thinking ahead to round two, and how I'd hate on those Chix.

The following Monday, the Chix jumped us as we boarded the bus at the main station. We weren't anticipating a fight that morning. They took us by surprise. We escaped without getting beated up. It was on.

The beef between Malene and our girl Styles turned into all-out war.

We fought everywhere. Didn't care who was with us or what we were doing at the time. We'd fight on the buses, in the shops, on the roads. Fights could kick off any time, any place, so we had to be vigilant. One time, me and Tantrum went into town to sort her out a new mobile. These days the Nokia 8310 had just come out, one of the phones that had the Bluetooth feature and FM radio. This was the must-have mobile. Me being me, I already had one. On this Saturday, Tantrum had £100 in cash money to upgrade to the Nokia. We bought the phone, all good.

On the way back to the bus station, Tantrum tried out the radio on the mobile, plugging the earphones in. Suddenly a hand reached out and yanked the headphones out of

Tantrum's ears. Spinning round, Tantrum shoved the girl who'd snatched her headphones and they started scrapping. We seen four girls rushing at us. A second girl tried to jump on Tantrum. I went up behind her and nailed her in the small of her back – boom.

The other two girls made to jump on me. I fucked up the first girl. Tantrum managed to shake the sket stepping to her and we focused on breaking away from the street. We had brawling skills, but four of them against us two was gash odds. A bus pulled up at the stop right next to where we were fighting. Me and Tantrum ran on board the bus as it left the stop. We caught our breath and checked our injuries. A few bruises and cuts, nothing bad. The moment the bus pulled away, me and Tantrum set about planning our revenge. How we'd do them, where and when.

We didn't have to wait long. We held a shubz to celebrate Split's birthday and invited bare boys and girls. Except, of course, the HBC. I rolled up with my girls and we're looking chooooong. Mad ice and chops, hair done proper, but no make-up; we didn't go in for lipstick and piercings. We had little VIP badges done up for each of us, and my girls looked neat.

A couple of hours later, the Chix blagged their way in. I counted fifteen of them. Ten of us N2L girls. We couldn't kick them out, because they'd paid their entrance money, and we didn't own the joint. Dubstep quaked the walls. Malene eyeballed me. Beefs simmered.

As the HBC lot raved, me and the girls knew it'd be only a matter of time until tings went bad. We stopped partying and hunted for weapons: we'd come to the club unarmed, not expecting the Chix to show. But they knew we'd be at the shubz, and reckoned on them bustin' tools. If they stepped to us, we needed to be able to defend ourselves. I went around the club, looking for anything that might be useful as a weapon. I found the perfect instrument: a glass ashtray. Solid, small enough to conceal and I could hold it in my hands and do some authentic hurt. Soon as we get out of this club, I thought, the girls are gonna attack us. We had to be ready to take them down.

At one o'clock in the morning, the shubz ended. For three hours me and my girls had trained our eyes on the Chix, waiting for them to step to it. They'd blanked us all night. The lights flared up and they left without giving us a second glance. Unsettled by their weird tactics, Nang tailed them to check what they were playing at. While the rest of us chilled in the empty club upstairs, I had the feeling that the Chix weren't done with us for the night. No doubt. You can't *not* fight someone when there's a major beef between you.

'They're waiting outside,' Nang reported back. 'They'll jump us the moment we leave.'

'All fifteen of 'em?' Tantrum asked.

'More. There's twenty-five down there, fam. Girls I don't even recognize.'

'You know what, let's have it out. I'm not scared. Come

on, fam.' I nodded towards the stairs. 'We're not gonna let them bully us.'

We all agreed. If we had to box our way out of the club, so be it. The club was on the first floor of a building with a narrow staircase feeding down to the main doors. We hit the stairs. No sign of the Chix. The club coughed us up outside. No one in sight. Maybe they've fucked off, I thought.

Two girls leaped out from behind a bush; a dozen came out from behind cars parked at the side of the road; now five of the biggest girls stood in the middle of the road, twenty metres away, goading us.

Nang turned to me as the HBC girls lined up across the road.

'Rah, for real, I'm gonna step to the biggest one.'

'You sure about that?' I said.

'Take down the biggest bully and the others won't rate their chances. It's either that or an all-out slog. One-on-one's a better bet,' Nang replied, dispensing more advice on street tactics.

'Cools. We're backing you up, cuz.'

'For real.'

The girl Nang had her eyes on was six feet tall and wide as a column of car tyres, with rough hands that looked as if they could grind up concrete. She busted a gold necklace with a pendant the size of a hubcap. Nang showed no fear.

'What you looking at?' Putting a knot on this girl.

'What do you mean?'

'You coming down here with this attitude and you *don't* expect me to lick you?'

'Wait here for a minute, then.'

'Fuck off,' Nang said. 'I'm not waiting for nothing.'

Another twenty girls appeared. They'd doubled their number and we're fronting up to about fifty girls, waving bats and poles. They charged at us like the hooligans in *Green Street*. Us N2L girls held our ground. We fighted the Chix. They were looking for action, and we gave them action. I licked some Afro girl. Styles rolled on the ground with another bitch, Nang had the hubcap girl in a headlock, squeezing her grip tight.

The Afro girl waved a bat at me, taking swipes at my arms. I blocked it and pulled out my weapon, the ashtray I'd secreted on my body from earlier. Taking a couple of steps back, I threw it at the girl as she ran up to me. She ducked; the ashtray flew over her head and smashed against a wall. The distraction bought me a few seconds. By now Nang, Tantrum and the other girls had broken free from the Chix and fled down the street. I sprinted after them, my legs shooting me down the street and round a corner. I risked a quick look over my shoulder and seen the Chix weren't giving chase.

We stopped at the end of the street.

'Where's Styles?' I asked.

'Shit,' Tantrum said. 'Where the fuck *is* Styles?'

'The Chix,' Nang said, catching her breath. 'She must still be there.'

We darted back up the street, to the scene of the dust-up. The HBC were in a circle, kicking and smacking a dark bundle of rags, thirty more Chix hanging further back and cheering in the road. I neared.

The bundle was Styles.

With the rest of the N2L girls at my sides, I charged at them, throwing fists and lashing out at anyone who wanted a piece.

Sweetz, the friend of the jezzy girl's boy who lived opposite our flat, also happened to be there that night. He came outside to see what the noise was, clocked the badness of the situation and hauled Styles away from danger. He saved her. If he hadn't helped, the Chix would've rushed us again. But when a gang boy gets involved, the girls ain't got no option but to leave it be. Sweetz had his affiliation and his status, and no girl could touch him.

The first ting I noticed was that Styles's creps were splashed up with blood like red polka dots. Then I clocked her face. She was gone. Mashed up. Her eyes were purple and puffy, her nose bloodied, her lips beaten black and blue. The other girls shook her, trying to wake her up. She didn't respond. Seeing Styles in a bad way distraught me. That's my bredrin. Hot, angry tears flowed down my cheeks.

We had a deep feeling for each other. If someone hurt my girls, that's the same as striking a blow at me personally. I say Styles was my bredrin, but really and truly, she was more than that. She was family. So were all my girls. We came from messed-up backgrounds where our families had problems, and we treasured each other like sisters. In this life, these times, we were all each other had. What they did to Styles put a lump in my throat.

I seen red.

A rage took control inside of me. I recovered a razor-sharp shard of the broken ashtray, gripping it like a blade, and jumped on to the closest girl. She toppled over, me on top of her, scraping the shit out of her face with the pointed end of the ashtray. I couldn't control myself. I was so pissed at seeing my friend knocked out, thought Styles might have been killed. I cut and cut that girl's face, the glass shredding the palm of my hand. The other Chix stared on in horror as I carved up her forehead, and by the time my girls pulled me off, it looked like someone had drawn noughts and crosses on her face in red felt-tip.

Maybe the reason the Chix didn't move to me as I assaulted their girl was that my cousin rolled with the mandem hard in her yute and her rep gave me some protection on the roads. My cousin had also beaten up Malene's older sister, Trinique. Had her in Battersea Park doing hopscotch and giving her bang every time she got it wrong. Making her do sick games, boxing her up bare times. My cousin tortured Trinique for long. Disrespected her.

Or maybe they just seen me over angry and thought pushing me harder might be bad for them and their rough faces. When I sliced at the girl, I zoned out. Went blank. If my girls hadn't dragged me away, I could've ended up killing her.

My fam meant everything to me. The way I see it is this. Some people have friends who won't lend them money or give them a place to stay when they're in bad times. Our fam? We'd kill for each other.

Three months later, I bumped into the girl I'd attacked in town. She'd had twenty-five stitches to her face. By the time I clocked her, the stitches were removed, but the scars stayed for life. One scar was six inches away from her eye, one above her eye and one on the side of her face at the temple. I sometimes bump into her today. She's got kids now. Well, past is past. But I'm not sorry for what I done. I had to defend Styles.

SIX

Guns 'n' respect

The feud with the Hard-Bodied Chix was ongoing. Every time I left my house I packed a ting in my hoodie pocket, knowing that one of the girls would probably step to me that same day.

My weapon of choice to carry was a snooker ball wrapped in two slipper socks. Easy to carry around, I'd stash it in my bag or my hoodie pocket.

The snooker ball had raw power. I'd seen the damage it caused up close in a fight with a girl I got into an argument with at a shubz. Few days after the party, I'd crossed over on to Styles's estate and bumped into this girl. We fighted. I gave her a serious boxing. When I was about done, she pulled a shank on me.

I swung the slipper sock above my head, building up momentum. The girl tried to duck as I lashed it and failed; the ball connected perfectly with her head. *Crunch*. My swing weren't even that hard, but the snooker ball took off her head. Smashed out two of her front teeth and busted her jaw. When I looked at my handiwork, I thought, Fuck, this girl looks like she's been hit by a lorry. She never messed with me no more.

The sight of the snooker ball intimidated bare girls.

Once, I found myself beefing on a bus with a Chix sister. This girl carried out a big American baseball bat made from silver metal. She only had one plan for the bat. To clobber me with it.

'Rah, you're on it? OK. Comes,' I said, motioning to her.

This girl moved down the bus, holding her baseball bat and tapping the end of it against the palm of her hand. The other passengers laid eyes on the bat and knew what was about to go down. Fights on buses in our endz happened constantly, and people knew better than to get in the way. They pretended to stare at shit out of the windows, hide behind their copies of *Metro*, fiddle with their mobiles. Anything but get involved with me and the girl.

She got to within a few seats of my spot before I reacted, digging a hand into my pocket and removing the slipper sock wrapped over tight round the ball. The girl got a sneak preview of the goods that'd shortly be rearranging her face. I swung it round my head like a bolas. Word must have reached this girl on the roads about the badness my snooker ball did to the other girl's head, because she stopped short and hopped off the bus in a rush, shouting about how she'd box me the next time she set eyes on me, reh-teh-teh.

My girls packed tools as well. Roxy carried a Taser gun she got through a friend of her cousin Sonita's. She showed it to me one day after school. I looked at this black plastic ting, like something the Terminator might use, a yellow cartridge loaded into the Taser. One pop of the trigger and some unlucky person would fry like an egg.

'Did you ask Sonita to sort you the Taser?'

Roxy shrugged. 'I just said I needed some protection.'

'And she gave you this?'

'Rah.'

Sonita had her own gang movements and knew Roxy was caught up in a big beef. She had experience of mad beefs and weren't about to let her go unarmed on the roads.

'Does it work?'

'Ain't tried it yet.'

'It's not exactly stealth, is it?' I said, holding the Taser and wondering how painful the shock would be. I imagined using it on Malene.

'I didn't want to carry a gun, but this is the next best ting.' Roxy was the tiniest girl in our gang, and despite the protection she received from Sonita's status, she had to take care of herself in case she got attacked.

We learned to share weapons between us. Roxy's Taser did a sort of pass-the-parcel from one girl to the next. I'd have it one day, Styles the next, Fierce day after that.

I occasionally carried a lead-filled boydem cosh or a pepper spray, but I had to be more careful about these items, because if the boydem stopped-and-searched me and found a cosh or the spray, I'd be in big trouble, as they're classified as offensive weapons. These were emergency tools. If I left the flat knowing that I'd be in a fight, a paid-up one-on-one, I'd take a tool along for extra force.

One-on-one fights was planned a few days in advance. Like, I'd get a phone call at night. Something would happen on, say, a Thursday. Someone in the Chix doing something to one of our fam. Violating Styles, or chasing down Tantrum and beating her up. I'd find out who done the beating. Although we was in a gang war, I'd know someone who had that girl's mobile number. Thursday evening, I'd call the girl up.

Sometimes the beef could just be over a couple of words. The worst cuss in our endz was 'Suck your mum.' If someone tells you, 'Suck your mum,' it's automatic beef. That person is looking to fight you.

On the day of the scrap, we'd organize where to take care of business. Mainly we chose the park, where there'd be bare exits, so if the fedz showed, we could easily scatter. Each time, I angled for the fight to come about on my estate. I felt safer in familiar surroundings, and if tings went wrong, I could call on people to chase the girl off. Rule number one of gang fighting is, never fight on another girl's endz. Make them come to you, or otherwise some-where neutral like the park.

The problem with parks is that when you're away from the comfort of your endz, anything can happen. They're big, wide-open spots; you don't know the layout as well as your roads. One of your girls can get shanked and no one would know it until long after the fight was finished. You had to be all eyes, treading carefully.

Once you hit the park with your fam, you're just wanting to get the fighting over and done with. There's no talking, nothing like that. You just see each other and boom – off you go trading blows. You fight in rounds. Your bredrin can't step to you. They form a circle round the two of you and that's it – boom. First round. When one of you gets knocked to the ground, that's the first round over. The other girl has to let you get back on your feet. Then the two of you box until one of you can't get back up no more. That's when the fight is over.

Gang fights between N2L and the Hard-Bodied Chix happened on the regs. The Chix did something on one of us; we badded one of their girls up. Every single time we'd fighted them, they looked to take revenge on us. We had literally hundreds of fights with the HBC. Back and forth, back and forth.

We were all still attending school and majority fights took place after school. As we'd be fighting in our school uniforms after hours, we had a couple of times where the next morning Miss Fredericks read out a letter in assembly to the entire school, saying that someone had seen bare girls fighting in town centre or at the bus station, giving it the lecture about respect and the school's good name. They didn't know for sure who it was, but I think the teachers suspected me and my girls of being involved.

At the age of fourteen, we started hanging around some of the boys in gangs. Boy gangs were more bigger than the girl gangs; most boys wanted to be living that G lifestyle. We chilled with two boys the same age as us, names of Sweetz and Tooth. Sweetz used to try it on with the girls endlessly. He had a bet going on with the mandem that he could sleep with all of us lot – Styles, Smiles, Roxy, Tantrum – before we left school. He didn't succeed in any of that.

I say any, but Sweetz did end up sleeping with Fierce.

When Fierce enrolled at Burnell, it had been a case of 'Who's this new girl?' Roxy brought Fierce into the circle and she took an instant liking to Sweetz. The liking went both ways – even though Sweetz later claimed otherwise – because one day I showed up in school and Sweetz was telling everyone that he'd had sex with Fierce in the playground at the back of the fields.

The reaction among us girls was, 'Urgh, that's slack.'

Breaking your virginity is all well and good, but you don't want to be doing nothing in no playground. Fierce denied that she'd ever slept with Sweetz. Way we saw it, having sex in a playground weren't exactly romantic, but that didn't mean she stopped being our friend, whether she'd done it or not.

Tooth had bare nicknames in school. He had a real sweet tooth, and we knew him as Sweetz's 'battie on bench', because if you got a bench, there's always a battie, an arse, or pair of jeans, depending on use of the term 'battie' – sitting on it. So if some boy was another boy's battie-on-bench, it meant they were over close. It ain't like he was a batty man – dat's a different ting. Just that he well looked up to Sweetz, over respected him.

Same as Sweetz, Tooth didn't get involved in robbery and such until he left school. Everyone used to love Tooth off; he was cute and jokey and light-hearted, but he could also be bad. He'd been a proper pest since day one, jarring us girls repeatedly.

Sweetz, Tooth and the others used to bad us up for our extra-curricular activities.

'Why you lot smoking weed? Why you lot tiefin'?'

Pretending they was angels at school. I shrugged.

'Can't help it, bruv, we're born bad,' I replied, tongue in cheek.

Because all of us lived in the same roads, we'd all walk home together from the afterschool club, taking a shortcut down the back through a cemetery that led right from our school directly back to our endz. A particular mandem by the name of Reef, in the year above us, had a rep as the school joker. That boy was the biggest joker among the lot of us. His style was to take the mick out of one person relentlessly, chiefing them to the end of days. He'd cuss and cuss and cuss for the whole trip home, taking the piss out of Bigs's weight by imitating this sort of waddling walk, cracking everyone up differently. Because we was all young and naive and laughing at Reef, we didn't see how Bigs got hurt by Reef's fooling. I'm still tight with Bigs, and if anyone tried that nonsense now, I'd stick up for her.

We did favours for the boys when the mood took us. A boy in a gang would have a problem with a girl in our endz. They'd be like, 'Rah, deal with the jezzy for us, innit.' Asking us to fight the girl, as the mandem can't be seen to be throwing punches and boxing her up.

Sweetz also got his name because he had a high opinion of himself and thought he was a lady's treat. We got to know him really well in school, as he lived two roads down from Roxy. In them days he terrorized the girls, pinching the girl-dem's arses. He had skin the colour of chocolate milkshake and strawberry lips that gave way to an easy smile capable of turning into a cheeky grin at the click of his fingers.

Sweetz had a problem with a girl we knew by the name of Bria. They used to date, and after Sweetz broke it off, she didn't like it and started running off her mouth, dissing him around the endz. Sweetz came up to me one day during lunchbreak.

'Ey yo, do me a favour and go to Bria's school.'

'What for?'

'Give that girl a beating. Say hello from Sweetz.'

'I'm on it.'

I didn't hardly know this fucking Bria girl, but if Sweetz wanted me to fuck her up, cools. He wasn't part of our gang, but he was affiliated to us and part of the mandem we'd call upon if we found ourselves in danger, and loyalty ain't no one-way street. Bria disrespecting Sweetz is like Bria disrespecting N2L, because he's our boy and the cuss is aimed at us too.

Roxy went looking for this girl at her school the same afternoon. Didn't find her. Fuck it, this girl's gonna get some, I'm thinking. It's a question of when. We reached out to the rest of our fam: anyone clocks Bria rolling in the endz, move to her. Getting to her at her school was gonna be difficult and I reckoned the bus station was my best bet for locating this girl. Every school in our endz was serviced by buses from the main terminal, so mornings and afternoons there'd be bare kids from various schools hanging about. The next day, I was at the bus station at three o'clock, and who I seen hanging but Bria. This is my chance now. She clocked me coming, seen I was ready to show her what time of day it was.

Bria didn't try to escape. She stood her ground as I approached her, looking at me like I was a piece of chewing gum stuck to the bottom of her creps.

'Yeah,' she said, 'and what?'

'Sweetz says hello,' I said back.

'Tch, fuck that boy.' She unfolded her arms. 'And fuck you too.'

Bria rushed me with such speed I was caught off-balance. She piled in with her fists. I lifted my hands up to protect my head from the blows and kicked at Bria's knee, booting it with the sole of my sneaker. She felt for her aching knee. I followed up with a stomp on her hand.

I stepped into Bria and smacked her about the head. Blood spots appeared on her nose and lips. A big crowd hollered as Bria tripped on herself, stumbling backwards. I clipped her on the ear and she landed on her arse.

'What is it now, Bria?' I said as her friends drew her away. 'What is it?'

Bria shook off her friends and stormed towards me, head down. She was gonna charge me in my chest. I smacked her fists against her upper back and pushed her to one side. Bria spat out blood and glared at me.

'Fuck me, Bria? Really and truly?'

I'd badded her up properly. I didn't feel sorry for that girl, or regret what I'd done to her. End of the day, it's all about respect. You don't go around after breaking up with someone slagging them off to everyone on the roads.

I walked away, glad I'd given Bria the beating she deserved.

The ting with street fights is, they're not like the fights you see in films, with two people fighting carefully and taking ten, fifteen minutes. In real life they're a few minutes long, a blur of hit-and-miss punches and kicks, a screaming crowd for background noise. When someone moves to you, all you're thinking is, I want to get this over and done with. I couldn't show fear, but inside I was always nervous going into a fight. You can't predict what's gonna happen: whether the girl you're fighting has a ting on her, or maybe she catches you with a punch and that's you out cold. I was a good brawler, and learned some solid moves from my girl-dem, but I also had luck on my side.

If Roxy or Bigs or Styles had been at the bus station that time, the result would've been the same. When you're in a girl gang, all your fam will step to someone that you've got a problem with, because they know you'd do the same for them.

Roxy bunked daily. She turfed up at school, signed in and signed right back out again. That way no one knew she was bunking. Roxy spent the rest of the day riding the buses, smoking weed and tiefing. Her skiving was so bait she had a teacher picking her up from outside her house each morning and physically escorting her into class. None of it worked. Roxy just didn't give a good fuck. She'd wander into my lesson for no reason, pull up a chair and talk to me like nothing was wrong, ignoring the teacher.

Roxy's attendance was bad enough that the school decided to ban her from lessons and dumped her in the Pupil Referral Unit, the centre for the baddest kids in the school, five of the worst offenders: four boys and Roxy. I'd pop along for a visit during lunchbreaks – the school banned her from hanging out with me and the girls too, but fuck it – and found her sitting at a desk being taught cookery by the centre teachers.

'Rah, ain't you gotta do coursework?' I asked.

'Nah, fam,' Roxy said.

'Wow.'

The Unit's supposed to be a punishment, but the kids don't give a flying toss, and from what I saw, neither did the teachers. Long as the kids aren't disrupting the normal classes, they're happy to leave them cooking Victoria sponge cakes all day. Roxy bunked the Unit, big surprise.

Eventually Roxy got kicked out. She went out for a spliff in the fields one day and Miss Fredericks happened to be monitoring the school grounds, doing her ting. She'd spied Roxy having a pull and marched over to her. Roxy dashed her spliff quick as, but the smell floated like a cloud in the air. Miss Fredericks reached her.

'Did I see you smoking . . . *marijuana*?' she asked.

Roxy could have just admitted to it, but she decided to take the piss. 'No,' she said. 'I ain't been smoking nothing. Must be the misty weather.'

Miss Fredericks frowned. 'I don't see any mist.'

'Don't you? Well . . .'

'Let me smell your fingers.'

Draw leaves a smell that's hard to get rid of. Had Roxy let Miss Fredericks have a sniff of her digits, she'd have landed in hot water. But instead of just saying no, Roxy went ballistic.

'Fuck off. You a dyke or something?' she said.

'I beg your pardon?'

'Smell my fucking fingers? You're gay, innit? I'm gonna tell everyone.'

Miss Fredericks most definitely weren't lesbian. But she seen that Roxy was prepared to take the piss for long; she told Roxy to go and wait outside her office. It turned out that a mobile phone had gone missing from Roxy's class and because of her rep for tiefing, she was the prime suspect. They searched through her stuff, but didn't find the phone, because Roxy hadn't stolen it. The one time she weren't guilty of something and no one believed her.

What they did find was a big bag of weed.

The news that Roxy had been booted out of school worked its way to my ear by lunchtime. Me and the girls rushed down to reception to find Roxy waiting for her mum.

'Cuz, everyone's saying you're gonna get excluded.'

'Transferred,' she said. 'If I don't, I'm excluded anyways.'

'Jokes, bruv,' I said.

Roxy smiled, but underneath I could see she was pissed. The glaze in her eyes from smoking bare draw had gone.

'Least you ain't gotta put up with more crap from Miss Fredericks' – me, trying to lighten the mood.

'That bitch,' Roxy said. Her smile burned away like a sparkler fizzling out. Then, 'Nah, she ain't so bad. She didn't shift me to the boydem. Can you imagine what would've happened then?'

'You'd be screwed,' I said, nodding. 'What school they gonna put you in?'

'All-girls' one.'

'For real?'

'Yeah.'

Roxy getting transferred only made us bond closer. The fam held us together and became the most important ting in our lives. Everything was N2L. We rolled as N2L. It weren't about Chyna or Roxy or Styles any more. Our reps was the gang rep.

Bored out of our skulls one night, me and Split rode on the bus. Split was the constant worrier. She fretted about this and that. Our fam used to joke that if Split had a million, she'd worry about losing it. That was the girl's vibe. She was a good, good friend of mine, though, and we chilled together bare times, listening to each other's music and comparing clothes.

We got off at the stop beside the shopping centre. Grabbed some wings, medium fries, Cokes from the McDonald's and boarded another bus, smoking and getting high on the upper deck.

We finished our spliffs and got off the bus in the middle of town. Snagged some liquor from an Afro-Caribbean food store up the road. An hour later, we were waiting at the bus-stop for a ride back when a group of boys came up to us.

'There's a house party up the road. You girls fancy it?'

'Whereabouts?'

'Freemantle Estate. You rolling, yeah?'

We were fourteen-year-old girls, a bit naive. And the boys look nice, so we're like, Let's get on it. Me and Split didn't know no one at the party, but we were up for an adventure.

Me and Split got piss-drunk at the party and chatted to various of boys. She danced with a boy bustin' in a white hoodie that had a picture of a yellow-eyed snake on it. Comes the end of the party, the lights blazed and Snake Boy wanted to take Split home. I told him, No way. Split was coming home with me. We didn't know this boy or what he was about.

Someone else said they were hitting a party in another block on the Freemantle Estate and invited us all to come along. We said yes. Snake Boy led the way, escorting us to this flat. He flicked on the lights, revealing a proper boy's pad: laminate flooring, leather sofa, thirty-six-inch wide-screen TV, Xbox, PlayStation, swish stereo and bongs. No sooner had we got through the door than Snake Boy pulled a gun out from under his hoodie, trying to impress us.

This was the first time I'd ever seen a piece up close. I was fixated by the barrel of the metallic black object in his hands.

'He's got a fucking *gun*, bruv,' Split whispered into my ear. Giving us his back, Snake Boy told us to make ourselves at home.

As we settled into the black leather sofa, we heard a crash so loud I jolted and Split jumped like a trampoline. Fifteen mandem piled through the busted front door and into the flat. Three of them rushed past us, grabbed Snake Boy by the neck and fighted him while he was stunned. They dragged him by his arms into the bedroom and slammed the door shut. Muffled shouts, screams and heavy smacks seeped out from the gap at the bottom of the door. I couldn't make out what the boys were saying, but I figured they were out to rob his stash. They'd followed us to his place and now they wanted the food.

The other twelve boys wouldn't let us leave and we had no choice but to stay put on the living-room sofa and wait for the robbery to play itself out. We didn't have no affiliation with none of the mandem present, and in our minds, this whole ting had fuck all to do with us. I smoked a Mayfair. Split, however, found it impossible to keep skelled. She was in full-on heart-attack mode, her voice shaking like a bag of loose stones, her legs jelly-wobbling. The boys were watching us, and no doubt if we panicked, they'd figure us as weak.

'Ohmigod, ohmigod, ohimgod—'

'Cut it, Split.'

'They're gonna kill us, bruv.'

'*Shut up*,' I told her between gritted teeth.

'Shall I say something? Maybe if I ask nicely, they'll let us go?'

'Keep your trap zipped,' I said.

One of the boys propped himself on the coffee table, his knees nearly touching mine. I was curious to see if he packed a gun.

'Who are you, then?' he asked.

I couldn't believe it. The boy was trying to chat me up in

the middle of a robbery, while his friends beated up Snake Boy in the bedroom not ten metres away. I replied in my best polite, gentle voice, cautious about being over friendly and planting ideas in this boy's head. Got to keep him sweet, I told myself.

'How can you talk to her!' Split belted out, in the most biggest hype mode of all time. 'You're robbing the house,' she screamed, 'and we just want to go home!'

The boy stitched his face into a grimace. 'Shut the fuck up,' he said. 'I'm having a nice chat with your friend.'

'Nah, everything's cool,' I said, keeping my voice and attitude in check. But underneath my steadiness, I worried that Split was in a major fit. We had to somehow get her out of there before she flipped. I beamed the boy my cutest smile. 'Can't we just leave, like, and maybe I'll call you sometime?'

The boy thought about this. 'Yeah, yeah,' he said, smiling enthusiastically back. 'All right. You two can go.'

We breezed out of that flat, never looking back and hoping Snake Boy was OK. As we hopped on to the bus, Split broke down in tears. The first time you see guns, you think, Rah, if that boy decided to point the gun at me and pull the trigger, I'm dead. Easy as someone bursting a balloon.

That wouldn't be the last time I laid eyes on a ting.

SEVEN

Dubz rep

I was walking down the corridor at school one day when I happened to pass a girl in the year below me running off her mouth at some tonked boy. She stood short, this girl, but what she lacked in height she made up for with her cussing skills.

'Fucking bumbaclot . . . what you giving it the 411 for behind my back, yeah? I ain't interested in your man, yeah. Fucking boy's butters anyway, yeah. I've seen old bangers got more class than that boy.'

This furious, rapid-fire stream of dissing gushed out of her mouth and I thought, This girl's got some potential, you know. I asked around. Turned out the girl had a little rep in her own circles and was known for the same kind of tings as me. Big mouth. Didn't care about authority. Took shit from nobody.

Couple of days later, I talked to her at lunch. She knew who I was, knew my rep, but she didn't appear intimidated. I liked that. We got chatting about this and that. She lived in a care home and had a tough upbringing.

Another week or two and she was like, 'Rah, can I be your younger?'

'Let me think about it,' I said.

When you choose a younger, it's got to be someone who reminds you a little bit of yourself. I saw my personality in this girl. When I was twelve, thirteen, I'd been doing the same tings, making the same mistakes, rolling with similar types of friends. I told myself, I could teach this girl to do tings differently and help her be more grown-up about tiefing and licking it. Like gang mentoring.

I called the girl over the next day at school. 'How's it feel to be my younger?'

Younger Chyna repped me to the max. In return I taught her what she really needed to know to get ahead in life: the best techniques for licking clothes, which shops had the swaggest security and how to rob people properly. You couldn't learn this from no classroom or read about it in some book, but in our endz, this stuff was important. I felt I had responsibility to Younger Chyna. I looked out for her and educated her on boys. And I protected her from beefs.

Younger Chyna had her own style, but if an older girl moved to her, I'd be there. Because my name already meant something in the endz, she had automatic status.

I also had a tiny affiliated to me. Tiny Chyna was two years below me, and twice as mouthy.

I didn't roll with my younger and tiny – they had their own crews – but when I hollered at them, they'd come to me in a shot. Having a younger and a tiny is a bit like passing on your name in a family. It's a way of making sure your street name lives on in the new generations. I also got some benefits from my little ones. As a show of respect, Younger Chyna would lick a phone from a girl, come to me and say, 'Rah, I got this phone but don't know where to sell it.' I'd shift the Nokia to the backstreet Indians, hand Younger Chyna half the money and keep the change. When Tiny Chyna licked clothes, I was guaranteed to get something out of it. Both them girls had mad respect and loyalty; they'd put their necks on the line for me, no questions asked.

Having youngers and tinies was good for sorting out beefs. If I seen a girl at school I didn't like, some dirty tramp who I wanted to box, an easy way of getting her to fight me was to get my younger to step to the girl and cuss her. Minute the girl answers back, I'm like, 'You're disrespecting my younger. It's on.'

Certain times, though, having a younger and tiny could be a bad ting. When they rep your name, they sometimes abuse your status, and, as the Older Chyna, I found myself getting into hypes for stupid reasons.

Younger Chyna rang me up one time. 'Come down to the park,' she said. 'There's a fight gonna happen.'

Course I'm gonna head to the park and look out for my younger. I arrived and I clocked bare olders and youngers from a couple of gangs, ready to lick somebody, drama in the air.

'What's this about?' I asked Younger.

'This girl was giving me a dirty look.'

'And . . . ?'

She gave it the screw-face. 'That's it.'

'Wait, wait. Lemme get this straight. This girl *looked* at you funny?'

'Yeah.'

'And now you want me to fight her?'

I explained to Younger Chyna that we could resolve that beef without having twenty or thirty girls beating the crap out of each other and boydem getting involved. Countless of times this happened: youngers and tinies using your name to cause trouble over nothing.

The boy gangs' youngers and tinies had extra responsibilities. Like hiding guns. If an older boy had a gun, they was reluctant to carry it themselves in case they get stopped by the boydem. So they tell their younger to hold on to it, someone who's too young to go prison.

We stuck with our youngers for long. To this day, some people still have youngers and tinies. One girl, the older's in her early twenties and the younger's just turned twenty, having been a younger for seven or eight years. My younger turned out all right, but my tiny remained mad after she left secondary school and got into bare trouble.

Being a younger or tiny is a privilege for them, because they're the only ones allowed to share your name. In the rules of the endz, two boys or girls can't share the same street name. If another girl went round calling herself Chyna, that'd be over beef. Fucking war.

Pulling on a draw one day in the school fields, my younger dashed over to me, out of breath and looking upset.

'There's some girl dubbing your name,' she said.

'What d'you mean?'

'Everyone's saying there's a girl in the Chix calling herself Chyna. And she been dubbing up the bus station mad like.'

My first reaction was, Nah, no way would any girl do something as stupid as steal my name. I thought nothing of it.

'Come down the bus station and see for youself,' Younger Chyna said.

So I did.

The bus terminal had several cement pillars the size of postboxes, which we dubbed on the regs. I laid eyes on the pillars after school, checking the dubz. And right there, plastered down the side of one of them in bright purple letters, was the word 'CHYNA' in a badly drawn dubz that looked jokes.

No way could I stand for this. Chyna was my tag, *my* rep. This other girl had treaded on my toes; I might do something on the roads and this girl could take all the credit for it.

'Word is she's dubbing bare walls,' Younger Chyna said. My blood was up. This new Chyna needed to be taught a lesson. The fact she was affiliated to the HBC made me doubly vexed.

I v'd her dub. 'V'ing' means spraying a big 'v' over the top of the dub. When you're in a gang and doing dubz and tags, that's your name and your rep. V'ing someone out is a way of dissing someone. I scrawled, 'The Original Chyna and Younger Chyna,' on top, letting her know who done did the v'ing.

A week goes by. Word reached my ear that Fake Chyna wanted to fight me because I'd writ what I'd writ and v'ed her out. Few days later, I got on to the bus at the station to go school. Swiped my Oyster card and hit the upstairs so I could bing up a spliff out of the window.

'Oh, bad girl.' Voice at my back. I turned. Found myself face to face with Fake Chyna. 'What you saying, bruv? What you saying 'bout me?'

She was backed up by Malene and bare other Chix. Her and her bredrin versus me. If the beef had been anything else, I probably would've scattered, but my name was at stake. I weren't about to give that up to nobody.

'Yeah, I v'd you out, so what?' I said. 'You tiefed my tag.'

'Nah, Bad Girl. That's my name. You're Bad Girl now.'

Fake Chyna was an ugly sket. She had a white face, pale as cow's milk and scarred with red spots and blotches. Ginger hair cut short and elephant ears bustin' supersize chops.

'There's only one way to sort this out,' I told her.

I felt for my slipper sock. Thought they was all gonna attack me, any second. That'd be just like the dirt Chix, thousands of them launching at one girl. They didn't play fair.

But Fake Chyna and her bredrin were glued to the spot.

No one rushed forward. I spied someone at my shoulder, turned to see who it was: Michael, Styles's brother. I loosed the grip on my slipper sock. He knew of our beef with her from Styles and, as luck would have it, happened to hop on the same bus as me. Michael had status and his presence made the Chix think twice.

Grinning, Michael propped an arm on my shoulder.

'It best be Chyna against you one on one,' he said, pointing his finger at Fake Chyna. 'Or I'll have to call the mandem, even tings up a bit, do you feel me?'

'Comes, then, let's do it,' I said to Fake Chyna.

She shifted on her feet. 'Not here.'

'Fine. Saturday, then. The park. No weapons.'

Fake Chyna shook her minging head. 'Can't. I'm not around then.'

'She don't want it' – Michael laughing, Fake Chyna glancing at Malene, but she had to handle this beef on her own; Malene weren't able to help her. I asked Fake Chyna when she wanted it repeatedly. The more I goaded her, the more I seen her as a coward.

'Fuck this,' she said, and barged past me down the stairs, bredrin backing her up, Malene knocking against my shoulder and laying on the kind of face that could blunt a sharp shank.

The next day at school, I heard from a friend that Fake Chyna had changed her street name. I continued dubbing my name.

Dubz was our ting in N2L. Our authorization and our signature seal. The more we sprayed, the more people in our endz knew about our fam. Each of us girls had a unique tag; as a group, we was always on the lookout for new tings to dub. I used to roll with a couple boys and one of them, Marcus, dubbed sick.

Marcus was a friend from school. He was affiliated with Sweetz's boys and we became good friends. Me, Roxy, Marcus and another boy would ride the trains on the London Overground network. Once we got to a certain station, we'd head straight to the end of the platform and jump the line, walking parallel to the slats. We learned which one was the live rail and by sticking to the gravelly part we'd avoid getting electrocuted. A hundred metres down the track, we'd come across a depot building. The railway network used little ladders along the tracks and Marcus being a climber, kind of boy capable of Spiderman wall-scaling, he'd put the ladder against the side of the depot and climb up to do the dubz. Create a big dub of all our names, with our names inside Marcus's name in mad cartoon style down the side of this building.

These times I dreamed of the whole world painted in our dubz. I wanted to graffiti up my bedroom walls, but my mum put her foot down. After school one day, Nang, seeing how upset I looked, asked what the problem was. I told her. The following day, she pulled me aside at lunch and took out a couple of A3-sized folded slips of paper from her bag. I opened them up and broke out into the most widest smile ever. Nang had artistically drawn our dubz styles on paper so I could Blu-Tack them to my bedroom walls. She added mad sketches of us next to each name – an overgrown baby with a dummy in its mouth and tears running from its eyes, repping Nang.

We used all kinds of tings to create dubz. Marcus mainly tagged with spray paints and had a lot of artistic talent; his dubz was Marc Ecko quality. Roxy used the most fattest marker pens she tiefed from school and broke off the end of the nibs to make the pen leak thicker lines. I sometimes used black and white boot polish, because you could layer the polish on thick on a wall and it'd really stand out.

Anywhere we went, we'd tag. Station platforms, bus stations, on the roof of the buses, around the estates, in the parks. Any wall would do, although some walls are better than others. Ones already decorated in dubz weren't good, because nobody's gonna see your tag against the million others on there. A clean redbrick wall, one with no tags on it and faces out to a busy road, was gold dust. I'd be out and about with my fam and one of us might clock a virgin wall. That's it – bang. Out comes the spray cans and the permanent markers and the boot polish and we'd be dubbing.

You could always clock a Roxy dubz because she'd spend hours at walls by herself, tagging the names of every single girl in the fam. Next day, I'd set eyes on some wall and see Styles, Smiles, Nangs, Tantrum . . . bare names splashed across the brickwork. Sometimes the mandem put us up on their dubz as well. We had such a mad phase of dubbing that certain days it seemed like every time we got off the bus or walked down a street, we'd clock our names. Every time I sprayed I felt more and more like Chyna was the real me. My rep was my life, and after a while no one in local endz knew me as anything other than Chyna. Only Mum called me by my real name. Even my sister and my cousins called me Chyna.

To this day our dubz are visible on the old estate in Wood Hall.

EIGHT

No more room for bad girls

Sweetz and Tooth were both part of a crew known as 3G: Grams to Grands Gang. 3G got into a serious madness with a bunch of boys that used to go to our school, a rival crew who rolled under the name Mash Boys, so called because a mash man is a gunman and that's what they dreamed of being. The Mash Boys and 3G would chase each other down with knives, axes, hammers, shotguns . . . anything that they could get hold of. The beef became so deep that every time someone from the Mash Boys laid eyes on Sweetz or Tooth, it escalated into a paid-up fight.

Two of the Mash Boys bredrin were Joker, Malene's boyfriend, and a boy by the name of Younger Shark, who I knew well. Roxy had gone primary school together with him. He had a hard face, didn't dare let his guard down, a rack of gold teeth that could fill a jewellery counter and deep-black skin. Shark carried himself in a way that intimidated a lot of people at school. Part of that rep, I reckon, came from his brother, Older Shark, who was in a gang called the Mash Men, the kind of older version of the Mash Boys. Older Shark had a notorious rep, and Younger Shark took it upon himself to keep up the name.

The rivalry between Mash Boys and 3G was intense. I'm

talking repeated heated street fights, similar to our run-ins with the HBC. The whole world heard about the beef between them two. Hundreds of dubz from 3G and Mash Boys sprang up throughout our endz, each crew v'ing the other one out.

One time Sweetz and his two cousins were waiting at the bus-stop. As the bus drew up to the stop, Sweetz clocked a bunch of Mash Boys onboard. Bare of them. Knowing that they were outnumbered and would get mashed in a dust-up, Sweetz and his cousins legged it. But one of his cousins was over slow, and the Mash Boys caught up with him and sank an axe into his back.

The cousin ended up in hospital for long.

Eventually Sweetz and Younger Shark decided to have it out in a fight and rocked it out at the back of the cemetery lining our route home from school. The graveyard splits into two at the middle point, with a gated alley in between, and a big crowd of us went along to watch. Sweetz and Younger Shark bucked up, with bare of us girls looking on, as well as their olders in Year 11. The rules for the fight were one-on-one, which meant no one was allowed to jump in. No weapons, no tools, just the two boys slugging it out.

One-on-ones hardly ever stayed that way, regardless of what had been agreed before the fight. The same for us girls. If Roxy, Styles or Pasha was in a scrap and the girl she was up against was licking her, the rest of us would soon jump in to lend a hand. But in the knock-up between Sweetz and Shark, they stuck to the one-on-one rule across three brutal rounds, both boys going at it heavily. They finished with no clear winner, both of them wounded, their faces bruised, their noses snorting cherry-red blood, their lips inflated purple, like bicycle inner tubes.

Younger Shark didn't come back to school after that, but I'd get to know his brother, Older Shark, a lot better in a few years' time.

In later years, their lives were to turn gash. Straight after they quit school, the same year as me, Sweetz and Tooth got sucked into all the stuff that they lectured us against. Another boy Sweetz was close to also got shot up. Sweetz took it really bad. Sweetz, who'd never touched a spliff before in his life, took to smoking weed hard. Later, he went jail for robbing loads of travel agents up and down London roads. One event is enough to make a person change, shift into rage mode and seek out the street life. His good friend Tooth went down for armed robbery. But that all came later.

A couple of weeks later, Fierce called me out of the blue. The operator asked me would I accept a reverse-charge call from the girl. I said yes, wondering why she'd rung my house line rather than my mobile. I caught the sound of cars rushing past, the beeps of car horns and distant boydem sirens.

'Where are you?'

'At my nan's,' Fierce said.

'What's all that noise?'

'Got the window open, innit.'

'Why you reverse-charging these calls?'

'My nan ain't paid the bill. Listen, can I cotch with you for a while?'

'Sure,' I said.

Fierce stayed in my house that night. One night became two. Two became a week, and before I knew it, Fierce had slept at my house for a fortnight. All the time I didn't question her about why she wasn't going home. I figured that she had some trouble; maybe she'd been kicked out and was sleeping rough. It didn't seem right to stick my nose in and add to her grief. My mum and me welcomed Fierce into the household and gave her time to get her head straight.

'You can stay with us for as long as you like,' my mum said to Fierce.

I'm cool. It's all gravy to me. I was happy for my mum to let Fierce into my home. She was my friend and part of the fam, and we're rolling anyways on roads.

My family treated her like a sister. She was given money to buy new trainers, trousers and bras. Had herself a nice TV in her bedroom. But as she made herself comfortable, I started to realize that Fierce was taking the piss out of my mum. These times she'd link with Roxy, be on her period and not come back home of an evening. My mum ran a disciplined ship, and if Fierce didn't show, she'd wait up past midnight for her. Finally, two days later, she returned at midnight to the flat bustin' in bloody trousers and knickers and I thought, Rah, I'm not really feeling her living at my house.

One day, I caught her wearing my dirty knickers. That got me vexed. I had to allow her. She'd not grown up in a normal family and didn't know them nasty tings you shouldn't be doing. Street rats, they don't follow the normal rules of life. Eventually, tensions got a bit much between us and Fierce left to go and live somewhere else.

She was a scatty girl, Fierce, but although she made me vexed, I didn't blame her for the tings she did. Like, she didn't have no mummy and daddy to say to her, 'Rah, do this and don't do that.' But the hype split us up. Me and Fierce didn't talk to each other, and she didn't roll with the rest of N2L as much as before. When we cotched together, I had nothing to say to her.

A number of girls in our fam faced exclusion from school. We had a troublemaking rep and the teachers picked up on it. They wanted us out of the school. Styles, Tantrum, Split, all them lot were sent packing. They shut Fierce out for a year, leaving me as the only one of the original N2L at school. Pasha and Smiles was around but in the year below me. The only reason I hadn't been excluded was because my mum over appealed to the school's board of directors when I fucked up.

For virtually the whole of Year 10 I was on appeal. They dumped me in the Unit and from that day on I stopped caring about being excluded. In fact I went looking for it. I pulled my Eskimo hoodie tight over my head and the teachers shouted at me in front of the school. I'd bust in black

Princess corduroy jeans to school, breaking the dress code and goading the teachers to send me home. The school, I reckoned, was looking for any little ting that might lead to my exclusion and I was only too happy to turn their wish into a reality.

Fuck this, I thought, as I sat in front of my computer in information-technology class one morning. This is shit. None of my girls are here, I got another year of this crap to look forward to, and fuck these girls in my class. There's bare jezzies coming into my school thinking that they're hot. I worked myself up into rage mode. I'm not having this no more, I thought. I'm one of the top girls in school and suddenly I'm surrounded by new girls acting all bad. Top of the list was a girl called Leah. I told myself, This jezzy needs to understand that this is my school. I got a reputation already and there's no space for more bad girls. Another girl, Stella, I didn't like the bitch; she went on about how she was hot the whole time. On top of that, a couple of white girls kept banging on about how they was good-looking even though they was pure wastegash.

But I couldn't fight all them girls same time. Instead I wrote a letter, with a short paragraph dedicated to each jezzy.

50 Cent had just stormed the charts with his G-Unit, so I came up with the idea of J-Unit: the Jezzies Unit. The letter read:

THIS IS OUT TO ALL THE J-UNIT IN MY YEAR.
LEAH, YOU LOOK LIKE SOMEONE TAKEN OUT
CIGARETTE BUTTS IN YOUR LEGS. TO THAT
GIRL THAT WANTS TO SUCK DICK IN THE
CORRIDOR FOR HALF AN HOUR, YOU KNOW
WHO YOU ARE. TO THEM WHITE GIRLS THINK
THEY'RE HOT, YOUR HAIR LOOKS LIKE
SOMEONE YAKKED IN IT.

I rinsed them countless of times. I signed it at the end, YOU
LOT JUST GOT BOYED OUT BY CHYNA.

I printed out 2,000 copies, 1,000 apiece from two different printers, quit the classroom and dashed them literally
from the top to the bottom of the school, in the corridors,
outside the school, down the drive, in the fields. When that
class bell rang, every boy and girl stumbled upon a print-
out. By lunchtime, the whole school had read it, my dissing's
all around town, and I'm ready for the comeback.

At two thirty the last bell sounded. School's out. Still no
one had moved to me. I thought, This is a bit fishy. Surely
Leah or Stella should have confronted me by now. The whole
reason for writing the letter was to see which one of them
bad girls wanted it the most. At last I got a reaction. Leah
decided she wants a bit. Out in the drive, she went fucking
mental. 'Who's Chyna, reh, reh, reh? I'm gonna fuck her
up, reh, reh, reh.' Leah was new to the school and didn't
have a clue who Chyna was.

I stepped in Leah's face. 'I'm Chyna. What about it?'

'Rah, meet me in town centre,' she replied.

'Cools.' I went back home first to get changed. Stella meanwhile had got the letter and run back home to her mum, who promptly marched into Miss Fredericks's office. I'd printed the letter at ten o'clock that morning. By six o'clock same night, I was told I weren't welcome no more at Burnell. My mum went ballistic, but I didn't stick around to catch the full brunt of her venom. I had a beef to settle. Leah rang my phone, told me to meet her outside McDonald's. I rolled with my cousin Zara, expecting fifteen girls to confront me.

By the time we arrived, though, Leah had breezed.

Two weeks later, my mum had a meeting at school. Somehow she managed to get me reinstated. Leah called my mobile, offering me out.

'I hear you're back at school next week.'

'Worried I'll write more letters?'

'Fucking bring it,' Leah said.

Me and Roxy headed to Leah's house and waited outside for her to show. She took long. Should've brought a weapon with me, I thought. Leah might come out of her house with a ting, and I ain't got nothing but my fists.

This called for a change of tactics.

Normally in a fight, you'd let each other get ready before popping off shots with your fists, but I figured I was at a disadvantage, so I bent the rules. I heard the jangle of the key chain as Leah fiddled with it, and the click of the latch as she unlocked the front door.

Here it comes, I thought. Best move fast, because if you fuck this up, you're not gonna get no second chance.

The door cracked open.

I pounced.

Leah had time to spot my fists flying towards her, but not enough to avoid me telling her what time of day it was. I didn't give her a chance to catch her senses. Two clean fists, right then left, the bony edges of my knuckles bashing up against her jaw. 'Urgh,' she moaned, and fell on to her back as the door swung on its hinges.

I'd dazed Leah. She weren't about to give in that easily, though. I didn't expect her to. You're fighting to protect your rep, because someone dissed you, and if you lose, everyone on the endz will be gossiping about how so-and-so's a soft touch. More people step to you, thinking, Rah, this girl's a pushover. That's why I fighted on the front foot, because you had good odds of winning with an aggressive style.

Back on her feet, Leah swung at me. She caught me on the shoulder. My instinct was to shuffle out of range, but I knew I had to put her down again. Ignoring the pain, I put a rapid set of punches – one, two, three – in her face. She crumpled.

I hoped the fight was over. Leah had four inches on me and long, stretched arms that could damage a girl's face. My plan had been to sock it to Leah quick and mean, burning her before she had a chance to strike.

For a second time, Leah pulled herself up. I noticed her left hand reach behind her. She whipped out a ten-inch kitchen knife from the back of her jeans.

My eyes settled on the tip of the knife. I sorely regretted not boxing her head in more when she was flat out. I should've moved in for the kill, I thought. I was afraid of getting shanked, seen other girls get stabbed and it looked fucking painful.

Leah charged me, slashing the knife towards my head. I almost froze with fear, then ducked at the last second. The blade swiped thin air. I had to finish this now, otherwise I'd be on the wrong end of that blade. Leah had a heavy swing, and as her arm went in an arc, I darted sideways and booted her in the chest. She crumbled. I booted her again. She stayed down. I grabbed the knife. Leah was out of it. I had her where I wanted her.

I could've ended the fight there and then, but the rage I'd first felt when my dad boxed up my mum and when Styles got attacked outside the shubz, it sparked up, like my insides was catching fire, my belly and my hands and my heart. I stood over Leah and raised the knife. I wanted to paint her red.

A hand gripped my wrist. A voice shouted for me to stop. *Roxy.*

She disarmed me, saved me from stabbing the girl and hurting her real bad. Maybe worse. I'd like to say my rage mode vanished, but it didn't. I still worked on Leah as she lay on the ground. Payback for spinning a dirty trick on me with the knife. She'd tried to attack me with a weapon, and she deserved an extra beating in return.

'And don't you ever pull no knife on me again,' I said to Leah as me and Roxy split.

The school told me I wouldn't never be coming back. Said they'd keep me registered at the school but I'd do my studies at a local college. I reckon they thought giving me the boot meant they'd wiped their hands of me. They probably didn't know how happy I was when I learned the news. Now I got more time to tief, I thought, and cotch with my fam.

Roxy began rolling with a girl called Paige, who she'd met at the all-girls' school she'd been transferred to. She told me she was scared about changing to a new scene because they didn't appreciate her status. But from the moment she sat in registration, all her stresses vanished. She recognized girls from the street, people she associated with on the roadside. She skived constantly, her and Paige.

Paige had jezzy status. With her short, wavy hair and distinctive Jamaican patois, Paige stood out from the crowd. Her family adopted her at a young age and took her in, but they let her basically run riot.

If Paige had a jezzy rep, I was known as a jezzy hater. I beated on jezzy girls, victimized slag-bags from school. If I spotted a slag in the park, I'd violate her. Take what she's got and chief her up. There was no way I would ever roll with nasty girls who fucked someone else's man, offering up their gash for anyone who wanted a quick pump.

One time Paige slept with the boyfriend of a friend of mine called Jessica. The fam supported me when I said I intended to move to Paige and cave her in. We found her hanging at the Foot Locker in town centre. Roxy was next to her. While bare of my girls threatened Paige, Roxy approached and tried to defuse tings.

'Leave Paige alone, cuz,' she said to me. 'She's my girl.' Meaning she'd back her up. Even if it meant trading blows with her own fam.

'You don't wanna be rolling with this slag,' I told Roxy. 'That girl holds the gold medal for sucking dick.'

'She's been good to me,' Roxy protested.

'That bitch fucked Jessica's man.'

'Shit happens, Chyna. The boy don't want Jessica and she's done with him, so what's the problem? Either way – Roxy, folding her arms – 'I'm not letting you lot attack Paige.' In Roxy's eyes, boxing Paige was disrespecting Roxy.

Before my girls could jump Paige, Roxy shoved her into the Superdrug opposite the Foot Locker.

'You lot come in here,' she said, guarding the doorway, 'you're gonna have to fuck me up first.'

No way could we set hands on Roxy. She was inner-circle fam. We checked for each other, rolled and had bare walls dubbed with our names together in the N2L crew. Secretly I was relieved that we didn't have to cause a major hype with

Roxy, even though I had a desperate urge to lick Paige for what she did to Jessica.

I tried to level with Roxy when we chilled away from the fam.

'That girl's gonna bring down your rep, cuz,' I said.

'Rah, the mandem know who I am, are you stupid?' She paused. 'You know what your problem is, Chyna? You and Paige are too alike.'

I frowned. 'What d'you mean?'

'You both think you're on it, don't you see? Look, she's facey, you're facey. She's rude, you're rude. She don't give a fuck, you—'

'This is some mind-game lark, cuz. Me and Paige is like chalk and cheese.'

'Chalk and chalk, more like.'

I cooled off, thought about it some more and realized that me and Paige did have a few tings in common. In my teenage years I was hostile and hyped, aggressive and flip. Unless I fronted, people would take advantage of me. I worried they'd smell any sign of weakness from a mile off.

I knew that in order to survive, I'd have to be on it 24/7, streetwise and tough. A lot of the girls understood this. Paige included.

NINE

Squashing it

The Hard-Bodied Chix maintained the heat on us big-time. The beef seemed like it had gone on since for ever with no end in sight.

A few months before the end of Year 11, Malene jumped Pasha in town on the weekend. With two of her Chix in tow, Malene boxed Pasha bad, mashed her peng face into something like a rotten apple. That proved to be the last straw.

As a battered Pasha described the Malene attack, I boiled up, over mad, ready to jump out my skin. When my girls was in fights, I couldn't stand by and watch; it was too close to my heart. My heart would be pounding, my palms sweating, I'd be feeling every punch thrown – and suddenly I'd join in, unable to let it go on any further.

The beef had brought our fam together, but that's not the whole story. You don't get the kind of love we had for each other simply through someone else hating on you. We'd created our unique family, somewhere all of us could feel understood and supported. These times I didn't tell my mum nothing about my goings-on. Roxy kept her life secret from her parents. Same for most of the fam. Styles had strife with her blood family. When the Chix attacked one of our bredrin, it hurt us emotionally. We all felt the pain. We'd been warring it for so long, we were tired – exhausted, even. I didn't want my girls to get hurt no more.

'How long's it been?' Nang asked.

'Long?' Roxy blinked. She took a long drag on a spliff, but the weed wasn't cheering her mood. 'You mean . . . the beef?' She shrugged. 'That shit's been long. Ever since Malene stepped to Styles.'

'And how long ago was that?'

'Four years ago.'

'Rah, long.'

We'd been in Year 7 when the hype went down at the original shubz. Since then it'd been constant warfare, all the way through to us hitting Year 11, fifteen years old, fucking back and forth, back and forth with the Chix.

'This could go on for another four,' Nang said, clicking the front part of her tongue against her mouth. 'Ain't no telling when this is gonna end. I don't wanna have to watch my back in town when I'm twenty, do you feel me?'

'You know what, fuck it,' I said. 'Nang's right. This has gone on too long. We need to end this beef.'

'But how?' Styles asked. 'The girls will keep fighting us. It's not like we can walk away.'

'True dat,' I said. 'So maybe we make them an ultimatum.'

'Winner takes all, you mean?' Nang asked. I nodded, handing her the half-smoked spliff. She took a big drag on it, giving off smoke from her nostrils. 'And you know what else? We should squash it today, bruv.'

I nodded. 'If we're gonna do it, let's do it.'

This time we didn't phone no one from the Chix. We didn't want to lay a warning that we was coming. Instead, we reached out to the rest of our fam and arranged to hook up that afternoon. With the full N2L girldem we marched down to the bus station. The HBC couldn't hide from us. Not this time.

We hit the bus station right after school's out. Bare girls from our endz clocked our fam rocking up and looked suspiciously at us, as if they understood what was gonna go down this day. The bus returned from Abbott. Malene exited, we steeled ourselves, peering out through the crowd of girls to count the other Chix, and . . . the last girl hopped off the bus, not a sniff of the Chix among them.

'Shit, cuz, Malene's alone,' Roxy said.

'Well, what are we waiting for?' Nang spat on the ground.

We stepped to her as a group. Malene saw us approaching and bricked it. She dug out her mobile and speed-dialled a number on her mobile.

'Fucking stay back,' she said. 'I'm gonna call my sister and she'll get every girldem in South on your cases.'

'Look' – I closed in on her. This was as near as any of us had been to a rival gang member in four years without hurling a punch or a shank – 'we don't wanna keep on doing this.'

Malene was silent. All by herself, enemy girls surrounding her . . . She was chiefed. A dozen pairs of hostile eyes burned holes in her. She studied our faces, as if trying to work out which one of us would box her up.

I pressed her. 'You're leaving school soon. Same for us. We can't go on fighting for ever.'

Malene shifted on her feet.

'So tell me,' I said, 'who's your beef with?'

Malene didn't answer. Our rivalry had gone on so long none of us knew what it was about any more. They'd violated Styles a few times and popped her chain, but that shit had been avenged again and again. The way of the roads is, someone beats on you, you beat on them twice. Send a message. But if that person's beating on you in *another* revenge, you forget what the original beef was about. It becomes endless beef after endless beef.

'Answer me, Malene.'

She snorted, eyefucking me. No doubt, if it was one-on-one, me and her, we'd be fighting, but circled by a posse of N2L girls, Malene had no choice but to take it.

'All right,' she replied, eyes flicking from girl to girl. 'I got a problem with her . . . and her.'

She pointed at Styles.

And Pasha.

Styles I understood, because in my eyes the Chix – really and truly Malene – was jealous of Styles. Styles's a very peng girl. You'd hear boys in class saying to each other, 'That girl is *choong*, blud.' That's why Malene hated on her. But Pasha? I didn't get it.

'OK,' I said. 'Phones your people and get them to come down to the estate. But on one condition: *you*'ve gotta fight one of these girls. No one else but you.' I jabbed a finger in her chest.

'Who's it gonna be?'

'Pasha.'

'Sorted, then.'

We met an hour later. The venue, a local estate near my flat, a new-build block where everything has a fresh lick of paint and is bright and clean. And somewhere neutral, where no gang owns these endz. The estate had a big field in the centre of it, like an arena hemmed in by the tower blocks. That's where we decided to hold the fight.

The weather was golden. Sun doing its ting up in the sky. Kids running after the ice-cream van or playing football in the streets.

As well as our fam, people who were affiliated with us linked up on the way over. Our olders, friends from other gangs, my cousin, Roxy's cousin Sonita . . . As we entered the estate, it felt like the whole of South was behind us.

Into the estate and we clocked the Hard-Bodied Chix straight up, forming a semi-circle in the field in the shadow of the blocks. Word about the fight had spread. Bare people gathered. Even the shotters took a break from selling food to the ill-looking cats. Cats are what we called drug addicts. I felt tense, caned a Mayfair to skell myself. Tar smoke tickled my throat.

'Fuck me, bruv,' Nang said. 'Is that Malene's *mum*?'

I squinted. 'It is.'

This ratty, titchy, light-skinned woman with a weave in her hair marched down to the field, Malene by her side. In the mum's hands was a present for her daughter: a monkey wrench wrapped in a kitchen towel. As they drew near, Malene's big sister, Trinique, gave her tips on what to do in the fight, how to move and swing the monkey wrench for biggest hits.

I turned to Pasha, seen how she was holding up. Looking at her, I thought to myself, Rah, Malene's picked the youngest one out of all of us, thinking she'd be the easiest target, pinning her hopes on defeating a younger girl. Malene knew Styles would've boxed her up. She'd bloodied boys' noses, was beautiful but deadly.

But Pasha's appearance was deceiving. She stood tall as Malene and had a similar build, although she was slimmer and more girlish in her shape than manly Malene. Pasha could get her own; she had a determined look in her eyes.

We formed our own semi-circle, creating a ring round the girls. Malene's mum ran her mouth behind her daughter, loud as a sound system.

'You wanna fight my daughter? She'll fucking lick you, pickney!' Reh, reh, reh, she banged on like this the whole time, trying to intimidate my fam.

'Don't worry about them.' I put my arm around Pasha. 'You're a top brawler. Go and do what you need to do, because we can't go jumping in there to help you.'

'I get it,' Pasha said. 'If you lot jump in, they're gonna say it's unfair and want more from us.'

'That's right,' Tantrum said back. 'And it starts all over.'

'Fuck that. I'm gonna drop this clown so hard she'll be hearing the sound of her beating for the rest of her life.'

Pasha moved to Malene.

First round, Pasha wasted no time and got stuck right in. Malene was bare-fisted, but I could see the mum clutching the monkey wrench and knew that at the first sign of her daughter in trouble, she was gonna give it her. Pasha side-stepped a blow from Malene, grabbed her from behind and hooded her, sending the girl to the ground before Pasha smacked her face with the smooth bone of her knee. *Crack.* Malene was stunned. The Chix bitched and shouted, and a few seconds later, Malene staggered back to her feet, her face splashed with surprise. She hadn't expected Pasha to be so talented.

'You fuck up my daughter, I'm fucking you up,' the mum said. She'd been shouting for long and her voice was reduced to a scratchy screech, like fingernails dragging along a blackboard.

Desperate not to lose in front of all the Chix, Malene got a second wind and teemed punches at Pasha, swinging this way and that.

'Come on!' Malene shouted.

Second round was scuffing, scuffing, scuffing. Malene connected twice, but Pasha ain't the kind of girl to go down under a couple of pops to the face. When Malene was done going wild with her hands, breathless and seen that Pasha wasn't floored, she shook her head. Malene had banked on a routine slap-up when she selected Pasha. She was wrong. Round two ended all-square. At the start of the third, Malene's mum chucked her daughter the monkey wrench.

'Smack her in the face,' she screamed. '*Fuck her up!*'

I feared for my fam. Licking a girl in a fistfight was one ting; beating on a girl armed with a monkey wrench, when you've not got a weapon, is ten times more harder. I remembered how upset I'd been when the Chix mashed Styles. I couldn't bear to see Pasha blown up like that.

'Maybe we should step to the Chix,' I said to Nang.

'Wait a minute. Pasha can handle herself.'

Malene leaned back and swung the monkey wrench towards Pasha.

'Are you ready? *Are you fucking ready?*'

Malene rushed towards Pasha, bringing the wrench down hard. Pasha jerked to the left, but not enough to dodge what was coming. The wrench thumped into her shoulder. Pasha stumbled. For a moment I thought she'd drop. If she goes down, I thought, I'm jumping in there to help. But Pasha managed to stay on her feet. In a snapshot she tore the wrench out of Malene's hands. Disarmed, she looked vulnerable. Glanced at Trinique and her mum as if to say, 'What now?'

Malene reached for the wrench, but it had dropped out of reach. Pasha socked one straight to her nose and followed through, knocking Malene on to her arse. Now she really went to town, sitting on top of her enemy, punching like a firing piston, fist after fist. Pasha beated Malene up so bad that the other Chix booed, forcing her mum to step in and drag Malene out of the way. Still running her mouth, but this time at her bloodied and bruised offspring.

Pasha heckled Malene as she departed.

The long-running beef with the HBC came to an end.

The crowd moped about, the youngers and tinies re-enacting the fight, the olders passing judgement on it. Everyone congratulated Pasha for giving Malene a licking she over deserved. That night we had a big celebration. I went home, got changed, left my endz for the first time without a shank or a slipper sock and met up with the fam. We smoked draw and drank vodka at a nearby hostel. Pasha's phone went haywire as bare people called asking for the score. She got increased status for flattening an older girl with a hardened rep.

The problem with beefs is, they're like boys. Soon as you're done with one, another shows up.

*

These times I had my first crush. I didn't like none of the boys in school. In N2L we used to hang with the boys but didn't check them out in a special way; I thought every boy in school was immature. Any way you put it, girls mature quicker than boys, and in my eyes, I couldn't be attracted to basically little boys.

With that kind of attitude, it was probably inevitable that my first boyfriend would be someone a lot older. Kendrick was in his mid-twenties, a notorious man who eventually got sent down for attempted murder. Stocky, skin like black leather, he resembled 50 Cent, decked out in his name-brand jeans and neat waistcoats, bare pairs of leather shoes. He was the Prada man: Prada shoes, watches, shirts, hats. When he went out, he was very snazzy, not like the boys at school, with their scruffy trousers, washed-out tops and hoodies tugged low over their faces. Kendrick looked sharp. His eyes were scary, fixed in his sockets like black moons.

Kendrick had a lot more status than the boys in school. He had his own place: open-plan kitchen and front room with laminate flooring and modern furniture, supersize TV and expensive hi-fi. I'd sneak out my mum's house when she went to bed at eleven o'clock, skip to Kendrick's place and come back at five o'clock in the morning, before she'd gotten up for work.

At first, I didn't want Kendrick to have my number.

A group of us knew a girl by the name of Sharise who

lived on the same endz as me. We'd chill at her mum's home of a night; Sharise's mum was an alcoholic, and long as we sorted her out liquor-wise, she'd allow us to smoke weed in her house. Sweet, I thought. No more pulling on draw out of my bedroom window and getting shit from my mum about 'skonk'. I'd turn up with £8 in coins so she could buy herself a bottle of £7.99 Sainsbury's own-brand vodka.

Now, because I lived close to Sharise, every single time I went home I had to go past her house. Bare boys shotted out the front. I got to know a few of them well.

Rips was a mixed-race boy who had this sort of playful, innocent look in his eyes. On the outside he looked like any other boy on the roads, bustin' his low batties, Adidas creps and hoodie permanently down over his face, but he had ambitions to break out of the endz and start up his own grime label, and when he was by himself, he'd be dropping bars and spitting riddims.

I vaguely knew this boy Wallace from when he dated Bigs. He was big-time flash and always looked nice and groomed, bustin' designer threads. Mummy looked after him. I liked something about him, though the fact he had a reputation for being a playa made me wary.

I had nothing but love for Safon, but I'd be lying if I said he weren't known as the tramp of the group. He didn't go in for fresh garmz; he'd sport the same pair of dirty old creps for long. Safon wasn't lazy – he just steered clear of the shotting game, earning nowhere near same sterling as the rest of the mandem. Safon's speciality was jacking rims. That work only pays out in dribs and drabs.

Kevin was known as the mouthy one. He was also the most biggest and successful shotter out of his mandem.

Stocks got his name from the fact he was the short and squat boy of the pack. His ting was comics. Incredible Hulk, X-Men, Spiderman, Captain America . . . Whilst the other boys spent their p's on motors and peds, Stocks was buying up collectable editions of *Preacher* or *2000 AD* and banging on about Iron Man's special powers.

Then there was Nugz, who inherited his tag from the fact he was a very big boy who spent half his life in Chicken Cottages and Dixie Chickens and loved his nuggets. He was a little-fish shotter and burglar. And he paid special attention to his hair. Busted stylish cornrows with a bit of a long plait at the back of his head.

Kendrick was their deela.

He asked Sharise who I was; she gave him the word. Then he wanted my number. I'd walk past their house and Kendrick would call to me, 'Come here,' trying to check me. I blagged it and walked on. I'd heard about Kendrick and didn't want to get involved. Girls told me he was a road man in the drugs business, that he wasn't the type of person to fuck about with.

One day, I was cotching in my room when my phone went. Number not recognized. I answered it.

Kendrick's under-low voice said, 'Come down, Chyna. I'm outside your house.'

'But . . .'

'I'm here. Come outside,' Kendrick said. 'I want to talk to you.'

My little brother, Devan, had the room with the front view, so I went into his bedroom and peered through the curtains. Parked on the road was a dark-green Golf GTI Mark 4 with tinted windows.

I found out later that Rips and Wallace, who shotted for Kendrick, gave him my phone number when he leaned on them for it. Kendrick could be a persuasive man.

I reluctantly went outside. We started talking. He said he liked me. I was confused, as I'd seen Kendrick as this big, tough, intimidating man. I didn't expect him to come round to some fifteen-year-old girl's place expressing his feelings and whatnot. When he asked me if I wanted to hang out, I said, 'Yeah, why not. Go with the flow.' And I know this sounds strange, but I wasn't scared. In fact, I saw it as a bit of a challenge. I liked to live dangerously and there was no man with a badder rep than Kendrick.

The rumours about Kendrick made me curious; if someone tells you that this person or that person is dangerous, some people will run away, while others will want to find out what that person's really like.

I also enjoyed the fact he was so obsessive about me. In our endz, every girl wanted to either sleep with Kendrick or be with him. He had everything a girl desired: he was ballin', had status and power; he looked fly. For long I was the only girl that turned him down. To have him chasing me felt good.

Once we linked, nobody could step to me in our area. *Nobody.* Anyone tried to mess with me, they'd get licked. As Kendrick's girlfriend, a little bit of his power rubbed off on me, and it went straight to my head.

He was also the boy who broke my virginity.

Quite a few of my girls had lost their virginity. They talked about their first times, the conversation going over my head. Then I got very curious about sex. Some girls told me, 'Go ahead and do it'; others said to wait until I was ready, not to rush it. I sensed that I was ready to break my virginity with Kendrick. My breasts had started to push out and I found myself becoming more and more interested in boys sexually.

For all his faults, Kendrick felt like the right man to have my first time with. I didn't want no little boy from school. If I slept with a school boy, he'd tell everyone how he done it, where he done it, what positions he did, how much times. That's all long, and it happened to each and every girl in that situation. I'd rather be breaking it with a man I'm in a proper relationship with, where I'm not uncomfortable and it's just another part of us being together. Kendrick had his faults, but I could trust him not to blast the news around town after I'd slept with him.

And to be fair, he was good about my first time.

So I liked him at first. But then, as he grew more casual

around me, I seen a darker side to his personality. I learned the truth about Kendrick. He was badder than most everybody, randomly beating up mandem from bare endz. One time he chased down some shotter who owed him £500. That level of p's was fuck all to Kendrick, but he liked excuses to go and mash people. When he eventually found this shotter, Kendrick knocked off his face with his pistol butt. Another time, Kendrick whacked some boy's ear clean off with the curved end of a crowbar.

He used to run his mouth at me. Unlike most girls, I wasn't scared of Kendrick and I'd answer him back if he cussed or threatened me. He never did nothing to me, but I felt like he was everywhere and I didn't have no room to breathe. Rah, I told myself, I shouldn't have started nothing with this boy. If I'd known the full story, no way would I have ever gone out with him. But what's done is done.

I tried to avoid Kendrick after that, cooling tings off between us.

TEN

Mad in da head

Of all the girls in our endz, Ashleigh was truly mad in the head.

Although she was never in the fam, Ashleigh had hung around with various of girldem of ours since the early days at Burnell. Back in Years 8 and 9, she'd proven herself an expert tief on the rob with me and Roxy. Her tricks of the trade – getting cash refunds on bras and whatnot – came in handy, but Ashleigh also had a rep as a street rat. Her mum was a heroin addict, and the kids of crackheads are often messed upstairs. She also had mad dress sense, proper Yardie style with every single ting loud and colourful and mad pattern combinations, floral prints and stripes and whatnot . . . She busted in over short skirts that barely covered her bum.

Maybe it was all the burnin' she attracted, but Ashleigh fighted bare girls, her versus three or four, and beat each and every one of them up. Boys used to get Ashleigh to fight other boys for them. No one actively seeked to scrap with Ashleigh, unless they had a death wish.

I'd sometimes bump into Ashleigh on the roads at Sharise's house. Sharise was the girl whose alkie mum we'd bribe with bottles of Sainsbury's voddie to smoke weed indoors. Wallace, Stocks and Nugz would shot from the house. There was always a gathering of boys and girls outside Sharise's, and as I walked past her place on my way home every day, I sometimes bumped into Ashleigh.

After dance class one day, this girl called Jelan said to me, 'You know your friend Ashleigh? Tell her to mind who she's watching.'

I figured that Ashleigh and Jelan had thrown each other screw-faces – and that Jelan had decided, since I saw Ashleigh on the regs, I should be the messenger.

I didn't get the chance – the next day, Styles seen Ashleigh about in town and said, 'Jelan will knock you out, you know. Mind how you looking at her.'

Ashleigh ignored the warning. Intimidating her was like trying to spit at the moon. She had it in her head that she was the baddest girl around, bar none. If anything, threatening Ashleigh only made her more stoked. The following day, she moved to Jelan, confronting her in the street accompanied by her mandem, full-on boying her up. Ashleigh took her phone; Jelan snatched it back. Little scrubble followed, and the phone dropped down a nearby drain. Having fucked up her phone, Ashleigh went one better and booted her on the bum as she stepped on a bus, shouting, 'Get on the fucking bus, rot girl.'

Jelan told us what happened at the next dance class. Ashleigh was absent. She collared me and Styles, blaming us for the hype. 'You told Ashleigh shit and spreaded lies about me,' she said.

'Nah, bruv, it ain't like that.'

'You'd best make this up' – scrunching her nose and resting her hands on her hips. She didn't believe a word of mine and Styles's protest.

'Make up what? We didn't do nothing,' I said.

'Just tell me where I can find Ashleigh.'

'If that's the way you want it,' I replied. 'But I ain't a part of this beef. This is strictly you and Ashleigh.'

We hit Sharise's house. No doubt, I thought, Ashleigh would be at Sharise's, doing her ting. Roxy and Styles tagged along. All of us smelled a big fight cooking.

Six o'clock on a Friday night, school's out and the weather was melting-hot. People in the streets shuffled along like they was drugged up. We reached Sharise's road, smell of weed greeted me, pungent and spicy. Thirty metres away and I heard the girls mouthing off and chatting with the mandem, 'So Grimey' by So Solid Crew playing. Among the voices I heard a scratchy, squealing laugh: Ashleigh. She was there, necking from large bottles of peach-flavour Lambrini.

Ashleigh was piss-drunk, so off her face that she had difficulty remembering who we were. Then she seen Jelan looking at her. She gulped the rest of the peach Lambrini and chucked the bottle into the street. It smashed into a hundred broken pieces, bits of glass starring the road.

'What is it?' she said, wiping her sticky mouth with the back of her hand.

'Watch youself,' I said to Jelan. 'This girl ain't right.'

'It's cool, blud. I'm a sort this out.'

'But, Ashleigh—'

'Screw this sket. I'm not gonna be violated like that.'

Jelan was in Ashleigh's face. 'What's the problem, blud? You intimidated me yesterday, but I ain't done nothing to you.'

'You flipping breathed,' Ashleigh said, rising to her feet.

Jelan went to open her mouth.

She never got the words out.

Ashleigh hocked shit up in her lungs. Spat out this big ball of saliva the consistency of slime. It landed bang right on Jelan's neck. She looked down in shock as this rank splodge of snot-coloured phlegm greased down until it reached the lining of her top.

Jelan spat right back, her gob smack-landing on Ashleigh's lips.

I'd never seen Jelan in a fight and had no idea what she was about. From what I'd heard, she was a good girl who went to college and such, and her ambition was to be a professional gymnast. She worked out, practised boxing and was well into her fitness. Jelan wasn't massive, but her body was built of muscle. Physically Ashleigh was weaker and normally I'd not give her a shot, but she had bare fighting skills. Bare times I'd seen her pick up a tool and stab somebody without blinking.

Ashleigh sprang to her feet and rushed Jelan.

Jelan smacked Ashleigh – bang – right to the centre of the head. Stunned, Ashleigh stumbled backwards, her eyes rolling in the back of her head as if she'd suffered a whitey. Jelan caught up with Ashleigh, dropped her shoulder, launched another fist at her. Something *cracked*, like a strip of wood breaking in half. The second punch crushed her. Ashleigh flopped, kissing concrete, her legs and arms spreaded. Then her best friend was kneeling beside her and shouting, 'Wake up! Wake up!'

She was conked out for Britain.

'Shit,' Styles said. 'You fucking killed her.'

I'm like, Oh. My. Days. Ashleigh was still.

'That sket ain't merked. She's just out cold,' Jelan said.

A minute later, Ashleigh's body twitched. She wriggled her fingers and toes. Like a zombie coming back to life. The sick feeling in my tummy, that we might be witness to a murder, vanished. We scattered, Ashleigh's friend shouting at our backs, 'Just you fucking wait!'

Their beef with us wasn't no gang ting, but the way they saw it, we'd set Ashleigh up, showing Jelan where she chilled so she could move to her. I saw tings differently. Jelan was gonna box Ashleigh up no matter what. Me and Styles taking her to Sharise's place didn't change the hate boiling between the two girls.

The wait was no long ting. We were in the last few weeks of school before we broke up for GCSE finals and Ashleigh had to act now if she wanted her revenge. Me and Styles were bait targets – Jelan were a few years older than us, in college, and Ashleigh couldn't get to her easily like she could us. I got a phone call from Ashleigh. Her voice on the phone was fucked up from where her jaws was swelled up. She sounded the way people do after going dentist.

'Rah, you set me up,' she said. 'This is your fault.'

'Listen to youself, Ashleigh. You're talking dumb.'

'You brought Jelan down to the endz.'

'Yeah, and you binned her phone. She wanted to see where you was. Why do I give a fuck what happens between you?'

'I don't forgets, Chyna. You and Styles, I'm looking for you. Come down Sharise's and see what happens.'

End of call. I went round to Styles's house and we smoked weed in her bedroom. We should have been happy to finally check out of the school system, but instead we were depressed. Both of us thinking the same ting: we've survived one beef and now we're diving straight into another one. I wasn't afraid of Ashleigh, but I didn't need the hassle of a dust-up with her, especially as I now heard she had a fondness for shankings. That's how she rolled. My game was about punching and stamping on people, but I never went in for shanking. When I saw people stabbed, my body cringed. But, Ashleigh liked nothing more than to shank you and laugh in your face afterwards. She'd cut you with whatever she could get her hands on. Blade, kitchen knife, screwdriver.

'Some boy been talking,' Styles told me. 'Word is, Ashleigh's gonna slice you up.'

'Nah, man, she's just hyping.'

'For real, fam. You know what else she said?'

'Don't tell me.'

'She's gonna draw you a clown smile.'

This is where the person cuts you from ear to ear. I've seen girls with the scars from a smiley face and they ain't never finding no man to love them.

'I said don't fucking tell me.'

'I'm worried about you, Chyna. Look out for youself.'

These times bare people called my phone. My fam, the mandem, other boys and girls. They're like, 'Don't go outside without us,' but I'm firming it, playing it cool. I'd been through my fair share of shit for longs with the Hard-Bodied Chix and no way was I prepared to suffer the same shit twice. Blanking my bredrin's advice, I showed my face around the endz by myself.

Of course, I knew what Ashleigh was capable of, but I told myself, I'm gonna face this threat down. With some people, there ain't no reasoning with them. You just have to deal with whatever shit they're throwing your direction, and be prepared.

A week passed. On the Saturday night, I went to a christening party for one of my friends who'd just dropped a baby. The dad was fifteen, the mum eighteen. People affiliated to my cousin Zara were there and they knew the boy's people. I made up my mind to go along. All my girls texted me, don't attend because Ashleigh's gonna be there. I felt a bit anxious inside. If me and Ashleigh got in a fight and she turned psycho, I might end up in hospital. She was a volatile girl, and I really didn't know what to expect when she clocked me. But I was determined not to let her ruin my social life. I firmed. I showed.

The party was held in a big hall the new mum and dad had rented out for how much hours. I arrived with Styles, the rest of my fam doing various of tings. Just us two feeling the vibe. Seated at a table at the other end of the room was Mz Wrong in de Head.

Ashleigh eyeballed us. She'd turned her chair away from the tables, giving her back to her girls, arms crossed, tapping her foot on the floor. Her electric-green eyes bugging me. I blanked her and chatted with my girls.

An hour skipped, and some boy approached me.

'Come outside,' he said. 'Now.'

'Why the fuck do I wanna go out for?'

I knew why, but I decided to play dumb. Buy myself extra time to think.

'Ashleigh wants to talk to you.'

Talking. That wasn't the only ting on the menu, I was sure.

'Chyna, let's breeze out of here,' Styles said.

'No, let's do it,' I said. 'No point running away from this.' I looked at the boy. 'I'll meet her.'

Styles tried to persuade me otherwise, but my mind was settled. The one lesson I learned from the HBC madness was, if you got a beef, crush it.

I didn't underestimate Ashleigh. Before we left the party, I pretended to go to the toilet, detouring into the kitchen. Raking through the drawers, I found the most biggest and sharpest knife and slipped it up the left sleeve of my hoodie, tip of the blade sticking out. This knife was sick. Fourteen inches, sharp as one of my dad's samurai blades at the end. Ting could slice through steel. Now I was tooled up and ready to confront Ashleigh.

Ashleigh waited for me at the end of the street with ten of her bredrin. Bare other people gathered around. As I drew closer, I felt for the handle to the knife, at my elbow, with my right hand. The only thought going through my head was, I'm going to have to shank this girl.

Ashleigh leered at me and Styles.

'Which one of you wants to get it?'

I brushed my hair out of my face. Took a deep breath, holding in my nerves, and said calmly, 'Which one do you want to give it to, Ashleigh?'

She stepped directly into my face. I felt the air hissing out of her nostrils.

'Do you really want it, Chyna?' she said. '*Do you really, truly want it?*'

'Listen, Ashleigh,' I said, fighting to keep my voice under control. I wanted to take the sting out of her anger. 'You're the one mouthing off,' I said. 'You need to tell us what you want to do, because none of us are sending out threats. No one snaked on you. If we didn't bring down Jelan, she would've come along with her own people and it'd be a different story.'

Ashleigh pointed her finger at Styles. 'She's the one that I got a problem with.'

That sent Styles wild. She dashed out her own knife. Styles had the same idea as me and tiefed her own blade from the kitchen. She thrashed it about, pointing the tip towards Ashleigh.

'What is it, Ashleigh?' she shouted. '*What. Is. It?*'

The knife, the fierce look in Styles's eyes, the pent-up fury in her voice . . . Ashleigh hadn't expected Styles to blow up like this. Ashleigh stood rooted to the spot, mouth wide, eyes extra wide. A bunch of the older boys flung themselves between us. They snatched the knives away from me and Styles. Dragged Ashleigh away.

Some time later, she got pregnant. I bumped into her in the street one day. She was out buying baby stuff from Mothercare. Had this big belly, as though she'd swallowed a watermelon whole. We talked, resolved our beef and became friends again. She had problems of her own. Drugs, boys in prison. But that's how life goes round our endz. No one gets an easy ride. And all these beefs is extra stress. You got to let go of them sometimes, otherwise you can't get on with your life.

The Ashleigh beef was the last major hype I had at school.

PART THREE

MANDEM

*'Just think where you'd be now . . .
if it weren't for me'*

– Wallace

ELEVEN

Girls-in-crime

Life changed after the HBC beef. Going out and licking it became a lot harder. Mobiles were fixed with blocking systems that made them worthless. Bare CCTV cameras and security guards swarmed every retail park and shopping centre. And my mum discovered I'd been tiefing, asking me why all my jeans and tops had little holes in them – from popping the tags. I'd blank her or blame it on the washing machine, but I reckon she'd sussed it out. Mums are like that. She was angry, but also embarrassed that she had a daughter who was out licking it.

Me and my girldem were shedding our tomboy phase. We ditched the Avirexes and wore tight jackets, trousers that showed off our figures. Out went the all-white Nike creps; in came pink Adidas kicks. I started dabbing on eye make-up and lipstick and did my hair in cornrows, slicking it back. We also busted handbags for the first time. Back in our tomboy days, everything was stashed in the pockets of our low jeans or tracksuit bottoms.

Now we was obsessed with getting the latest DKNY, Juicy Couture and Warehouse handbags and purses. Just as important as the kit we added was the stuff we ditched. Gold went out. I lost the sovereign rings from each finger. Dropped the big chops. The only bit of gold I kept was a ring that covered three fingers and said, 'BITCH,' along the front.

Bustin' our new look, we attracted bare attention from the mandem. We enjoyed the smiles and compliments, but we weren't changing it up for the sake of the boys. On the roads, we matured more quick than the good girls at school who went home to Mummy and Daddy each night, revised for their GCSEs and planned to go university and blushed when some boy so much as looked at them across the street. You had to grow up over fast in order to live our lifestyle. With our new styles and garmz, we made a big impression. Now every boy wanted to be with us. It was a case of push out the old girls, here come the new girls.

These times I welcomed a new girl to the fam. Her name was Candice, and she was a crazy-in-the-head mixed-race girl who fought bare man due to her heavy build, with arms like steel cables and broad shoulders stolen from Deebo in *Friday*. Candice was very loud and very rude. I was very loud and very rude. We clicked, shared the same interests in music and garmz. She was the sister I never had.

In the daytime, Candice had to go to the YOT, Youth Offending Team, to do her community service. She was on probation for this, that and the other, but she didn't give a shit. Same as me. We were a couple of bad girls, although Candice was bigger than me, and she probably held the upper hand when it came to intimidating people. We'd call each other our girl-in-crime. And we pushed each other to do more badder and badder tings.

I introduced Candice to Rips, Stocks, Wallace, Safon and Nugz, and she soon began clicking with Safon. I linked with Wallace. Styles hooked up with Rips.

Wallace had his attractions. His mum was from Barbados; his dad came from America but walked out on the family before Wallace could even walk. Twenty years old, he was only a little bit taller than me at five foot seven, but what he lacked in height he made up for with strength. Wallace had a barrel chest and powerful arms, but he also had class. He owned neat rims and a ped, and had his own little movements and money. When he asked me out, I blushed.

I knew of Wallace's rep. He's what the girls call a gyalies. A playa, in other words. Word on the roads was that he still linked up with his ex, a girl by the name of Breelyn. I'd heard of this girl, didn't really fucking know her or anything, and although I can tolerate a lot in a boy, having another girl on the radar ain't happening. Before we got together, I had a sit-down conversation with him where I told him, 'Look, I know you got this previous with Breelyn. Truly I don't give a shit about her. Just don't fuck me about. Don't hurt me.' He gave it all the talk, said those days of chasing the girldem were behind him. And I believed him.

Way I saw it, Wallace represented a nice change from Kendrick. But we had a problem: Wallace shotted for Kendrick. As his basic boss, Kendrick treated Wallace and the mandem like shit. He'd call up his friends and get them to rob his own shotters.

Although I'd kept my distance from Kendrick, he didn't take too kindly to me and Wallace linking. Wallace wasn't worried about dating a girl who'd been with his deela – his basic boss – but I had major fears. After all, I'd been close to Kendrick, and I knew what he was capable of.

When he learned I was close to Wallace, Kendrick took action. He started randomly beating Wallace and robbing him of his food and money. He nicked his car and parked it on double yellow lines so it'd be towed. Then he'd ring me up and brag about what he'd done. I wasn't impressed, and told him what I thought of his stunts.

In Kendrick's eyes, he still believed he had ownership of me. One day, me, Candice and Bigs were in Wallace's Beemer. We arrived at Rips's house and Safon, Wallace and Rips told us to wait in the car while they retrieved something from the house. As we waited, four long, sleek cars speeded down the road towards us. The cars stopped outside Rips's house. My Nokia buzzed. Wallace.

'Drive my car,' he said. 'Get the fuck out of there and whatever happens, don't open the windows or unlock the doors. You feel me?'

'What's going on, Wallace?'

'No questions, Chyna. Now go.'

Wallace's tone was urgent and he weren't one to panic without a good reason. I did what Wallace asked, revving the engine and shifting the Beemer into first gear. My foot was suspended above the accelerator when I heard a distinct *tap, tap, tap* against the window, like hailstones.

The Beemer's windows were dark-tinted. Three shapes I took to be men presented. They were dark outlines, the faces of two of them obscured by the man in front, pressing his face against the window.

Kendrick.

He gripped a gun in his right hand. Tapped the window with the barrel of his ting – *tap, tap, tap* – quicker now, impatient, aggressive. I gripped the steering wheel with both hands, faced forward, knowing that Kendrick wouldn't be able to see me through the tint.

'If you don't open this door,' his voice carried, 'I'm gonna put a shot through the glass.'

I was petrified, didn't want to disobey Wallace, but same time, no way was I gonna get duppied because of some stupidness. I pressed the selector. As the window lowered, I seen the barrel of the gun, the endless dark hole at the end six inches from my face. The static, menacing look on Kendrick's face departed when he laid eyes on me. He smirked.

'What you doing in Wallace's car?'

Kendrick had been planning on tiefing Wallace's rims. Looking beyond Kendrick, I spotted the other four cars were taken by Kendrick's mandem. The Beemer was the last motor on the road. The front door of Rips's house was busted off its hinges. His mum screamed from inside as bare boys stormed the house.

'This ain't Wallace's no more,' I said, inventing a lie on the spot. 'He sold it to my mum and I've taken it out without her knowing about it.'

'Truth?'

'Cross my heart.'

'And hope to die.' He blinked. His moon eyes seemed to swell up. 'That's how it goes, ain't it?'

I didn't answer.

Kendrick turned his attention to Bigs in the back seat.

'You spreading lies that I raped you?' he said.

'Nah, man, you got it wrong' – Bigs shifting in her seat. A week ago, she'd claimed Kendrick raped her. In our endz there's lots of rumours running about, and it's hard to work out who's lying and who ain't. Kendrick, though, looked so outraged I figured he was telling the truth.

'Everyone on the endz saying I fucking raped you.'

'I swear, Kendrick, I didn't say nothing.'

'Step outside so I can box you up.' The way Kendrick said it, he almost made it sound inviting.

'Stop hassling Bigs,' I said.

He ran his tongue around his mouth. Looked at his shoes. Laughed at them, as if a joke was stickered to the toes. Tucked away his gun. 'You saved Wallace's bacon today, you know that?'

Kendrick left me and the girls to it. His mandem breezed

out, my hands clinging to the steering wheel like I'd die if I let go of it. My head was in pieces.

'Bruv, you've got to get that man out of your life, because, you know . . .' Candice said.

Otherwise I'm gonna end up killed, I thought. The headache for me was how to lose someone as vicious as Kendrick without him retaliating and making my life hell.

In the end, the boydem did me a favour by arresting him for armed robbery. I changed my mobile number. Moved on.

With Kendrick out of the picture, me, Wallace, Candice and Safon had good times together; driving to Southend and hitting the rides at the fairground. Sometimes we smoked draw in Candice's room. We'd hear her mum's footsteps on the stairs and the boys hided under the bed, Diane banging on the door and shouting, asking who was in there, us swearing blind no one.

It was Candice who introduced me to the world of motors. She taught me how to drive. We'd tief her mum's car at night. Diane was a scheduled person, had dinner at seven, bath at eight, in bed by ten o'clock on the dot. So we knew that at ten thirty Diane would be out for the count. Candice nicked the keys from her mum's purse and off we went, racing around the endz in a silver Jeep, me getting a crash course in steering and braking.

If Diane's Jeep weren't available, we'd hotwire rims.

Candice had the skills to speedwire. I remember reading somewhere that a good car tief can jack a motor in thirty seconds or thereabouts. Candice was good to go in *twenty*. This girl's fingers worked in fast-forward.

Candice taught me what cars to look for – old standard-shape Rover 100s and Fiestas and XR2s. Banger cars, we called them. You could break into these ones simple – they didn't have built-in alarms or immobilizers. Your brand-spanking-new Benzes and Beemers aren't worth the time of day to a car-jacker. You need to have the key fob because it's all about computer chips these days and the engine won't ignite without the chip present at the wheel. No fob, no drive. But older models, now, these have potential.

I had the role of lookout, scouting for boydem while Candice forced open the door by slipping a knife into the actual lock itself, or smashing the window in, her hoodie wrapped round her fist. Once inside, she'd pop the case from under the steering wheel, strip the wires, do the right ting in the right order, and rev the engine.

We'd cut loose from the yard in our jacked motor and ping it far, Candice driving like an F1 racer, down to Southend or Brighton, where we'd get piss-drunk on the pier and sleep on the pebbled beach. Drive home next morning. Neither of us had a licence, and neither of us gave a fuck, although Candice was the madder driver. She had her own Volkswagen V5 with blacked-out windows. Her rims were listed on the boydem computers as a runner: a car that's on record as out-running the boydem. Candice got a thrill from gunning the boydem as a sort of hobby. They'd chase her; she'd skid her V5 round sudden corners and accelerate down busy thoroughfares, winding left and right, left again, until she shook the cars tailing her.

Another bit of fun we had with motors was to join the boys at a ting called the Cruise.

Once a week, a text message is sent to all the people in the Cruise network, telling them to meet at such-and-such a road on the Saturday night at eleven o'clock. Cruises weren't open to anybody; you had to already be 'in' with associates before they'd admit you, in case you were undercover boydem. Cruises are a white tradition. All the white boy-racers attend, girlfriends by their sides. You get the top, top drivers from the area competing with each other for cash prizes.

The road had to be far from Central and boydem patrols, and at least a mile in length. The dual carriageways connected to the M25 hosted majority Cruises. First time we attended, the Cruise resembled a scene out of *The Fast and the Furious*. A hundred BMW coupés, Audis, Jaguars, Ferrari F335s, Porsche 911s blinged up and revving their engines, raring to go rip up this length of tarmac. Some boys rode on bikes, Ducati Monsters and Aprilia Tuonos, performing wheelies, stoppies, street skis and flips where they'd stand on the bike while doing fifty, sixty per and lift one leg up behind them.

If anyone wants evidence of how talented some boys on the endz are, they should check out the Cruises. Many drivers was highly skilled and polished behind the wheel, doing tings that could get them Lewis Hamilton p's with the right guidance.

We rolled to the Cruises with Stocks, Kevin, Nugz and Safon. They put in for a race each week. For them, it was a chance to show off their rims and driving abilities, especially Safon, who had mad skills he learned on the streets when jacking rims and out-racing the boydem. The races ran on through the night until five o'clock in the morning, or when the boydem interrupted it, whichever happened first. They were great fun, but they could also be really dangerous. I saw four people die at the Cruises. One biker boy tried to pull off a trick, lifting his front wheel off the ground and putting the bike vertical, so that only the back wheel was on the road. The boy got it wrong and fell off. Bike collapsed on top of him and the telescopic fork slugged directly against his head. No helmet. He died instantly. Later, a man in his fifties got killed after a car crashed into him. Man was just in the crowd watching the race and then boom. Dead.

For a while I managed to stay out of trouble. I went to the Cruises, cotched with the boys and kept it sweet. But my run of form ended one night. I was minding my own business when one of my friends from the endz, girl by the name of Vashonne, rang me as I lounged in my pink pyjamas. It was ten o'clock; the night had real bite to it, like sheet metal pressed against my skin. I was cosying up in the warmth of my room when Vashonne's number displayed.

''S'up, cuz?'

'You'll never guess what,' Vashonne said. 'I've just got my insurance money through.' A few weeks previous, a drunk driver had collided with Vashonne's rusted old motor. She was fully comped and planned to spend the insurance money on upgrading to a new set of wheels, meantime using a Vauxhall Astra hire car from the insurance company.

'What car you gonna buy?'

'That's the ting. I've just been speaking to a boy who's friends with Renell,' she said, Renell being Vashonne's girl, although I didn't know what she was about. 'This boy says he's got just the car for me. Peugeot 307, two-litre engine, normally five grand second-hand. He'll sell for two. Me and Renell just done a HTI check and everything's legit. We're gonna go pick up the rims tonight.' She paused. 'Only prob-lem is, I'm gonna drive back my new rims and not sure what to do about the Astra. I was wondering, Chyna, can you drive back the hire car?'

I thought about it. I had nothing doing and I never said no to a bit of an adventure, especially a trip to another part of South. 'Yeah, cools,' I said.

I still didn't have a driving licence, but the hire car was fully insured and me and Vashonne had the exact same birthday. Plus she had a licence. Anything happened and the boydem decided to stop me, I could say her name.

'Come and pick me up in half an hour, give me time to get dressed.'

'I'll be round sooner than that, cuz.'

I arched my eyebrows.

'I'm about thirty seconds from your house.'

I barely had time to throw on my jacket over my pyjamas, put on a pair of slippers and grab my keys and phone. The cold hit me like a truck. I felt it in my bones. Jumping into the back of the fifty-eight-plate Vauxhall Astra next to Renell, I settled in for the ride.

'Where are we meeting these boys?' I asked, rubbing my blue hands.

'On their estate.'

'Shit, are you stupid?' I leaned forward between the front seats. 'You're seriously gonna take two grand cash on to some estate you don't rightly know? Call the boy and tell him we'll meet him at a petrol station.'

'Yeah, I should've thought about that,' Vashonne said, slapping herself on the forehead and rolling her eyes dramatically. 'The boys are gonna run us up because we're girls and we're *always* getting jacked.'

Renell joined in. 'They're gonna rob your car, your money, take your phone . . .'

'I'm a be like, "Please don't run me up, bad man."'

'Ain't funny,' I said, crossing my arms and refusing to join in the laughter. 'You girls are meant to be street – you should know better.'

'Please, please, Mr Bad Man . . .'

'Very funny, cuz.'

We reached the estate and parked up in front of a basketball court, tarmac playing surface and chain-metal nets, deflated Spalding ball under the hoop. To the right of the hire car, an alleyway channelled between two tower blocks that stood either side like giant Lego blocks. Wire fencing stretched over the balcony windows, worn duvets and T-shirts hanging from clothes racks.

Vashonne killed the engine and flicked off the headlights. The world seemed alive with shadows. Two boys came out of the alley and approached our car. One of them, a light-skinned boy with dragon tattoos on his hands, rapped his knuckles on my window. I pushed the slider. It made a *whirring* sound on the roll-down.

'Which one of you is Renell?'

Renell waved.

The boy gave her a slight nod back. 'The car's outside my mum's garage. But here's the ting. Not all of you lot can be seen at my mum's. Only two of you can come.'

I felt uneasy about the set-up, but Renell and Vashonne seemed OK with it, so I agreed. As I'd be driving the Astra on the return trip, Vashonne and Renell decided they'd go to make the exchange. The dragon-tattoo boy escorted the girls. The second boy, black and with a face locked in a sneer, climbed into the back of the Astra. Just me and him. I sat in the front and shouted for Vashonne to give me her car keys to keep the engine running, otherwise I'd fucking freeze.

I sat in the driver's seat, engine purring, heating system working overtime, binging a spliff out of the window. My fingers were numb with the cold. The boy in the back seat tried on the small talk.

'You know anyone in our endz, then?'

'A couple,' I replied.

'Like who?'

I laid down the names of some people I'd affiliated with. Each time I mentioned a name he nodded his head and said in a voice slow as treacle, 'Safe.' That's how it played for five minutes. Me talking, the boy's head moving up and down like a bobblehead doll and repeating after himself, 'Safe.'

The heating system did a naff job of warming the car, so I dashed my spliff and moved to roll up the passenger-side window – and clocked Renell pacing up the alleyway towards me.

Renell, but no Vashonne.

The light-skinned boy draping a heavy hand over her shoulder.

Behind them another boy was fast approaching. Skin the colour of desert sand, he was a good six inches taller than his friend, looked like a basketball player. His hoodie popped low, he wore a cowboy-style handkerchief that covered his nose and mouth. Before I could understand what was going on, he circled the Astra, stopped at my window, reached in and snatched the keys out of the ignition.

They shoved Renell into the back seat. Same time, the conversational black boy shot out.

'Chyna, get in the back and don't say nothing,' Renell said.

'Fuck you mean, *don't say nothing*? This boy just took the keys.'

I struggled, but the boys dumped me in the back. Me and Renell swapped confused looks as they rooted through the glovebox, scrambled about under the seats and ripped out the floormats, investigating every nook and cranny of the Astra.

'Where's the fucking money?'

'Where's Vashonne?' I said back.

Renell pulled me close. Whispered, 'Vashonne scattered.'

'She *what*?'

Renell explained that when she, Vashonne and the dragon-tattoo boy had disappeared down the alley, the handkerchiefed boy came up behind Vashonne and made a tug for her Nike bag. He grappled with her, Vashonne struggling to hold on to her bag. His strength won out, and when the bag came loose from her hands, Vashonne ditched it and sprinted in the opposite direction. The boys hoped to find the p's in the bag. Wrong. They thought they must be in the car. Wrong twice.

All three boys crammed into the Astra and took us for a ride through random South endz. They drove insane in the membrane, burnin' the tyres, wheels spinning it, worse than any experience in the Cruises, us in the back, clinging on to the handles as they trashed the Astra. Eventually they parked up in another area of their endz. Big block of flats overshadowed the car, brown as coffee-stained teeth. Acres of scrubbled, dog-shitted parkland sprawled in front. The boys exited the car, having turned it inside out looking for Vashonne's two grand.

I overheard the boys discussing what to do with us next. One of them said they'd take us country, strip us naked and leave us in some fucking farmer's field. Another threatened to whip us, scar our faces.

Suddenly there was this pause of silence. The boys stared out to the field. Me and Renell chased their eyes to see what they'd scoped.

Flickering streetlamps washed the field lime green. A short, skinny black girl stood in the middle of the green a hundred metres away, clutching an Iceland food bag. We clocked her, she clocked us and she broke into a run. I seen that she weren't Vashonne, but from a distance, she was similar enough to fool the boys. The light-skinned pair burst down the field after her.

I flipped open the passenger door.

'Where the fuck you think you're going?' the black boy said.

'I'm gone, mate,' I replied, banking on the fact the boy couldn't abandon the rims – at least not while his two friends were busy chasing the girl with the Iceland bag. I tilted my head at Renell. 'You coming?'

She was.

The boy looked helplessly, angrily on as we breezed out, winding through the estate until we emerged the other end. Found ourselves in the wrong side of South at the wrong side of midnight, me and Renell thinking, Fuck. This is bad endz. Bare yutes on every corner and I'm in pink pyjamas, big fluffy slippers on my feet.

As we belted it past the Tube station, two boydem vans veered into sight, lights flipping, sirens buzzing. The shotters outside the KFC edged back into the shadows. The boydem pulled over next to us. Wanted to have a word. Said we'd been victims of a crime. And I realized, Vashonne's called the boydem.

'I'm not no victim,' I told the officer.

'Your friend's still missing,' he said. 'Aren't you worried about her?' Trying to reverse-psychology me.

To be honest, at that point my mentality was, Fuck Vashonne. In our endz the last people you ever, ever contact is the boydem. In my head I formed a plan. It went something like, get home. Call my fam. Speak to the mandem. Find out who run us up. Sort them out. Way, way at the very bottom of the list was, call 999.

'How about a ride-around?' the boydem man suggested. 'Maybe we can find your friend.'

I looked at his car like there was a bomb strapped

underneath it. Had this nightmare image of me sitting in the passenger seat as we cruised the endz, every flipping gangsta boy eyeing my face and wondering what the fuck I was doing riding with the boydem.

'Come on,' the officer said.

'Is the windows tinted?' Renell scratched her elbow.

'Yes,' he said, a jagged smile working its way up the left side of his face, the right-side muscles refusing to play along. 'Yes, they are.'

Me and Renell had no choice but to accept the ride. We slinked in the back, our eyes almost level with the bottom of the passenger windows as we accelerated past bag of yute after bag of yute. We located the Astra on some back road, abandoned and stripped of its tings. My phone, which I'd left in the car, was also missing.

The boydem dropped us off in our endz. I told him to take me to a road the other side of the endz, so my bredrin wouldn't see me coming home in a boydem car. Borrowed a mobile, made a couple of phone calls and found out who the boys were. The black boy was some eejit called Skittles.

I woke up the next day to find Vashonne banging on my door. She explained she'd kept the two grand stuffed down her bra, which is why the boys had no luck finding it in her Nike bag or the Astra. Vashonne didn't need telling that she was over lucky. She'd walked into a trap the minute she agreed to meet the mandem in their roads. If she hadn't legged it, the boys would probably have got around to strip-searching her. Vashonne ought to have been thanking her good fortune, but she wore a serious face, her eyes deading me out, as if I'd cussed her mum and nan in the same sentence.

'You set me up, Chyna.'

'*What?* Are you fucked in the head? I got the name of the boy who did. It's Skittles.'

'Nah, nah,' Vashonne said. 'You and Renell set me up. Know what, fuck you, Chyna, and fuck your fam. I ain't speaking to you no more.'

We never spoke again.

TWELVE

No letting go

That summer I took four GCSEs. Missed the others because, like, five minutes before, Candice would ride into the school and tell me she was hitting Brighton beach, and I'd be like, 'Cuz, I'm on it!' Keep it moving.

My mum got letters from the school saying I'd fucked up my GCSEs. Tings was icy between us. Because I stayed out for long, my mum was isolated from me and she probably felt like she couldn't do nothing. Not without any evidence. Like, she probably had a good sense that I was smoking weed, shotting and tiefing, but she didn't know the ins and outs of what I got up to.

I enjoyed spending time with Wallace. We had a good laugh; he treated me right and made me feel special. I used to spend days down at Wallace's place, not really doing much, just liking the feeling of being in his company. He represented a big change from Kendrick, and I think I just wanted to be in a normal relationship after the experience of my first boyfriend.

There's certain tings street boys do when they rack up stacks of paper. He'd take me down to the car showroom and ask me to pick out a motor for him. Looking back, I think, Fucking naive, but these days I'm a sixteen-year-old girl linking with man and I'm like, Rah, this man's spending so much time and money on me, he must really think I'm something special. Most girls fall for that stunt at least once in their lives, I believe.

After a great honeymoon period, I got to see the flipside to Wallace. This was after my mum booted me out of the house.

I did a robbery one day with Roxy and a girl by the name of Clarissa. No comeback for three months. We thought we got away with it. My mum went on holiday and left my auntie to look after me. While she was away, the boydem raided my house. Five o'clock in the morning, I was cotching upstairs in my room with Wallace, Safon and Clarissa when I heard extra banging on the door, heated shouts of 'Boydem!' They arrested me and Clarissa and Roxy. I didn't worry about the boydem, they had nothing on us, but I did stress over my auntie. I pictured her on the phone, my mum a thousand miles away, fucking ballistic.

When I got back home, my auntie said nothing. She'd not spoken of it to my mum neither. On the day my mum flew back, I was out chilling. My phone rang. Mum.

'Your aunt's just told me what happened,' she said, her voice so cold you could've used it to freeze a lake.

'It weren't nothing to—'

'Don't come back to the house,' she snapped, cutting me off. 'That's it, do you understand? I warned you before, girl. I've had it up to here with you. I don't want you living under my roof any more, end of.'

'But, Mum . . .' I'd not seen her behave as distant as this. I felt less like a daughter, more like some stranger off the road.

'I know everything already, *every little detail*. Save your breath. I don't care what you do. Just don't bother coming back to the house tonight, because you're not welcome.'

'*What?*'

'I'm kicking you out, girl. This is it.'

I walked in a daze to Wallace's house and stayed there for the night. Being kicked out scared me. Grim thoughts crowded my mind. Where am I gonna live? Where's my future gonna go? I was also angry. Some families might chuck out their daughters when they're bad, but my nan and granddad bought up five children and had nuff problems with them, and never once did she kick them to the kerb. I thought, Rah, I know I'm bad, no denying that; but in my eyes, the problems I had, they was fixable.

For long my mum didn't call me and I didn't call her. I had nowhere to go apart from Wallace's. Every day of the week his mum went and bought me fresh knickers and garmz from Marks & Spencer, sorted me out with a whole new wardrobe. If it hadn't been for Wallace and his mum, I would've been slumming it on the streets.

Three weeks passed. Not a word from my mum.

Eventually I thought, Fuck this and I picked up the phone. She answered sixth ring. Not a flake of warmth between us.

'Yes?' she said. Not, How are you? Or, I've been worried. Just, Yes?

Fine, I thought. If that's how she wanted to play it.

'I want to come around and collect my stuff.'

'No, girl. That's not happening. Everything that's in my house stays here.'

'But, rah, I want my stuff.'

'That's not my problem now, is it?'

Call over. I couldn't believe how frosty my mum had turned towards me. Instead of making me feel regretful and wanting to make it up to her, I became colder in return. Any hope of me returning home fizzled out. Her tone – and mine – was flat as day-old cola.

That evening, me and Wallace had an argument.

Like Kendrick before him, Wallace began to turn over possessive, not giving me room to breathe. I reckoned Mum for a control freak – telling me I couldn't wear skirts in the summer, not approving of me sleeping over at friends' houses and lecturing me about the badness of smoking cigarettes and weed – but Wallace was off the fucking scale. Pretty soon, he got really controlling. Put down bare ground rules.

Can't go out partying with the girls.

No wearing them high heels.

Don't be talking to no boys neither.

His piss-take rules led to heated arguments. At these ages I wanted to go out and party with my girldem, roll in nice wheels and drink liquor till I was legless. And yet I lived with a boy who had a massive influence over me, pinning me whenever I went out. At first I tolerated his controlling ways. He's took me in, I reasoned. Made me safe, kept me clean.

I came to depend on this boy, and that in turn made me vulnerable. Each time Wallace laid a new rule, or asked me where I was going, I weighed up the situation in my head. What if I fucked him off and he kicked me out? Where would I go then?

All the time, Wallace reminded me of this fact: 'Just think where'd you be now, Chyna, if it weren't for me.'

He made me feel that, somehow, I owed him my life and my happiness. Wallace dominated my mental side. He was an expert manipulator. I depended on him, and he was well aware of that fact – and that made me feel horrid. Now I look back, I think a lot of what drives some people to crime is a sense of vulnerability. Why d'you think it's kids from poor backgrounds who want to get rich quick? Because they ain't got no support network. Some rich kid wants to buy a house? Here comes Daddy with the money for a deposit. If a nice middle-class girl comes up short on her rent, she's got family she can go to. Not us. We live on the edge.

I split from his house at six o'clock that evening and waited outside my mum's house until three o'clock in the morning, when I knew she'd be asleep. Creeping up to the side of the house, I sneaked through the small gap in the downstairs bathroom window and, walking on the balls of my feet, silently made my way to my bedroom. Stuffed every-thing into two big suitcases stored at the top of my wardrobe. I took all the clothes from their hangers, each pair of shoes, my toiletries, the works. By the time I was finished, my room was barren except for my TV and hi-fi. If I'd had some way of carrying them, I'd have taken them too. I opened the big window at the back of the house, nudged my suitcases through the opening and bailed out.

Wallace knew I planned to break into my mum's house and his car was parked round the front. Clarissa was there too, sitting in the back. She'd also been kicked out of her home, and although we weren't good, good friends, being sort of homeless created some common ground between us.

Pasha rang my phone as I dumped my suitcases in the boot. She'd heard about the drama with my mum and offered me to sleep at hers for the night.

'Rah, get up early tomorrow. Me and my mum will help you find a hostel.'

That was me taken care of, but I worried about Clarissa. Like me, she had nowhere to go. I said to Wallace, 'Clarissa needs somewhere to stay – why don't you put her up in the spare room at your place?'

'Yeah, yeah,' Clarissa said.

'No,' Wallace butted in. He peered into the rear-view mirror. 'No way.'

I couldn't understand why Wallace didn't want to help Clarissa out. He repeated it again and again. 'No, no and no.'

So Clarissa would be staying with Pasha too. Off we went to her home to corral her stuff. Her bags had been chucked in a dustbin out the front of her house. We collected her bags and returned to Wallace's car. He'd planted our suit-cases at the side of the road.

'You'll have to get a taxi, Chyna. I'll shout your fare,' Wallace said. 'Ain't got time to take you both to Pasha's.'

'What?' I said, trying to figure why Wallace was behaving strangely.

'Got some tings to take care of, innit.'

I thought he might have some shotting to do, a place to be. These boys don't have fixed schedules. I shrugged and took the £20 for the cab fare and off we went to the taxi rank. There's a twenty-four-hour Tesco a short hop up from the rank and my stomach was hollowed out. I'd not had a bite to eat since breakfast and it was now half four in the morning. I entered the Tesco Express, thinking to buy a sandwich.

Wallace had his back to me at the checkout, holding bags of nibbly bits for a night in. Next to him was a girl.

I recognized her immediately. Known her for long.

Sharise, the bitch. The girl with the alkie mum whose house Wallace shotted from.

I'd caught him red-handed. I was angry – angry to the point of feeling weak, as if someone had drained all the energy out of my body. I staggered up to him, thought I might faint with every step I took. A weird sensation came over me. I didn't know what I was going to do next. I thought back to that moment when me and Wallace first linked. *Just don't fuck me about.* That's all I'd asked. And now . . . this.

'You all right, Wallace?'

He spun, flinched, retreated, hands in the air, like he thought I was about to deck him.

'Yeah, I'm all right,' Wallace said, trying to style it. 'What's up?'

He tried to dress it up as a friend ting, but Sharise was an ex of his, and I didn't buy his cover story for a second. His eyes gave him away. They fixed on the floor like he'd dropped something.

'Why the fuck are you coming Tesco twenty minutes after dropping me off, saying you had business to take care of and buying nibblies with your old girlfriend, Wallace? Answer me that.'

He was baffled. Not a word.

I turned to Sharise. 'You all right, Sharise? Know what you're doing here?'

'Yeah . . .' she began.

''Cos you're not in a relationship with Wallace. So what is it?'

She put her hands on her hips and pouted. 'I'm his girlfriend.'

I looked to Wallace. 'Is that right?'

'I don't know,' he mumbled. He managed to scoop his eyes off the floor and meet mine. 'I was gonna take her home, I swear—'

Sharise's eyeballs tore strips off Wallace. *'Take me home? Is that it, now? You said you were gonna take me to your house.'*

There's moments when life stings you so bad you're lost for how to respond. In the movies, people act upset when someone close to them dies, or a relationship breaks up. The truth is, you're hurting too much to react. People in real pain, they do nothing. I'd placed my trust in Wallace and he'd trampled on it.

'Know what, Wallace, I'm not gonna fight a girl over you. I'm gone.' I gave them back and left the store, walked up the road from the Tesco, digging my nails into my palms so hard I thought I was going to bleed. Clarissa behind, trying to comfort me. When I couldn't hold in the pain no more, when it hurt so much I was struggling to breathe, I found a spot of pavement, sat down and cried.

No one had hurt me like Wallace did that day. The cussing in school, the fights with the Hard-Bodied Chix. I was homeless, broke and my heart treated like a cheap toy. Pasha put me up for the night. Somehow I stopped crying, feeling alone in a cold, unfamiliar bed, missing the warmth of Wallace's body even as I hated on him, and fell asleep.

That was the worst day of my life.

I woke up the next morning to twenty-six missed calls from Wallace. I didn't return them; couldn't face speaking to that sleazebag. Three months into our relationship and he'd played me. Fuck this boy, I thought. He's bad news.

I moved out several days later into the shared accommodation house. I didn't tell Wallace where I was living. Far as I was concerned, me and him were history.

Me and Wallace got back together a few months later. He took me out for lunch and we had us a second sit-down conversation. Over tomato bruschettas and Four Seasons pizzas in Pizza Express he said he was truly sorry for what he'd done, he wanted to make it up, prove to me he could be a good boyfriend. He was charming and sounded sincere, and I had missed him as well, despite his cheating. I agreed to give him a second chance.

When you got nothing in this world and someone loves you and does nice tings for you – and Wallace could be a real gentleman – then it's hard to let that person go.

A year into our relationship, tings had been good, Wallace was behaving himself, as far as I knew, and I was out shopping in town on a beautiful sunny Saturday. As I strolled into River Island, I bumped into a man on the way out.

Kendrick.

He paused. I paused. The silence was long.

'Thought you went down,' I finally said, my voice cracking like sandpaper.

'Remanded. I was found not guilty.'

'How long you been out?'

'Same time as I been looking for you.'

'And . . .' I was almost too scared to ask. 'How long's that?'

'A while.'

'Oh,' I managed.

Kendrick was stiff. His moon eyes had me on lockdown. I had to appease him, so I sold him a pack of lies. Told him that I was to blame for the relationship turning swag. Rah, I was too young. Rah, I wasn't ready. Rah, my mum moved me to Brighton. The words coming out my mouth were rubbish, but I wanted to keep Kendrick sweet.

'Gimme your number,' he said.

'I'm not sure that's a good idea.'

'Give me your number,' he said again, reminding me that in Kendrick's world, there's no such thing as no. 'And don't be giving me no fake number, because I'm gonna check it.'

Forced into a corner like that, I had to give my real number. On the way home, I took a roundabout route in case he had someone following me, and went into the nearest Carphone Warehouse, bought myself a new SIM card, chucked the old one in a bin and went straight to Wallace's house. I broke down in tears. Wallace attempted to comfort me with the macho talk, but he weren't in a position to protect me. I'm fucked, I thought.

That Sunday, I lay in bed with Wallace dreaming of a lazy day. A fry-up for breakfast, pancakes and eggs and slices of bacon and cooked tomato. And then a trip to the shopping centre in the afternoon. My thoughts were punctured by someone pounding on the door. I checked the alarm. Seven o'clock in the morning. Who's out and about this early at the weekend? I wondered.

A voice boomed through the front door, 'Open up, Wallace, we need to talk!'

Kendrick.

Despite me and Wallace linking, he still did business with Kendrick. I'm not sure why. Maybe Wallace had nowhere else to source food. Maybe – more likely – Kendrick got some sort of kick out of bossing around his ex's boyfriend. While they still had a business relationship, tings simmered. I knew it was only going to be a matter of time before it came to a head. Now that time had come. I thought, No deela does their work at stupid early on a Sunday. They sleeps in the day and works at nights. What was he doing here at this hour?

'You should answer the man,' I said to Wallace. 'He ain't gonna leave you be.'

'But he'll see you.'

'So what? He probably already knows. Kendrick's bad, but he ain't dumb.'

Muttering under his breath, Wallace slipped on a pair of batties and went to open the door. I slipped on a dressing gown and binged up a spliff to skell my pulsing heart. The chain rattled. The door creaked. The floorboards groaned as Kendrick made his way for the bedroom. The spliff worked its magic. Kendrick entered and instead of being a nervous wreck, I was borderline comatose.

Kendrick met my eyes and a crackling laugh escaped his mouth like an unwanted burp that he couldn't hold in. Every muscle in his body seemed to laugh too, taking me by surprise. There's a dozen reactions I expected from Kendrick – furious, violent, sinister – but laughing?

'This your new boyfriend, then?'

I said nothing.

'This your new boyfriend?'

I said nothing, smoked.

'Do you feel safe here?'

I smoked, said nothing.

'Leave the room, Wallace,' Kendrick said. 'I wanna speak with Chyna alone.'

Wallace protested, but a man who buys his food from someone else and gets robbed by that same someone randomly ain't in a kosher position to protest. I nodded to Wallace, *It's OK. I'll handle this.*

Enough fucking about, I thought. The weed had blown away my fear like so many cobwebs. I exhaled, looked him in the eyes and said, 'Look, Kendrick, I'm with Wallace now.

There ain't no going back to me and you. Why don't you just move on?'

Kendrick maintained his nice-boy act, flashing the smile, his voice smooth as an aromatic candle. 'You should be with me, not this shotter fuck. Come home with me now.'

I stubbed out the spliff and shook my head.

'Now, why would I leave with you? I've moved on.'

'Come on, Chyna. Me and you.'

'No.'

The more times I said no, the more ruder Kendrick became. I reckon no one had ever told him 'No' to his face in such a direct way, and he couldn't handle the fact that some sixteen-year-old girl was refusing his demands. Humiliated, he gave me his back, swearing to himself.

'I only came to see if you was here, you know,' he said, glancing sideways at a spot on the wall.

He left.

I never saw him again.

THIRTEEN

What love is all about

At sixteen I had an abortion.

I missed my period, made myself sick with worry and went to Superdrug where I purchased a Clear Blue tester. When the digital display flashed PREGNANT 2-3, I cried. I suppose lots of women cry when they read a positive result, because they're happy to have a baby inside of them. I cried scared tears, not happy ones.

Wallace craved a baby with me. That much was bait. He talked about children daily, but I didn't want a kid. Not then. Not at that age, when so many other girls were dropping babies and being ditched by their baby fathers.

I told Smiles the result. She was fam, and I could trust her to keep a secret.

'Don't worry,' she said, 'we'll take care of it, and Wallace never has to find out.'

Together we went to the local sex clinic and registered for an appointment. Smiles came with me to the scan, where they confirmed I was pregnant and established the age of the foetus. And she came the following week when I booked in for a trip to the abortion clinic.

My experience was horrible. Teenagers and parents mingled outside, kicking gravel and smoking cigarettes. The atmosphere was like a funeral. Smiles wanted to come in and support me, but the woman at reception said she wasn't allowed. Family only, they said. She didn't understand. To me, Smiles was fam.

The abortion people took me upstairs. They directed me to a room. It was cold as damp snow, and the air smelled strongly of disinfectant and tasted bitter on my tongue. I clocked a bed with a curtain railing round it.

They told me to lie down on the bed.

I lied.

They put me to sleep.

I slept.

Five minutes later, I woke up without a baby.

They used a suction pump to suck the baby from inside me. When I came to, I was way, way bad. Imagine the worst period pain you've ever had and times it by a million. One of the women saw me looking needled and asked how I was feeling. I think I replied, 'How d'you fucking think?' Someone handed me some leaflet crap and said it was important that I read it. I binned it. Leaflets wasn't gonna make the pain go away. If I'd known what was going to happen though, I wish I had read it – tings might have been different.

I walked out the main door. No. That's a lie. I wobbled and swayed, clutching my belly as if I'd been shanked.

Smiles was waiting for me outside.

'Don't worry, cuz,' Smiles said. 'The worst of it's over now.'

I thought I might puke. My right hand covered my mouth. My left clutched my stomach. I felt as if my insides had been scooped out. 'Maybe.'

'You've had the abortion. What can be worse than that?'

'Hiding it from Wallace.'

When I got back to my shared accommodation, Wallace was there. He asked where I'd been. I ducked and dived his questioning, brushed him off by saying I didn't feel so good and couldn't tolerate no weed or liquor. But as days went by, I got iller and iller. It became impossible to hide. I knew Wallace had his suspicions. The constant vomiting, the high temperatures and the weakness in my bones. Something wasn't right. A week after the abortion, I checked myself into hospital.

Smiles drove me to the A&E. The doctors performed a load of blood tests and explained that I'd contracted a viral infection from the abortion. They needed to keep me under observation for a while. All the time I'm thinking, Please don't let Wallace find out.

'You should call the father. He'll be concerned,' the nurse said.

'I'll be OK,' I replied.

I had a lot of time to think while I recovered in hospital. Mostly I thought about me and Wallace. We'd been together for eighteen months and our relationship was headed down a slippery slope. I thought, Rah, this boy's taking the piss out of me. He's got me sitting at home. If I walk left or right, he controls it, and if I don't listen to him, it'll be a fight. Not an argument-fight, like normal couples have, but a fistfight, like the ones between my dad and my mum.

These times I decided to make some space for myself. Although I had my own little room and stuff, I really wanted some distance between me and Wallace. I'd hopped from Kendrick's bed to Wallace's, and men were beginning to fuck with my head. I was exhausted, pent-up, cornered. More than anything, I needed a break.

Wallace became ten times worse after he got tagged and couldn't go outside after seven o'clock at night. Sometimes I'd chill with Safon while he busted shots around the endz. Safon had moved on from purely car-jacking now. The game had become much more dangerous with the new security systems and he was left with no choice but to join Wallace and Stocks in the shotting game. We'd grab some munch in Burger King, innocent chilling between two good friends. This pissed Wallace off. He rang up my mobile one night while I cotched with Safon and called me a slag, said he was gonna hurt me. I was like, Whatever. I got bare threats from Wallace these days. He didn't scare me. There's only so many threats you can chuck at a seventeen-year-old girl before she tunes out.

That same night, Safon dropped me outside my house. As I got out, a motor swerved alongside, crowbar jutting out from the passenger-side window. The bar raked against Safon's driver-side. Glass crunched. I had no idea what was going on. Safon wasted no time breezing out, the other car making itself scarce. I asked myself, Would Wallace actually do that? It seemed too much of a coincidence, coming so quickly after our tiff on the phone.

For a whole week Wallace maintained his cussing. There are nicer tings a boy can tell his girlfriend. Ignoring him, I went to cotch with my girls on the Saturday night. Weed, wine, DVDs, some chat. Me, Smiles, Styles, three of us jamming.

We'd just finished watching the bit in *Training Day* where the Mexicans pull a gun on Ethan Hawke when Breelyn, Wallace's ex, rang me.

'Where's that bitch Smiles?' she said. 'I'm gonna fuck her up.'

My fam instincts kicked in. I passed the spliff to Smiles and shot to my feet. 'Who the fuck do you think you are, calling up my phone and saying you're gonna step to my bredrin? Listen, Smiles's my girl—'

'*You* listen, Chyna,' she said. 'When I tell you what that girl's done, you're gonna want to fuck her up as well.'

I was thrown. 'What you talking about?'

Breelyn was quiet for a moment. 'She's with you, innit? That fucking jezzy's right next to you.'

'So what if she is?' I asked.

Breelyn went off on one again.

I cut into her rant. 'Listen, blud, why don't you comes here and we'll sort out whatever needs sorting, yeah?'

I told Breelyn where to find us. Hung up and turned to Smiles. She had her eyes on the TV, avoiding eye contact with me. Styles stood up and announced she was off to go and buy some more Rizlas from the Indian man's shop.

'Before this girl comes round,' I said, when the two of us were alone, 'do you want to tell me what she's banging on about?'

'Truly, I don't know,' Smiles said. She lit a cigarette and ran a hand through her hair, chops jangling on her wrists. 'She's probably off her head, that's all.'

Fifteen minutes later, Breelyn fronted. I met her outside. Bare girls gathered in the street. I clocked Candice, Bigs . . . a dozen girls in total. They looked pissed. I folded my arms and nodded at Breelyn.

'What's going on?'

'I was round Wallace's this morning—'

I felt like someone had struck a match under my heart.

'What the *fuck* are you doing at my man's place?'

'—and I saw all these texts on his phone,' Breelyn said, blanking my question. I was straight-up gobsmacked. Her words hardly registered. All I could think was, The only reason for Breelyn being round her ex-boyfriend's place first ting in the morning was if . . .

They were sleeping together.

I frowned as Breelyn handed me her Samsung and explained that she'd copied dozens of texts from Wallace's phone to hers.

Texts from Smiles to Wallace, and Wallace to Smiles.

Bare of them.

Babes, you still comin to my house?

Yh stop phonin me im in here with Chyna xx

OK how long til you leeve her?

20 mins xx

I needed answers, because it definitely looked like Smiles – my good, good friend, my *fam* – and Wallace were two-timing me. My mind was split down the middle. Wallace – I knew what he was like. He had form. I thought back to Sharise. How naive I'd been to believe Wallace's lines about staying faithful. But Smiles? Part of me couldn't accept it. Not Smiles. Not the girl who supported me during the abortion.

I needed answers. Only one person could give me them. Wallace.

Breelyn tagged alongside me towards Wallace's pad. I couldn't even look her in the eye. She definitely had to be sleeping with my man, I had that figured out from the off. Smiles hovered nervously at my back. What with the twenty or so other girls present, she was basically forced to come down to Wallace's against her own will.

'Breelyn's chatting shit, blud. I ain't never meshed with your man, I swears,' she said over and over.

'Allow it,' I shot back. I didn't look at Smiles, but I felt the waves of panic coming off that girl.

We reached Wallace's house and shouted for him to

come down. When he showed, Breelyn confronted him with the texts. He raised his hands in the air and shook his head. 'No, no, no, it ain't like that.'

I moved to Wallace. He blanked the other girls and dropped his hands.

'Tell me the truth,' I said, my lips trembling.

Wallace sank to his knees. He wept like a baby, begging me to take him back and saying that he didn't even like Smiles, calling her a slag while she stood not ten feet away.

The pain clawed at my belly. I felt sick. Wallace had cheated on me bare times, but somehow doing it with Smiles made it worse. He'd violated me. Took the ultimate piss. Flipped my world upside down, and nothing made sense any more. I wandered away, tears swelling up at the back of my eyes, biting my lip to stop them streaming down. It's over, I told myself. For good.

My relationship with Wallace was broken, but the first cracks opened up in our fam. The loyalty and sisterhood we'd worked so hard to create had been shattered by Smiles. I didn't speak to her for five years. She could never be bredrin again.

I got my revenge for what Wallace done. I had to get at Wallace where it hurt. So I thought to myself, What does Wallace love more than anything else? Himself, obviously. But something I could attack . . .

I called Candice. Hadn't seen her since the Cruises, before I had my abortion and caught Wallace two-timing me with Sharise. I gave her the heads-up on my man predicament.

'What are you doing right now, cuz?'

'Nothing,' she said, chewing gum. 'Why, what's up?'

'Pick me up in your V5. There's something I want to do.'

I decided to show Wallace exactly what love was all about.

Me and Candice rocked up to a nearby Tesco service station and bought a jerry can of petrol. We drove on towards Wallace's house. He lived at the bottom of a steep hill and normally parked his car – a brand-spanking-new three-door BMW 330 Coupé Sport – at the top. Space was limited on his road and the only free parking spots tended to be at the top of the hill. Wallace lived five doors down from the hill and from his bedroom window, I remembered, he didn't have a clear view of his rims.

I smashed in the driver's window and poured the petrol underneath the engine, on the roof, on the seats. When I'd finished, the car was dripping in petrol and the fumes choked my throat. From my back pocket I fished out a box of matches, lit one for underneath, one for the top and chucked two more matches inside with the rest of the box. Then I turned away and sprinted towards Candice's V5.

Boom!

The sound was like a whole army of Yardie men firing niners at the same time. Windows totalled. Flames licked. That Beemer burned up for real. The heat scratched my back as I hit the V5. We breezed out, Wallace ringing my mobile a minute later, crying his heart out about his barbe-cued BMW.

The score weren't settled yet. I stormed over to Breelyn's house, knowing that she and Wallace must have been sleep-ing together. She may have blown the lid off the Smiles and Wallace cheat, but I had to deliver some payback to this girl too.

Breelyn used to be with a boy called Nasha. I say 'be', but truly she was just sleeping with Nasha these times. They weren't boyfriend-girlfriend. They weren't holding hands and eating at Nando's. Breelyn lived in a bait house, one of those places where Nasha would stash his guns, shot food from there and whatnot. There'd be bare people down there, and I planned to confront her. Have it out properly.

Out front, I noticed this boy checking me.

He stood tall, six foot three, and with big, thick-fingered hands and a high forehead. I was instantly drawn to his eyes. Where Kendrick had dull, black moons, this boy's eyes were amped, on fire. They seemed to stare right through you. They were eyes you were afraid of and fell in love with at the same time. I suddenly lost my rage and felt myself blushing up. When this boy looked at me, it felt as if my toughness melted away, and something inside me said this wasn't the last time me and him would randomly meet.

The boy's name? Rashid.

FOURTEEN

The food chain

These days I'd go to Nang's house and jam it, smoking a casual spliff and chatting about plans for the future now we was all grown-up and left school. Nang told me she was shotting weed, but her real ambition was to carve out a career for herself in a legit job. I checked her maybe only once a month, but the love we had for each other was like, you don't need to see someone to know that she's your girl. That's how we had it.

Karma was less kind to Smiles. One day she went out the front of Rips's house and someone tried to shoot up Rips. Bullets zipped. When the shooting was over, Smiles noticed her ear was bleeding. A bullet had skinned her. One inch further across and she'd have taken a round in the face.

Meantimes I started rolling with Older Shark, the brother of the boy in the Mash Boys crew that beefed with Sweetz's 3G gang. I met him through Younger Shark, and I was on the rebound from my friction with Wallace, desperately seeking out a change of scenery. I linked with him at a good time – or a bad time, depending on which way you look at it.

Older Shark's real name was Leon. He was trouble from the get-go, but he was also caring and smart and funny.

Leon was twenty-one years old, but that only made him seem more attractive to me. We hooked up, liked each other, hit it off.

Leon treated me with respect. He had this soft, kindly face that reminded me of a younger Jamie Foxx, and when he was pleased with something, he'd bust this big smile, teeth white as paracetemol. He never raised his voice or threatened me. Made me feel a proper lady.

He also introduced me to a whole new world of crime.

Leon was a deela specializing in crack cocaine and heroin. There's a scale of drug deelas. At the bottom of the food chain are the shotters, the kids standing on street corners, or hanging around the stairwells in the estates, dealing small quantities to cats on the roads. They're the foot soldiers. Shotters get paid an OK amount of p's, way better than they'd earn in a McDonald's anyways, but it's nothing compared to the higher-up deelas, the ones who work in keys – what we call kilos. They're the men who buy it wholesale and distribute it among the shotters. They get most of the money back from the shotters, and the rest the shotter gets to keep as profit.

So when I say that Leon was in the drugs game, I mean he dealt in big bits of food. Because of this, he made good p's. Because of this, he made a lot of enemies.

There's another ting you should know about Leon, and the game he played. In the world of drugs, what people don't realize is that deelas are robbing each other *all the time*. Deelas see that another deela's got a nice new set of wheels, or is splashing his p's on nice clothes, and they think, Rah, someone's made a stack of money to be easily got at. Or maybe they hear that a deela's got a big delivery of food and is hiding it on his person or in his car. So they go and rob that person.

Leon was a deela, but he also robbed other deelas when he needed the money. Or sometimes when he just felt like it.

One day, Leon robbed a boy from a local gang called the Swear Down Crew.

A Swear Down Crew boy by the name of Tyrell approached Leon and asked to buy some food off him. My boyfriend had the drugs, but noticed the boy was off his face and he figured he could capitalize on some robbing action. With a few of his mandem to help, Leon set the SDC boy up. Tyrell was told to go to a certain place and wait for Leon to arrive with the food. When he and his mandem showed, the boy got the fright of his life – one of Leon's friends pulled a gun on him.

They kidnapped Tyrell and demanded to know the whereabouts of his food stash. Tyrell was stubborn at first and gave them a screw-face and nothing else. For two days Leon held him hostage, beating him up, threatening him, torturing him. At last they broke his spirit and he gave up the address.

Leon and his mandem drove to a special place, the kind of joint where a boy keeps his drugs. Deelas usually hide their food in another house, because it's too risky to store it in their own pad. Sooner or later the boydem are bound to come and search their home, but if they don't find nothing, they can't press charges. The special house would belong to a girl that the deela wasn't dating, just sleeping with. That was a typical arrangement for boys. They'd be seeing some girl and one day ask her, 'Oh, babes, can you do me a favour and keep something for me?'

Nine times out of ten, the girl wants to make the man happy and agrees, not realizing that she's becoming an accessory to a crime and putting herself in jeopardy. For the boys, storing stuff around girls' houses is better than boys', because a boy might try and sell the drugs himself. And besides, most of the girls weren't known to the boydem.

Leon and his mandem rode to the special house. He told Tyrell to phone his girl, pretend like everything's gravy, and get her to bring down the food and p's and dump it in Leon's car. The girl would suspect nothing. Them sort of boys always live on the edge, and a boy asking for all his food to be brought to him out of the blue ain't less ordinary than shitty weather in England. This girl handed over the £10,000, half in drug value and the rest cash, and not a question to go with it. Once they'd collected the goods, the mandem released Tyrell back to his people.

Leon didn't mention a word of this to me until two days after. We was cotching in my room, watching *Scarface* on TV, when he piped up, 'Guess what I did the other day?'

'Robbed a bank.'

'Try again,' he said. He grinned but avoided eye contact, preferring to inspect the tips of his fingernails.

'Won the lottery.'

'Almost.' On the TV, Al Pacino snorted a mountain of coke. Leon loved this film. He must've seen it a hundred times. 'I robbed Tyrell.'

'You did *what*?'

'Did him for ten grand.'

'Tell me you're fooling, Leon.'

He lost the grin. I'm not the kind of girl who hides her expressions, the opposite of dainty or dull. Someone wrongs me or pisses me off and I'll wear my screw-face. A blind man can tell when I'm not feeling it.

'You *know* the SDC boys. Fuck, you *talk* to Tyrell every week.'

'It was a spur-of-the-moment ting. The boy was off his face on dis and dat. I thought I might as well help myself to his takings. Ten grand, Chyna.'

'They're practically your bredrin. What you did . . .' I searched for the right word 'that's . . . that's . . . snakish.'

'Ten grand,' his voice trailed.

The SDC boys swore revenge. As if robbing one of their bredrin weren't plenty bad, by hostaging the boy, Leon had humiliated SDC. For a high-level deela, Leon lacked affiliations since the Mash Boys crew he rolled in had split up. No gang creds made life hard for the two of us. The beef was between him and these other boys, and he had no one he was able to reach out to for protection.

Leon steered clear of the Swear Down Crew endz. He vanished into thin air. The Swear Down Crew searched high and low for Leon, but when he went underground, it was impossible to find him. They grew frustrated and, with no mandem, they needed another way of getting to him.

His girlfriend.

They called me on my mobile one morning, asking where my man was. Leon being a roguish and canny opera-tor, he'd anticipated the Swear down Crew boys might approach me and had briefed me on what to say. 'If anyone ever calls you asking where I am, tell them we're not together any more,' he told me. 'Say you hate my guts and you deleted my number from your phone.'

'OK.'

'But, Chyna' – Leon held me close and searched my eyes – 'you got to say it like you mean it.'

'Think I can do that,' I said, not letting on how vexed I was at Leon tangling me up in some stupid drama.

A week later, I got a phone call from a boy in the Swear down Crew. I'd spoken with him a few times down the years, but we weren't the kind of close where he'd casually ring me up to see what's what.

No time for small talk, this boy cut straight to the chase. 'What's the deal with you and Leon?'

'We broke up,' I said. 'I told your mandem last week.'

From the get-off, this boy knew I was spitting bullshit.

'Chyna, Chyna,' he soothed. 'Think about what you're saying. You'll only make this harder for you and him. We want to talk to Leon, that's all. We're just a couple of boys who need to sort some business between us.'

'Wish I could help, but . . .'

The boy huffed down the phone. The line hissed. 'OK, if you want to play this the hard way, 's up to you. You know what that means, yeah? We'll kidnap you, take you to the motorway and strip you naked. Fucking hold you there until Leon shows.'

'What?'

'Any time you want to talk,' the boy said, his voice sweet, as if we was good friends.

The Swear Down Crew made it clear I had to watch my back. These boys weren't in the joking business. If they said a threat, they meant to do it.

These times I made an attempt to sort my life out by applying to study at college. I was seeing other girls going to college and studying. Thought, Rah, maybe I should be doing something else with my life. I applied to study child-care, but even enrolling was a bitch with the SDC beef playing on my mind.

During enrolment I had to rush to get home each day before it turned dark, because if the boys were planning to kidnap me, they'd have to do it in the evening, when the streets was pitch-black and the roads empty. As the daylight

hours shrank, I relied on friends picking me up and dropping me right outside my front door. If no one could offer me
a ride, I wouldn't go home. After a few times like this, I
thought, Fuck it. Childcare diplomas ain't designed for
Bonnie and Clyde people. I quit the course.

I was now drifting between rented accommodation,
bedrooms in house-shares and bedsits around South, with
the rent paid by the local council. I'd settled on a bedsit that
had a nice feel to it. Even here I didn't feel safe. SDC boys
hung around outside waiting for a chance to jump me. The
only comfort I had was knowing they wouldn't rush the place
because a dozen other people lived in the house, men and
women, and they'd have to fight their way up a couple of
flights of stairs to get to me. They sweated it out at the end
of the street and their presence guaranteed I wouldn't sleep
a wink all night.

My girls would invite me out to some exciting party and
as I dressed myself up, I'd receive a call from a fucking SDC
boy saying a bunch of them were waiting at the end of the
road to kidnap me. I'd peel back the curtains and spot a
monster group of boys standing around smoking weed. I
had nowhere to go, no one to ask for help. Leon, as my
boyfriend, was the person I'd normally lean on, but because
of his beef with the Swear Down Crew, showing his face
would put him in danger.

This waiting game played itself out for long. After eight
weeks, it'd become a sort of weird routine for me, having to

plan ahead and check when it was due to get dark on a certain day. Worrying all hours that I'd get snatched.

As Leon couldn't visit me, we'd go to the Waldorf Hilton in Central. Obviously the Hilton's £269 a night and we'd be there for a week. More p's blown. Leon bought me a Tiffany cushion set with the earrings, bracelet and necklace made of sterling silver and decorated with freshwater pearls, price tag £899. It was nice to be took to the Tiffany store on Bond Street, but these tings didn't make me happy. I was getting more and more depressed about my life. I felt like I was missing out on fun times, living in fucking hibernation.

'Don't you like it?' Leon said as he handed me the Tiffany set, lying on the queen-size bed at the Hilton and nursing a glass of Bollinger.

'It's pretty, no doubt. But you know what I'd like more?'

He blinked.

'Not having to worry about being dumped on a motorway,' I said. I was dressed in a waffle bathrobe. It was fluffy against my lathered skin. 'You shouldn't have robbed those boys.'

'Too late now,' he said, examining the calluses on his hands. He had rough hands. Street hands. 'It's not like I'm gonna roll to their endz and give them the stuff back, is it?'

Especially when you're spending it, I didn't say. But that's the way it is in the endz. Quick money is *quick*. It comes in quick. Goes out even quicker.

October became November. My studies were fucked and so were my living arrangements. My room became a part-time home. Leon's mum allowed me to crash at her house for a couple of nights a week. She didn't have much space, and I was grateful to her for the sacrifice. On the nights I slept over, I was able to chill a little. I'd wander outside after dark and feel like a normal person.

Morning came and I'd have to return to the nightmare.

The madness dragged on until circumstances forced Leon to confront the beef head-on. When you and someone you're beefing live in the same endz, a showdown is inevitable. You can't run and hide for ever. Leon's moment came when he and Tyrell bucked up one day at a party in South. Leon was there. So was Tyrell. Soon as they clocked eyes on each other, both boys knew there was gonna be a fight. In the early hours of the morning, the party finished and Leon made to leave. Fifty boys were waiting for him outside. The Swear Down Crew mandem. One of them pulled out a gun. Tyrell charged at Leon and the two started fighting.

Shots were fired. I don't know who by, because I wasn't there and Leon didn't want to talk about it. All I know is what they reported in the news: two boys shot, one in a critical condition.

No one got arrested. The CCTV cameras faced the wrong way, is what I heard. The boydem had evidence Leon was at the scene of the crime because they could tie his car to the area, but the boydem didn't have anything to pin the shootings on him.

To this day, Tyrell's on the lookout for Leon. In his mind, it's a case of when, not if. Right now, Tyrell hasn't had the chance to nail Leon in a one-on-one encounter. He might see him in his daily life, but having a chance to do something to Leon ain't a case of clocking someone in the street and stepping. Leon knows bare people have beefs with him, and he makes sure he's always with someone. Tyrell ain't the only one who wants to beat him up. He's robbed countless of people, sometimes for thousands of pounds. None of them boys ever forgets. If all his friends suddenly left him, he'd be fucked. He has to live with that knowledge daily, for the rest of his life.

That's the risk of life on the roads. Rob someone and you might get away with it. Maybe nobody says nothing. Maybe the boy you robbed walks right by you in the street. But you can guarantee that person's watching you, holding out for an opportunity to make you bleed. When you hear a story on TV about some boy getting shot over nothing, that's bullshit. In our endz, no one gets shot over nothing. It's always to do with something happened in the past. Might be years ago. I've known a boy who robbed someone a decade ago, when I was in fucking primary school, and ten years later, the victim targeted the robber's friend with a MAC-10. They crashed their motor into the boy, splitting his leg in two. *Ten years.*

Despite the aggro he'd caused with his robbery, I still wanted to give Leon a chance.

Then Wallace bounced back into my life. He stalked me, harassed me. Made my life miserable. Knocked on my door at three o'clock in the morning when I was in bed with Leon, checking to see if he was in the house with me. Feeding Leon lies.

'When she's not with you, Chyna's with me,' Wallace told him.

These lies messed up my relationship with Leon. I tried to cut Wallace out of the picture, but he knew where we lived and unless I moved again, he was gonna carry on making life hard. I think deep down he'd never really gotten over me walking out on him. A man with a lot of pride like Wallace, a woman doing her own ting is a bitter pill to swallow.

Leon couldn't buck up to Wallace. To do so would mean Wallace's bredrin coming back at Leon. Rips, Stocks, Nugz, Kevin . . . Without representation, Leon would be up against bare boys. If life had been hard living under the threat of the SDC, boxing up Wallace would bring a world of shit down on Leon. So he had no choice but to take the shit streaming out of Wallace's mouth. Take it, and try to ignore it.

After several months of 3 a.m. wake-up calls and lies, Leon had enough.

'I'm not feeling it, Chyna,' he said.

'It's because of Wallace, ain't it?' I said back. 'Let me try and sort shit out. Get him out of my life. We should give this another chance.'

I liked Leon, I really did. Sure, he had rushes of blood to the head and made mistakes, but he was a nice boy with his heart in the right place. Really and truly, if Wallace was out of the picture, me and Leon would have stayed together. But that's the hand life seemed to deal me. I thought I'd found a bit of happiness and somehow it was snatched away from me.

'He ain't gonna surrender,' Leon said. 'You know he'll keep coming and coming. I want to believe you, but . . .'

Me and Leon never got back together.

Wallace bided his time.

PART FOUR
SHOTTING

'I got these endz on lock'

– Lickman

FIFTEEN

Supply and demand

My relationship with Leon might have ended, but seeing up close the massive p's in the drugs game, it got me thinking, Rah, enough of this tiefing and street-robbery nonsense, bringing in £40 or £50 a time. That's for the youngers. The real sterling is in selling hardcore drugs on the endz.

Crack. Cocaine. Brown.

Our fam became looser as boys played a more important role in our lives. Pasha was in the year below us at school, so I checked with her at the weekends. I hung around with Roxy and Styles the most. Meanwhile Nang had given up the weed shotting and was trying to work a nine-to-five job to make ends meet. Bigs was doing her ting. Smiles was out of the picture.

I was desperate to get a shortcut through the paper chase. I didn't see no other way of me getting access to the tings I wanted: slick rims, designer garmz, big house . . . Some boy from our endz stacked up £1 million in p's and relocated to the country with his Porsches and phat wardrobe. I thought, Rah, why not me?

As a paid-in-full weed fanatic, I spent a lot of time at a woman's house in a part of South that used to be rich but had fallen on hard times. Her name was Courtnie and she lived above a corner shop on a tattered main road, all cracked pavements and crumbling red brick, with a car showroom opposite. An over big woman with three pickneys and an addiction to Oreo cookies, Courtnie rented out her flat as a weed house. Sort of like a crackhouse without the crack.

Courtnie smoked bare weed. She'd smoke a ben in just one spliff, no Golden Virginia or Cutter's Choice to dilute the mix. The convenient location and her weed dependency meant all the local shotters used her house as a base – someplace they could set up shop, keep their food and money there, with the showroom a legit spot to link with people. In return, Courtnie got free weed.

Wherever there was weed, there's where you'd find me and Roxy, my smoking partner. We'd cotch at Courtnie's with the mandem, Safon and Rips, Nugz and Stocks. These times I still saw Wallace and sort of dated him and sort of not. We had an on-off ting going on.

Courtnie's flat was filthy. Dirt and food trampled into the carpets, stringy bits of rolling baccy sprinkled on every surface, heap of unwashed pots and pans sitting in the sink. Bare man jamming in the living room and kitchen. One of her daughters suffered from eczema and her problem was made ten times worse by the rank living conditions. Whenever we went there, Roxy used to make her bed, shaking off all the dead skin she'd shedded and helping her apply the lotions.

Because of its rep, Courtnie's flat was bait. Everyone who knew anyone knew about the flat. It was a highly exposed and very dangerous place to be. When we rolled up at her house, we didn't need no key; I'd kick the door and it'd swing open, on account of the reg times other mandem had raided the flat.

A notorious boy by the name of Straps and his boys shotted out of Courtnie's flat. The rest of South lived in permanent fear of getting run up by Straps's mandem. That made me more interested in these boys. Boys were literally so shitless they'd leap out of the windows of Courtnie's flat, fifteen feet to the street below, injuring themselves and hobbling on busted legs for their fucking lives. Wallace once got robbed by Straps and his bredrin on the stairs as he entered the flat. They stripped him naked and stole a half-ounce bag of weed on his person. For Straps's boys, it was all in a day's work.

One raid turned into a street fight. Me, Roxy, Styles and the mandem left Courtnie's flat to go and chill in the boys' motors. We crossed the road to five cars parked beside the showroom. I sat seated in the back of a metallic-silver Volvo S60, Roxy by my side. I lighted up a spliff. Clocked two black boys outside the door to Courtnie's place.

'Who the fuck are they?' Roxy asked.

We'd been in Courtnie's pad about every day. Knew the faces of every shotter and smoker. These two boys – I'd never set eyes on them before, but I guessed what they were about to do.

They booted the door in.

No one dared chase the boys. Straps's mandem packed guns and weren't afraid to spray them.

Two minutes later, the boys exited and made a beeline for the boys' rims.

More than two boys. I clocked thirty other boys sieging us from the left and right. I panicked. We got to breeze out of here, I thought, before shit kicks off. Roxy shouted at the driver to put his foot on the pedal. He was already on it. Passenger doors slung open, the cars revved up and skated into the middle of the road, but our driver hadn't checked for traffic, and two buses from the opposite lane of traffic blocked his exit. Horns blared.

I spotted Straps in the road, making his way to another of the mandem's cars. Barrel of a niner gleaming in his hand. Our motor swerved to avoid him, arrowing towards the buses.

We braked. And lurched. Our Volvo screeched. The buses stopped inches from the hood of the Volvo, brake-lights having an epileptic fit, shunting us forward, bashing our skulls against the backs of the front seats.

Crack! Crack! Crack!

Gunshots. I'd no idea who was doing the firing – Straps or one of his bredrin. I weren't hanging around to find out. Out of the car! I scattered with Roxy. We sprinted to the other side of the road and down the street, putting as much distance between ourselves and the guns as possible.

'Where's Styles?' I asked Roxy.

At the corner of the street, we seen Styles fifteen metres ahead of us. We called to her. Instead of joining us in our getaway, she ducked into a Polish food shop. We'd turned the corner and were twenty metres down a sloping hill, waving and shouting at Styles for her to come with. Straps stormed into view, chasing Styles inside the shop.

'What the fuck?'

The shop door was open. I caught Straps shouting at her, 'Think you can diss me, yeah?' Straps booted Styles in her back. 'I checked you, and now you linking with that piece-of-shit boy? Going out with someone I *knows*? Fuck you.'

Shit, I thought. I hadn't even realized Styles knew Straps.

Thirty seconds later, he breezed out of the shop and went back to what he was doing. Robbing the mandem. We grabbed Styles, dozen boys in the background, running around the street, dashing in and out of Courtnie's flat.

Seeing them boys licking off shots, maybe I should've been scared away, but I was still interested in rolling with them. Spending time in a dirty flat smoking weed and driving around in Fiat Puntos was good fun, but I could see where I'd end up if I stuck at that lifestyle: in the same state as Courtnie, bare pickneys and mandem in my life, getting robbed and shit on.

Whilst other people's instincts might be to run the other way, I got to know Straps better these times through Styles. How we grew close was that if shotters in Courtnie's flat badmouthed us or threatened to beat us up, I'd call Straps.

Get him and his friends to rock up and flush out all the p's and weed from the joint.

People seen Straps as a loony who did crazy stuff on the regs. He was, without doubt, the most hyped character on the roads. Straps instilled fear wherever he went. He looked a lot older than his sixteen years, his face hard-edged, his eyes like blackened bottle caps and stubble stickered across his jaw. He looked more like twenty-six. When Straps wanted something, he took it. If he asked for some boy's bag of weed, that boy weren't about to fire a comeback his direction.

He had himself a rep as a violent boy, expert at bullying people and getting what he wanted on tap, no questions asked. One time me and Straps happened to pass a bus-stop where two black boys were perched on the plastic bench, a couple of large Pizza Hut boxes on their laps. The pizzas gave off a powerful smell of spicy pork, pepperoni and onions. As we walked on, one of the boys shot Straps a dirty look.

'Safe, you got a problem, blud?'

'Nah, man.'

Straps weren't done.

'Nigga, gimme that pizza,' he said. Before the boy could answer, he snatched the box out of his hands and passed it to me. 'Help youself, cuz.'

'Why you breading for?' the boy said.

'Because of the way you looked at me, nigga.' He spat

on the ground. 'Look at me like that again, you won't have no eyes left. Fucking guide dog'll do the looking for you, feel me?'

'Fuck you, bumbaclot.'

Chiefing Straps is a bad, bad idea.

'You'd better run the other direction,' I warned the boy. By this point Straps was growing angrier and my instincts told me, There's only one way this is gonna pan out. But the boy ran off his mouth and Straps swung for him.

Getting punched by Straps, I reckon, is sort of like someone swatting you with a paving slab. He had the hardest punch of anyone I knew. This boy dropped like he'd been hit in a drive-by, blood streaked on the hot concrete and wetted over the bus-shelter glass. As if the man had yakked blood. We blew out. I was amazed at how Straps had conked the boy out with a single punch.

None of Straps's random violence frightened me. When you're on the roads and you're tight with someone, you see people in a certain way. I'm sure that if a stranger walked down the street and clocked Straps, they'd cross to the other side of the road – and not just nine-to-fivers, but gangstas too. Ting is, they see this big, scary black boy, but they're only looking at one side of his personality. Instead of being scared of Straps's violent temper, I always felt protected around him. I knew he'd got my back, wouldn't let nothing happen to me. I knew his uncle, his mum, his sisters. They were good to me. We had love for each other like that. Straps was the closest I ever had to a real brother.

A lot of boys in the street lifestyle get a rep for being bad. I'm sure they deserve those reps. But them same boys can also be kind and considerate and loving. I knew Straps would never do anything to harm me, that he looked on me as fam. Anywhere we went, people asked who I was, Straps replied, 'That's my little cousin.'

That didn't stop Straps from being a ticking time-bomb. Hanging with Straps meant accepting that any situation, anywhere had the potential to explode. One time we was watching TV in a friend's flat. He had this gun in his hand, a smaller piece on the roads like the Baikal .22 pistols that were getting popular with the boy gangs. Out of the blue Straps went gun-crazy and spun the trigger on his finger, freaking me. I shielded a sofa pillow in front of me and told him to stop fucking about.

'Leave it out, Straps. It's gonna go off.'

'Nah, cuz, it's cool.'

Boom!

The sound was deafening, like a carburettor backfiring inside my head. For a minute I only heard a high-pitched ringing in my ears. Straps laughed and made light of it. Guessing that he'd shot up the ceiling, we hunted around for the bullet. Nothing seemed to be broken. I looked at the window.

A neat hole the size of a 10-pence coin was punched into

the glass. The bullet had travelled right past me, two or three inches from my face. From that experience, I knew what guns were about and what kind of lifestyle I was deep into.

I also started seeing big shipments of drugs. Not no little bits of weed that I used to shot to my friends at the bus station, but huge boxes of cocaine and crack.

Straps was my first affiliation in the more extreme South mandem, the Front-Line Soldiers. In our endz 'front line' means the main road, where all the action is, where everything's going down. Calling themselves FLS was the boys' way of saying, *Rah, we on our own ting. We in a war.* I started seeing and hearing of the FLS a lot more around town.

These times me and Wallace had gotten back together, although tings were a bit strange between us. We were in a kind of on-off phase. He'd cheat on me, I'd ditch him, not speak to him for weeks. Then something inside of me clicked and I'd take him back. I don't know why I kept doing this. I might've been lonely, or a little naive, or too trusting. Or I might have just loved him to the point that I couldn't let go. My head was all over the place when it came to Wallace. I couldn't think clearly. Problem is, once you've let a man back into your life, it's like lending money to someone. You make it easier for them to come back again and again.

We had a break-up routine. I'd cut him loose for two-timing me. He'd beg on his hands and knees for a second chance. I'd let him off the hook. Wallace went back to his old habits and I pushed myself further into denial. Thinking, This time it'll be different. Or, He doesn't mean to cheat on me. He can't help himself. He loves me. That's the most important ting.

When me and Wallace weren't linked, he'd go to his ex, Breelyn, and sleep with her for a little bit. I had no evidence of this, but I knew it was true all the same. Boys are forever reckoning themselves smarter than girls, able to outwit us whenever, but the reality is, we're experts at finding out the truth. After a few weeks with Breelyn, I'd buy Wallace's bullshit apology. He'd pee her off and come back to me. I'd get the full speech about not making the same mistake, wanting to be faithful to me and, somehow, it used to work on me. Wallace could be over charming on his day, and when he beamed his smile and looked at me with his honeyed eyes, I found it impossible to say no to him.

The only way I can really explain me and Wallace is, when we used to be good, we was good. When we used to be bad, we was bad.

I kept my friendship with Straps secret from Wallace. If tings were simmering between us, it'd only make Wallace angry if he knew I rolled with a boy who'd robbed him countless of times.

Another boy also came on to the scene these days. His name was Rashid – the boy I'd met at Breelyn's place.

Rashid was part of the FLS and used to rob Wallace on

the regs. So I began hearing more and more about this Rashid boy, and becoming intrigued by him. I remembered those intense eyes and the confident, skell way he carried himself, like he was a king. The more I got word of Rashid's movements, the more he was on my brain.

Around these times Cheese, a good friend of Wallace, got shot in a street hype. He'd shelled out phat notes for a new Mercedes CLK Coupé in all black. A week before the shooting happened, Rashid robbed Wallace and Cheese. Bang – drama.

On this given day, Cheese took his Benz for a cruise through the endz. As he reached a junction, he eyed Rashid and a bag of mandem standing on a street corner next to a Chicken Cottage. Cheese couldn't let this opportunity of revenge slide. Slowing his Benz, Cheese rolled down the electric window and began cussing these boys differently.

'Yo, wasteman,' Cheese shouted. 'Think you can rob me and my bredrin?'

'Drive on, drive on!' Rashid shouted back, sensing that tings was getting out of hand.

'Rob me like it's anything? Fucking come down my endz again, bruv—'

'And what?' – one of the other mandem inching towards the Benz. 'Brother, I'm warning you, drive on.'

But Cheese maintained with the abuse. He was all 'wasteman' this and 'bitch nigga' that, chiefing up the bag of mandem and thinking, I'm safe, I'm in my Benz.

Cheese – and Rashid – not realizing that one of these particular mandem had a gun on him.

In broad daylight, on a main street, with a church bang right next to them, this boy took out his gun and unloaded two shots at Cheese at close range. The bullets pinged through Cheese's thigh and knee, leaving him with a little bit of disability. He can't do certain tings now. Boy paid a high price for running off his mouth. Maybe that price seems too high, but that's the way it goes down on the endz. A lot of people I know would say, 'Rah, Cheese got what was coming to him. You can't be running off your mouth like that.'

I was noticing Rashid's name on the roads more and more frequently. Like, he did heavy tings. He was much more higher up in the game than most boys and lived a reckless street lifestyle.

My relationship with Wallace finally snapped when he had to go court after he was arrested for driving while serving a ban. Wallace had to face up to the probability of going prison.

Roxy and me attended court to support him, but we didn't know which courtroom to go to. I rung his phone. He didn't pick up. I thought, Rah, this is suspicious. We explored the court, going from room to room and looking for my man. At the end of the corridor, I stopped in my tracks.

Wallace had his back to me, holding hands and kissing some girl.

Breelyn.

Seeing her here, now, as the girl Wallace leaned on for comfort, set fireworks off inside my head. I followed Wallace into the courtroom and got into a big hype.

'I'm gonna fuck you up,' I shouted at Wallace as he sat in the dock, unable to look me in the eye. 'Fucking coward! Look at me!'

'You'd better get this girl out of here,' the judge said. An orderly yanked me out of the room as I vented my rage.

Next stop, Wallace's house. Nugz lived with Wallace these times and whenever we'd had a split or issues, Nugz had always been the one to defend Wallace and comfort me, acting as a peace man. He'd tell me, 'Rah, Wallace's only got eyes for you. He don't love no one else.' All this. My thinking now was, Nugz must've been saying these same tings to Breelyn. I had a hype with him, called him a two-faced shit.

Wallace got sent down. I wasn't sad to see the back of him; he'd caused me plenty of pain. My attitude was, good riddance.

To make extra p's, I'd go out with Straps's crew and shot with them of a night. I quickly learned that shotting isn't glamorous. For one ting, your customers are addicts. You'd get a cat come up to you, hardcore junkies begging with you for a hit. If the government really wanted to stop kids taking drugs, all they'd have to do is dump a cat in front of the class.

Cats look deadout. They're skin and bone. They don't

shave or wash and their faces are covered in spots and scabs. Teeth yellowed, white scum on their lips. Their faces are so skinny their eyeballs look like they're about to pop right out of their sockets.

I can spot a crackhead immediately. Not just by the way they look, but how they walk. They got this stiff-legged way about them, like they're balancing on stilts. Wooden. But we dealt with them because they were our customers, and once the money's in my hands, I'm like, Rah, I'm earning serious p's.

Shotting food is a learning curve. Crack's easy to get the hang of, but brown is awkward because it's like dust. If you wrap it in cling film, it'll stick. The ting to do was buy a packet of Rizlas, fold them in half and tip the brown into the Rizla paper, wrap it round and then put it in a plastic bag.

The hardest ting to learn was how to keep the pebbles in my mouth. Pebbles are rocks that are wrapped up really tight, making them over small; you can hide them in your mouth. Every shotter has to practise this trick until they're good enough to hold a conversation and not no one realize they've got three or four bags of rocks on their person. I held them under my tongue. Once I seen the crackhead and checked that the coast is clear, they gave me the money and I spat out the rocks. Concealing the rocks in my mouth was important, because I had to react fast if the boydem arrested me. Swallow the rocks and they wouldn't find any drugs on my person.

At first, my shotting earnings was all right, but not great. I made between £500 and £600 a night. Half of that money had to go back to my link to pay for the consignment, leaving me with £250 or £300 for seven or eight hours' work. Compared to what the boys were making, that amounted to hardly nothing.

Still, the money went as quick as I earned it. I saved no p's, blew my profit on nice clothes from places where it was hard to tief, treating myself to name brands like D&G, Gucci and Armani jeans. When I was younger, I'd go out wearing five pairs of tracksuit bottoms to help keep me warm against the cold, especially in winters, when we'd be out of doors for long. These times I went for the girly stuff, jeans and tops, instead of the hoodies, woolly hats and tracksuit bottoms I used to wear. I threw down bare p's on liquor and had to support my own weed habit. To live that sort of lifestyle, I needed to have access to big p's. I started thinking about making my way up the shotter food chain – becoming a deela in the future with my own people and consignments.

As I got better at shotting, I started to build up lines.

Building a line is hard work. Selling drugs ain't no simple ting of standing on a corner and whistling until a crackhead shuffles over. To build a line, you need to cultivate, recruit, market and befriend.

The secret to building a line is finding the best place with the most amount of crackheads. In South and North, this ain't as easy as it sounds. In most places where there's crackheads, there's bare shotters too, and they don't like new people muscling in on their roads. You've also got to give the crackheads a reason to come to you rather than deal with the boy on the other side of the street.

An experienced shotter can instantly tell what's a crack goldmine in London city. Location, number of estates, type of shops – and the people. After shotting for six months, I got to recognize crackheads from the get-go.

One top crack-spot was the Hill. The Hill straddles two massive estates and is lined with tired-looking people, kebab houses, second-hand furniture shops and bookies with groups of Yardie men standing outside smoking cigarettes and hopped-up Chinamen betting with their last 20-pence pieces. The Hill had all these, plus a prison looming opposite.

The Hill is Crackhead Central.

The downside to shotting on the Hill was the relentless heat from the boydem. That place was hotter than a sauna. Proper rodded, with more boydem on the roads than there is people. The area came with a bad rep. You had to really watch yourself in these endz.

I also had to be careful about treading on deelas' toes. Wherever you build a line, selling to the cats, there's gonna be a man nearby who will disagree with your right to bust shots. The first days I started shotting on the Hill, I had a couple of boys coming up to me. They pointed to some crackhead I'd just sold a couple of rocks. The shotters acted mad, like I'd spat on their trainers.

'That's my crackhead, cuz. What d'you think you're doing?'

'Supply and demand, bruv.'

'Fucking mind your own cats. Mine comes to me for food.'

'What you telling me for? Ain't my fault they choose to deal with me.'

A dozen shotters worked the Hill, and because I was a girl, slim and peng, they thought they could push me around. I had nothing to worry about; none of the boys never laid a finger on me. They took out their frustrations on any 'cheating' cats. Bottom line, every shotter was out to steal every other shotter's customers and no one could pretend to be righteous. Besides, attracting crackheads to your line took a lot of hard work and you had to be resourceful.

There were two ways of reeling in junkies. You could set the price of your rocks lower than the other shotters in that area. Obviously there's a limit to how low you can go, because you need to make enough p's to settle your debt to your deela. As well, you got to make it worth your time and energy spent grinding.

The second way to attract cats was to shot top-quality crack. If the other deelas are dishing out swag stuff, the crackheads are going to switch to you, because they're getting more value for their hit of crack. Rule number one: a cat's only loyalty is to the food. I was working with a deela who took his cut, and the food I got was OK quality. Decent, but not great.

I'd get my food once a week from this man, meet him somewhere local. Going to his place was out of the question. You never knew where the deelas lived, because many shotters would be tempted to go there and rob the man of his drugs. The trade-off point was on neutral turf, like an alleyway near my house, somewhere not bait, where me and him both felt relaxed.

At first I had to pay for the whole package of food up front. In the beginning, I was new to the deela and he didn't know fuck all about me. That worked for me, as I started off buying small bits of food. I didn't know how much I could realistically shot on the Hill, and there's no point me going for a big package if I couldn't get rid of dinky little bags of the stuff.

Happily for me, business was soon booming on the Hill. On a typical day, I'd get there around four or five o'clock in the afternoon to work on building my line. Armed with my shots of brown and heroin, I'd find a cat scouting for crack and try to recruit them to my product. My style was to play it nice. Although the cats are total wastemans and I got no respect for them, you got to pretend to be on friendly terms with them. I'd make small talk with the cat and tell them I was a shotter new to the endz and they should think about buying from me. My trick was to give them a free sample of the food. Nine times out of ten, the tester sealed the deal. As most cats have been addicted to crack for longs, they could instantly tell the quality of my product.

'Here's my number,' I'd say, giving them a burner I used, a pay-as-you-go mobile like them ones used by the Barksdale boys in *The Wire*. 'Tell your friends if they want the best brown, give me a call and I can sort them out, yeah?'

Now, crackheads being crackheads, they're always looking for better-quality food, lower prices and whatnot. They hang around other crackheads, and all they ever talk about is crack: where they get it from, how good it is, where they're gonna get their next hit and how they're gonna tief to pay for it. So I knew that by doing business with one cat, they'd mention my name and maybe three or four other cats might call me that night. You'd get the next and the next and the next.

That's your line.

Being proactive about my line also meant I didn't have to fuck about on the roads for long. Suppose a crackhead buzzed my shotter mobile and said, 'Gimme three rocks.'

'Cools,' I'd reply, cotching round a mandem's house or in a nearby McDonald's. 'Meet me at the phone box outside the Chicken Cottage in fifteen.'

I took two precautions before meeting the crackhead. I'd bust a knife, and I'd make sure someone else came with. Either a mandem I knew hustling further up the Hill or else one of my girls. The need for some company meant that I started working with Paige, Roxy's girl from school, the one who almost came between us because of her jezzy status when we confronted her outside Superdrug. I'd made my peace with her after school, realizing that, rah, we did have a bit in common, and she also had experience of the shotting game.

Sometimes me and her took turns to work the streets, her doing days, me nights.

Being more broke than Lehman Brothers, tiefing shit is always on the cat's mind. A cat does three or four rocks of a night, seven days a week. That's a £60- or £80-a-night habit, or about £500 a week. I'm sure they looked at me and Paige and thought, Hmm, seventeen-year-old girls? I'll rob them. Once or twice we went to meet a cat and found they wielded a bloodied needle in their hands as a weapon. 'Course, they couldn't aim for shit and they couldn't run either, so getting away was easy.

The line expanded. Business boomed. I'd bust twenty or thirty shots a night, turning around my week's supply faster than a Tinie Tempah freestyle. Gradually I went in for bigger bags of food from the deela.

After I came up with the p's the first few times and proved myself reliable, I managed to build up a good level of trust with the deela and he let me get the drugs on a consignment basis, the same arrangement I had with my cousin in school for buying bags of weed at the age of thirteen. Except now the drugs were harder and the p's bigger.

The sterling flowed. We built up a far line. I linked up

with my fam at the weekends, going out to raves and parties, but now we were sipping on cocktails and investing in designer threads.

One day, I was shotting with Paige on the Hill when this man on the other side of the road eyeballed me. He was a man, not a boy, early twenties, decked out in low batties and a black hoodie with a grenade symbol drawn on the front. Yankees cap on top, sucking on a lollipop. His hoodie was down, revealing a line of cornrows on his head. I could see the man had a knife scar on his neck, the scar tissue pink and plasticky, like an upside-down Nike swoosh.

He'd been shotting on the roads, like us, but today he didn't pay much attention to the cats. Instead he trained his eyes on me and Paige. Trying to freak us out, I guessed. Then he crossed the street. Boydem sirens echoed in the distance.

'Heads up,' I said to Paige. My hand instinctively felt for the folding-blade knife in my jeans pocket. If the shotter thought he could rob us, I'd draw him a fucking twin for the scar on his neck.

'Yu the yutes been stealing my cats.' The boy had a pure Yardie accent. He talked dull and steady, like hot tar being poured on to a road.

Out the corner of my eye, I saw Paige move for her own blade up her sleeve.

'Here's de ting.' Yardie Man licked his lollipop. 'This is

my yard, and I don't take kindly to squatters. How about yu work with me?'

'And why would we do that?' I asked.

'Simple, girl. I got these endz on lock. Sure, yu got some business off me, but de kind of proposition I'm making, yu eiter make more coil with me or yu make shit.'

I thought about it. It mightn't be so bad, partnering with this Yardie. The quality of my food wasn't off the wall. If we went into business with him, he'd guarantee top-drawer drugs, because he had a connect that reached directly back to Jamaica.

'What if we say no?'

Yardie Man took the lollipop out of his mouth and pointed the sticky red end at me. 'Then yu both fuck off.'

We didn't have much choice.

'Yeah, all right,' I said. 'What's your name?'

'Lickman,' he said. ''Cus that's what I dos if people dare to cross me.'

We didn't know what we was letting ourselves in for with Lickman, but he was right about us earning more p's with him. The first week of our partnership, I racked up £1,500 in profit. This was what I'd dreamed of, the kind of p's where I could buy a car, go to the bestest clubs and get the most richest bottle of champagne.

Now we was flossing.

'Grand five hundred,' I said to Paige, counting my p's. 'This is the big-time, fam.'

'We're not even getting *started* yet,' Paige said. She always had her eye on bigger game. 'Look at how many cats there are. Millions, bruv.'

That's the ting about shotting. The p's are great, but everything else about the job is waste. I hated dealing drugs. The work is boring and the hours are long. You work harder than a nine-to-fiver; my phone was on 24/7 because if I turned it off, my cats would think that I'd gotten arrested. For three weeks they'd stop phoning me and take their business elsewhere.

On the streets, trade could swing from bustling to barren. Maybe one day you're bustin' thirty, forty shots, and the next it's a struggle to move five or six. The winter was easily the most miserable period for shotting. My ears and toes would be so cold it felt as if someone was lighting matchsticks under them. I'd be tired and hungry. Time didn't pass; it crawled. And I was conscious of the fact that every time I went to sell some food, I had to be lucky to avoid arrest.

But I loved the money. That feeling of walking away from a ten-hour grind having shotted forty pebbles, bare grand stuffed in my back pocket.

I guess there's a lot of people in the world got jobs they don't like doing. You just get on with them all the same because you need the money. Drug deelas are no different.

Some of the p's I earned went to compensating for crackheads who came up short. You had to walk a tightrope between cutting the cats a little slack now and again, and allowing them to take the piss out of you. I'd get a call late at night, middle of fucking winter. Some cat wants a couple of rocks. I'm cold and tired and want to go home after grinding it for twelve hours solid. But money's money, right? So I'd meet the cat and it turned out he'd have £8 on him in dirty coinage. Pounds, twenties, tens, twos and ones. He's £2 short. But I didn't want to lose the cat's trade, he's a regular customer, so I took a hit, pocketed the £8 and told him next time to come with the right money.

Following day, seven or eight cats tried tikking me a few pounds. After that I got tough and told them no money, no food. I worked out that if ten cats came up £2 short on each rock, I'd be down £400 in a month.

For cats who were flat broke, they could always turn their flat into a crackhouse. One day, Lickman, me and Paige were offered the chance to use a cat's house as our base for shotting. We wasn't sure, but Lickman said it'd be a good ting, as shotting on the endz in January and February was gash.

'Yu get so cold yu'll be wondrin' if de cat ate yu toes,' he told us.

The place was on the third floor of a block of council flats off the Hill. The stairwell was grotty, a permanent smell of shit wafting in the air. You had to watch carefully where you're treading, what with the puddles of piss on every landing. The one working lift had bloodied phlegm marks up and down the walls and graffiti scrawled into the metal grille next to the controls. You had to fight your way past millions of crackheads shuffling from floor to floor, and smacked-out prostitutes hawking for business in the stairwells, sucking dick behind the block for £20 a pop.

The flat was just as grotty on the inside. It had one bedroom, a kitchen with bare dirty plates and Domino's boxes, armies of ants on the floor and a bathroom where the white tiles were smeared brown. I hadn't seen a home this gross since me and my mum lived in the safehouse. But if these rooms were filth, the front room was over nasty.

'Dis yu new base,' Lickman said. He waved his hand across the room, like he was an estate agent showing me around a box.

Four crackheads slouched on a dirty, stained sofa. The coffee table in front of them was covered in teaspoons, orange juice, Rizlas, bits of rolling baccy and cigarettes cut in half, Doritos packets and needles. On an armchair to the right a skin-and-bone man injected himself with brown. In the far corner was the kitchen, where all the shotters hung out. You had to cross the dirtiness of the front room to hit the kitchen. The shotters used the kitchen because the window overlooked the entrance to the block and they could keep a lookout for any boydem.

'What d'yu tink?'

'Not the Ritz, is it?'

Lickman widened his eyes. 'What yu talking 'bout? Dis here is de five-star crackhouse!'

One of the cats on the sofa leaped to his feet and hopped to Lickman like he was dancing on hot coals.

'Man needs to get his pay,' Lickman said, handing over one £10 bone. That was the man's daily payment for renting out his flat to us. His girlfriend tried to get a peek, but the man shielded the food from her.

I set up my office space at the kitchen table. Shotter phone, cigarettes, my personal weed stash, the rocks.

Soon as I produced the food, the other cats got excited. This, I saw, was the B-side to crackhouses. They were a great way of keeping clear of the heavily rodded endz. But crackheads talk about crack and nothing else. A crackhouse is brimming with junkies zoned out of their skulls and casting their mind ahead to their next hit. And you're in the middle of these cats, holding a grand's worth of food on you. I had to be on point with these cats every minute, because they'd try and make small talk with you, hoping you'd dash them a free rock.

I was always hyper-aware not to touch anything in that flat. Once, I happened to be in the front room and some pound coins tumbled out of my pocket and down the back of the sofa. I considered that money lost. The idea of rooting around that dark fold at the back of the sofa never crossed my mind; there was a good chance the cats dumped needles down there. Soon as I got pricked by a needle, it'd be over for me.

The cats sometimes made an effort to strike up a

conversation with me, but crackheads' lives begin and end with crack; nothing else enters their mind. They'd see me and be like, 'Oh, give us a ten-pound draw. I'll get the money to you, I promise!'

If I refused, they got down on their hands and knees and begged.

This time I didn't get taken in by their pleading. Not since I let a few of them off the hook and degraded my profit. Now, if they came to me with £9, I'd say to them, 'No deal. You go and get the extra pound, then we'll do business.'

I weren't the only people working for Lickman – he had a set of workers doing separate shifts. Because crackheads are on it day and night, a professional deela needs to have shotters on call 24/7. Sometimes six or seven o'clock in the morning would be the busiest hour of the day; other times eleven o'clock at night, right after the cats burgled someone's house. It varied; crackheads don't really stick to a schedule like the rest of us.

I developed a stupid crush on a boy around the endz by the name of Aishy. He was a little baller, shotting hard food – crack and brown. When I got around him, that's when I knew what it was all about, because Aishy used to make money differently. I've no idea what his name meant, and I never thought to ask him. I just accepted him as Aishy. He stood at six feet four and made me look like a midget, with skin like ground coffee betraying his Ghanaian roots and a heavyset, toned style to him, as if he spent hour upon hour in the gym.

The ting that attracted me to Aishy was his style. Because he was a baller, he had the p's to dress nice. Normal yutes dressed up in Nike and Adidas, shopped exclusively at Foot Locker and JD Sports, but Aishy wasn't on that: he rolled in Iceberg, Versace, Louis Vuitton, dropping bare grands on these type of name-brand threads at Selfridges.

Aishy also did some shotting for Lickman. He worked the opposite shifts to me. If I did nights, he grinded in the daytime. But Aishy lived on the Hill; when I turned up for work, he might still be around the block. If mandem live on their block, they're not leaving, because the boydem can't do nothing about them hanging about their own endz.

'Rah, that boy's looking at you,' Paige said to me.

'What? Don't be stupid.'

She stamped out her cigarette and blew smoke into the sky. The smoke mingled with clouds that looked like bags of plain flour. You couldn't tell where the cigarette smoke ended and the sky began.

'He looks nice. You should talk to him,' Paige said.

'Yeah, another Kendrick, dat's what I need in my life,' I said, dismissing her advice with a wave.

A week later, London city was in a cold mood, the kind of cold that makes your bones chatter. I guess it must have been fate, that weather, because when it gets chilly, the shotters retreated inside to the crackhouse and the stairwells inside the block, sitting around, listening to dubstep on their phones to pass the time, rubbing their gloved hands to keep themselves warm.

Me and Paige tried to avoid spending too long in the crackhouse. Fifteen, twenty minutes at a time. We entered the crackhouse. Aishy was sat at the kitchen table, rolling up a spliff. This was my first close-up look at the boy. He had a thin, long face and big, worldly eyes. He looked like a younger Jay-Z.

''S'up, choong?' he said.

'Safe.'

'Rah, what's your name?' he said.

I told him. Knowing a little about Aishy, I asked him what he did with himself.

'Bit of this and that,' he replied, trying to play it cool. 'I do OK for myself.' Shotters generally avoided telling people too much about their activity. They didn't want word to flow around the roads that they were swimming in sterling. He angled his head at me. 'I've seen you around . . . You're in with those N2L girls, ain't you?'

'Something like that,' I said, playing it cool right back at him. 'I do OK for myself.'

'What you doing tonight?' he asked.

'Working here, innit.'

He nodded slowly. Rubbed the tips of the long, red Rizla paper between his fingers. 'If you want, I can keep you company. I'm about to clock off for the day, but . . .'

Aishy had a sharp ped, he was officially licensed and everything, and he used to drive around the endz. One day, we bumped into each other and started talking. We was both inquisitive about each other; I'd noticed him around the endz, Aishy likewise, but we'd never had the opportunity to have a proper chat.

We talked some more. He was confident, cocky, a bit rough around the edges. And no Kendrick, which was an automatic plus point in my book. Against my better judgement, I took a shine to Aishy.

When my shift was done, I couldn't stop thinking about him. Aishy had explained that he was a big-time deela, doing eighteenths, big blocks of crack, whereas we operated on a strictly small-time basis. According to Paige, the word on the roads said that Aishy was involved in a rivalry with a bag of big boys on the road, and that he was dangerous to be around. I didn't listen; I had a love affair with trouble.

I spent more and more time around Aishy. He'd pick me up from my house in his car, a brand-new Alfa Romeo Spider 2.0, a convertible with sports rims and leather seats and a built-in GPS.

We went on bare dates, to Cineworld or Nando's or Tiger Tiger, or grabbed a takeaway Chinese or Indian after a hard day's grind on the Hill. After long, we made it official.

Our working arrangement wasn't a problem; because

Aishy was a big-time deela, he'd only appear in the crack-house for a few minutes to check on his people, then disappear for three or four hours. Anyway, I wasn't down with the idea of spending time with my man surrounded by crackheads. Not seeing him around the Hill weren't a problem.

Aishy's rivalries were beginning to give me sleepless nights. A regular stream of threats were aimed at him, and with every passing day it became bait that Aishy had a number of enemies and was a serious target for particular mandem. I had to share my worries with someone. I checked my girl Roxy and told her how I felt.

'He's a target for the other boys,' I told her in our local Tiger Tiger. A plate of king prawns lay uneaten in front of me. I didn't touch the glass of rosé. Roxy grazed on a plate of nachos layered with guacamole. 'They rob Aishy bare times.'

'That's a shotter's luck, bruv. You know that.'

'Yeah, 'course,' I sighed. 'But, like, they *violate* him.'

A week later and the threats to Aishy became intense. And then, on the eighth day, I rang his phone of an evening. Some boy answered.

'Yeah?' this boy said. I recognized his voice, but couldn't place the face.

'Why you answering my man's phone?' I asked, vexed.

'Chyna, is that you?' He sounded surprised. 'It's Manu.' Manu was a friend of a friend. I knew of him, seen him on the block a couple of times. 'Ring me back in five minutes and you can speak to him.'

The fact the voice was halfway familiar skelled me down a little.

'Where's Aishy?'

'Ring in five, Chyna.'

Manu hung up, leaving me to bite my nails and wonder what the fuck was going on with my boyfriend. I counted down the minutes and, on the dot of the fifth, rang Aishy's phone for a second time.

I don't know why, but I sort of expected Manu to answer again. Instead, Aishy came on the line. Wind blustered in the background, drowning out his voice.

'Where are you?' I said.

The wind blotted out Aishy's reply.

'Are you outside? You walking?' I asked the question because Aishy never walked anywhere. That boy drove thirty seconds in his Spider to Burger King if he felt hungry. Aishy had grown up in a very poor family and for him, walking was for broke people. He took great pride in his Spider.

'Speak to me, Aishy, fuck—'

'I got robbed,' Aishy said, and I went quiet. 'My face is like out *here*.'

'I'm worried, Aishy. Tell me what's going on?'

'You know I went to the mansion?'

'Yeah,' I replied. Aishy had told me that morning he was off to go and meet his bredrin at a private estate in Kent. As he drove his Alfa Romeo inside, Aishy explained, the doors closed behind him and his friend went inside. The mandem greeted them, but not with handshakes and hugs: one of them shoved a shotgun into Aishy's face and told him and his friend to hand over the money.

'You had p's on you?' I asked.

''Course not,' Aishy said. He paused. 'My friend had to be escorted to his pad to get the money. But here's the ting. He somehow escaped on the way back. Boy left me alone up there, Chyna.' Aishy's voice cracked like ice. He sniffed. I pictured tears in his eyes. He cleared his throat and went on, 'They boxed me in the face. Then they burned . . . They took a blowtorch to my ears.'

My eyes welled up.

Aishy had been released once Manu realized he was my man. They booted him out of the estate, kept his wheels and dumped him at the nearest train station. Aishy bought a ticket and turned up at London Victoria. I raced to the station and found Aishy slumped on a bench outside WH Smith, holding his face in his hands. I took him to the nearest hospital.

As we huddled tight on a couple of wobbly chairs in the A&E room, surrounded by bloated alkies and screaming babies, Manu had the cheek to ring my phone.

'I didn't know it was Aishy,' he pleaded. 'I wasn't in the room, Chyna. I stopped it soon as you called. Come on, you've got to believe me.'

I hung up on Manu.

Aishy's problems ran deeper than his fucked-up face. Once a shotter's been robbed, the word gets around the endz that he's a soft touch. Some deelas gets violated almost every week. If one man thinks you're vulnerable, every person on the roads will think the same ting in no long times.

His mistake had been to roll in his Alfa Romeo. That's the problem with being a successful shotter. Soon as the endz clocks you cruising around in brand-new wheels, they'll suss out that you've stacked up bare p's. Peoples think, Rah, if you spend thirty grand on a car, how much you got tucked away in a safehouse somewhere? Spending major p's is what every shotter dreams of. But it also makes them targets.

Months passed.

Gone three o'clock in the morning, at the fag-end of a shotting shift, I returned to the crackhouse over tired. I'd been grinding the whole day. I needed some shut-eye before breezing back to my endz. The cats who owned the flat had a set-up where they allowed shotters to use a bedroom for catching forty winks, which we'd do for an hour or two at a time.

I was working the shift with another boy that night, by the name of Samuel. We sometimes paired up, one of us cutting and calling while the other delivered the pebbles.

'I'm grabbing some shut-eye,' I told him.

'Safe. I'll look after the food.'

I left him on the sofa. He looked shattered and I wondered if he needed the sleep more than me. Samuel was bustin' a pair of fleece ski gloves to combat the biting winter weather. He tucked the bag of rocks inside the glove and I left him watching late-nite horror films while I collapsed on the floor next to the bed. As I say, I wouldn't touch anything in that flat if I could avoid it. I shuddered when I thought about how long it had been since the couple changed the sheets on the bed. It wasn't unusual to see fat cockroaches the size of a thumb, scuttling along the floor and up the cobwebbed, stained walls.

Two hours later, Samuel shook me awake. He was on a major hype, sweating and speaking so fast I couldn't keep up with his stream of words.

'Seckle, bruv,' I croaked, rubbing sleep out of my eyes. 'What's the problem?'

'That cat's gonna get duppied man, fuck . . .'

I noticed something in his hands. The ski glove. The fingers had been cut out. Palm too.

'You've got to be kidding.'

'I'll spray that wanker when I see him,' the boy said.

The cat in the front room had patiently bided his time till Samuel closed his eyes and, armed with a pair of scissors, carefully cut around the glove, removing the patch where the boy had clenched the food. I figured they must have been extra concentrated to have removed the drugs without the boy waking up.

I lifted a hand to my temple. A headache tapped against the sides of my skull repeatedly, like a hammer.

'How much rocks did they take?'

'The lot,' Samuel said. 'Whole bloody ting.'

'You mean a couple of pebbles or—'

'*Everything*. We got not a rock left, Chyna.'

I finally understood what Samuel was saying.

'Everything,' I repeated. 'So that works out to—'

'Just over a grand five hundred,' the boy said. I looked at the angles, trying to see how we could fix this mess. As it stood, we were down a grand to the deela. A grand's not a tiny amount of cash that the deela would ignore. Like shotters, deelas know a weak rep gets transmitted around the endz like chlamydia. Lickman weren't about to grant us a payment holiday.

'How much you got on you?'

I dug my hands into my pockets. 'Three hundred. You?'

'Hundre' fifty.'

My shotter phone buzzed. Lickman wanting to collect his money. I had no choice but to answer.

'What's up, girl. Yu got my coil?'

'Yeah, yeah,' I said, making it up as I went along, the boy lifting his eyebrows like the Golden Arches. 'But I got a problem to sort out this morning, so I'll come pay you tonight.'

Lickman breathed down the phone so hard I thought my head might explode. He was quiet for, like, ten, fifteen seconds. Finally, he said, 'Tonight, den. Everything best be cook and curry on de stack.'

'Rah, it is.'

'Mi come soon.'

Call over.

'OK, this is what we're gonna do,' I said to Samuel, thinking fast. 'We'll take the p's we got now, borrow some sterling, get some rocks from another mandem. We'll lick it extra hard. That should make up the money we lost.'

'I'm shattered,' Samuel said. 'And it'll take all day for us to bust enough shots to make up Yardie Man's money.'

'That makes two of us wiped, but I can't think of another way of getting the money. Or do you want to call Lickman and tell him we don't have his p's?'

'Fuck no' – shaking his head fiercely.

Lickman was no different to other drug deelas. Whoever shotters buy their food from, they know the risk they're taking. If they lose their drugs somehow, or get busted by the boydem, it don't matter. They're in debt to the deela. And deelas aren't like banks or aunties. You can't ask them for a bit longer to get the p's. If you don't have it, they'll target you and your whole family.

I'd seen Lickman box down people because they owed him money. Soon as them words came out of a mouth – 'I don't have it' – boom, he launched his fist like a torpedo and dropped the boy. He'd been known to torture deelas, using pliers to squeeze their fingers. It was a ting where we had to do whatever it took to make the money for Lickman.

We grinded twelve hours that day, licking shot after shot after shot. Lickman showed at ten o'clock that night and we gave him every penny of debt. He counted it, said nothing, left. Me and Samuel couldn't even look at each other, knowing how close we'd come to being fucked.

A month later, I was chilling at the crackhouse when another shotter rang me up and asked me to bust a rock to one of his customers. I'd worked the night shift and it was six o'clock in the morning, the sky rinsed in pinks and reds, me slumped on the sofa, my body flatlined. Last ting I wanted to do was bust another shot, but he begged and begged and said I could keep the money; he just didn't want to lose this cat's trade. I'll bung it, I thought. Just this once. I popped a couple of rocks under my tongue and went out to hook up with the cat.

Deal done, I wearily returned to the estate. Fifty metres away, I clocked splotches of light dancing along the front, bright red and blue strobes.

Boydem.

I got as close as possible, crouching at the corner of the nearest flats, thirty metres from the front of the crackhouse block. I counted a dozen riot vans outside the main entrance, flanked by five boydem cars. Boydem decked out in riot gear, packing riot shields and black helmets, hammered down the metal front door to the block and stormed the stairwell, yelling for people to put their hands above their heads.

No, I thought. Not the crackhouse.

The boydem came back out the entrance, leading out Lickman, the cats and the shotters.

Behind a couple of shotters, I spied Aishy.

He stepped through the toppled entrance in handcuffs. I looked on, numb and helpless, and chewed up inside. I wanted to run out and rip those handcuffs off Aishy, but the minute I came into view of the boydem, they'd arrest me too. I couldn't save Aishy. And at the same time, when you're on the street, you take on a self-preservation mentality. It's everyone for themselves out there, and I'd be lying if I didn't say that even as Aishy was escorted into the back of the boydem van, a part of me thought, If I hadn't gone to bust that shot, it would've been me taking that trip down to the station.

Seeking a shoulder to cry on, I hung out with Paige at the playground in the endz we grew up in, me on the swings. Paige hadn't been working that shift in the crackhouse. Me and her, we was the only two who'd escaped arrest. We smoked draw and shared a bottle of Smirnoff, lost in our thoughts about our lucky break – and poor old Aishy.

'These endz are getting hot,' I said. The vodka scorched my throat and helped me forget the pain of seeing Aishy in cuffs, and of my own selfish reaction.

'You thinking what I'm thinking?'

'Build a new line?'

'You know dis, fam.'

We hung about in the park for maybe an hour or so,

until it started to get dark. Paige finished off the last of the voddie and threw the glass over the other side of the playground. It smashed on the ground, breaking up into a thousand stars.

The judge refused to grant Aishy bail. I don't know why. He went straight to jail. I promised to write him letters, but truthfully the affection between me and Aishy had died, and my heart wasn't in that relationship any more. Lickman the Yardie was deported to Jamaica. He left the country with me owing him about £3,000 for a consignment.

The very next day, I made up my mind to deal someplace else.

Me and Paige had a few grands' worth of Lickman's brown left over. We sold it on to shotters in our endz. We didn't want to be seen on the Hill no more, and anyway, if you've got big bits of food, it's far easier to sell than it is to shot. Instead of grinding for ten or twelve hours surrounded by whinging crackheads, I'd ring up shotters I knew.

'Safe, what's up, cuz? Me ain't heard from you in longs.'

'Been busy, bruv,' I replied. 'Got some food if you're interested.'

'How much?'

'This price for this much. But I got bare people asking for a slice. You want some action, gimme a ring back quick.'

'Nang, nang' – the boy doing the maths in his head, working out how much profit he could make from shotting this quantity.

In a month we'd offloaded a lot of the package of food Lickman had left as an unexpected present. We were ballin' it now and had everything we ever wanted. The latest threads, bare phones and accessories. Paige bought herself a white Fiat Punto. Because we was rolling in p's, we could afford to be less bait on the roads. We cooled tings off and shotted weed instead of crack and brown.

Once you got a rep for selling drugs, it's very hard to shake it. Everyone knew me, and everyone was aware that I shotted. People came to me daily looking for a bit of this and a bit of that, and that can be a good ting and a bad ting. Good because you're making more sterling. Bad because I had that status, so some people thought they could rob me, people thinking they can disarm me on certain packages I've got. Although lots of people knew I shotted, I was cautious about not too many people being aware. Ain't no quicker way for a boy to make p's than running up a shotter girl.

There were a few steps I took to make myself safe. I made sure I never did have a lot of p's on me. If I was bustin' bare paper, questions would be asked. How'd I get a hold of this much paper, what am I doing to earn it, rah, rah, rah. And if I carried too much weed, at the first sign of it, some-one would pipe up, 'Tik me a draw, cuz.'

'Tik' means lemme take the draw off you and give you the money later. Sort of like a bank loan.

'Tik' really means you probably ain't gonna see that money any time soon.

Because my friends were usually the ones asking for a tik, I found it hard to turn them down. It was seen as rude if I said to them, 'Nah, man, I can't tik you a bag of weed.' But a bag was £10. If I tikked five bags in a day from my stash, across a week I'd be down £350. And maybe only £100 would come back to me, long time later. Meantime I'd be trying to manage my cashflow back to my deela and the debts mounted up. Rather than refusing to tik people, I busted a minimal amount of weed. Rude for them to ask for a tik from a tiny bag of drugs.

I never kept hard drugs in my house and I was always on point about this. If the boydem raided my property and found drugs, I'd be done for. I got around this problem by wrapping up the brown inside a Tesco's bag and hiding it underneath the flowerpots at the front of the house, or tucking it underneath someone's wall, where I know no one would disturb it. I was less cautious when it came to weed. Majority of the time I didn't mind bringing weed into the house. Never saw a big problem with that.

SIXTEEN

Going country

What with all the heat from the Met, London was no longer the town to make money.

Bottom line, if you were in the drug-selling game these times, London wasn't about it no more. People were going prison, boys' houses were getting raided daily, and estates were attracting a lot of negative publicity. Faced with the squeeze, I spoke to a connect via Stocks about moving to some new endz. He recommended I go country.

Country is like different endz outside of London city. Southampton, Bristol, Cambridge, Cardiff. Apart from seaside places like Brighton and Southend, I'd never really left town before. My world was my bredrin, and they lived in the space of a few miles in South. The world beyond – I couldn't tell you nothing about it. To me, North seemed far, East seemed far, West seemed far far.

Southampton was the end of the fucking world.

I was amazed at how many crackheads could fit into such a small place. The council estates were our territory. They weren't as big as the blocks in London, but a lot of crackheads lived in these flats, enough to give us good reason to operate down there.

The deela, Leroy, had already set up a line in Southampton

and he offered me and Paige an in by travelling down with him and shotting off his supply. Plus we could get rid of the leftovers of Lickman's heroin. We thought it was a good opportunity to shot and not have no heat from the boydem, and for Leroy, it meant having some company in endz where he didn't know no one. As well, a couple of girls rolling with him made Leroy look less bait. If you're in a place like Southampton, majority white, and you see three black hoodie men hanging around, people automatically think, Drug deelas. What a cheek!

We'd set off for Southampton at sun-up, Leroy driving, us girls in the back smoking draws, shuttling to a crackhead's house in the centre of town. We always made it a two-day trek to save petrol money and the hassle of shooting to and from London city.

The crackheads we mostly stayed with weren't your ordinary cats. They was a family: a man and a woman and their ten-year-old boy. The boy had no idea who we was, probably figured us for friends of his mum and dad. But his presence meant the crackheads refused to invite billions of cats and deelas around. Good news for us: the crowd was just them, me, Paige and Leroy. The sofas were cosy, comfortable to crash on, and splitting a £10 bone to the mum was much cheaper than laying out sixty sheets a night at the local Travelodge. We had a sweet schedule. Shot on the Southampton endz. Drive back up to London. Freshen up and throw on some clean garmz. Travel back to Southampton. Shot some more.

I maintained this hard grind for six long months. Between each trip I was so dog-tired I'd just lie on my bed and drift.

Southampton got rodded. On one trip to the endz, I'd rented out a room at a local hotel, rather than staying at the crackheads' flat.

Paige and Leroy were out shotting. I was having a time-out, flicking through the cable channels in the hotel room. The room was a standard hotel suite: two single beds plus a fold-out sofa bed, out-dated furnishings, cigarette burns on the carpet, the air musty, recycled. I was far tired, but I couldn't sleep. A half of brown rested on the desk and a voice inside me told me that I should hide it somewhere less bait.

I took the bag of brown, tucked it into my jeans pocket, grabbed the hotel keycard and put the lock on the latch. Scoped the corridor. Twelve thirty in the morning and nobody about. I scaled one flight of stairs, then another. On the second landing, I stopped and listened for footsteps. At the corner of the staircase, a lamp was fitted to the wall with the shell in a U-shape. I ditched the brown inside and hustled back to the room to get ready for bed, my mind at ease. Hadn't even closed my eyes when someone knocked at the door. I peered through the spyhole and seen one of Leroy's delivery boys who'd come down for the trip with us, boy by the name of Nathan.

'Four more rocks to this lady and I'm done,' he said as I unlocked the door.

'Call it a night now if you want.' Nathan looked wiped.

'Four shots is four shots.'

I was having trouble tuning into the conversation, eyes half closed. 'True dat. All right, bust them tonight.'

Four rocks worked out to £40. Once the clock ticks midnight, there's an unwritten rule among shotters that anything over £20 is a deal, but below £20 ain't worth the hassle. Every time you go to bust a rock, you run a risk. Maybe the cat's gonna rob you. Maybe the person you're selling to is an undie boydem officer. It happens. The risk has to be worth your while.

'One ting,' I said as Nathan headed to the door. 'Don't be playing over loud grime in the car or smoking no weed, you feel me?' Nathan had been driving around Southampton in a rental car, and as he had less experience than me and Paige, he behaved a little naive. I'd seen him breezing on the road, phat Roll Deep tracks blaring out so loud the pavement vibrated, air reeking of weed. In a place like Southampton, White Central, he risked drawing attention to himself.

'Yeah, yeah' – Nathan waving his hand at me.

Few hours later, Nathan got pulled.

Lights blazing in his rear-view, Nathan dashed his shots rather than gobbling them. They searched him, found the pebbles – and the keycard to our hotel room.

Six o'clock in the morning and I woke up to a crash, boydem officers circling my bed and ordering me to get dressed. I rubbed the sleep out of my eyes, not quite believing what was in front of me. On the side table, I'd left a small £10 bag of weed for my personal spliff-smoking. The boydem wouldn't give a shit about that, but they might suspect I'd stashed a big supply of heroin.

'We're arresting you on possession of cannabis,' one of the officers told me, 'and intent to supply Class-A drugs.'

They didn't find no hard drugs, but they were still able to charge me with Class A because they'd seen a plastic bag on the floor.

That don't sound incriminating, but when you cut up heroin, you're left with teeny pieces, each about the size of a pea. Before you pop them in your mouth, you need to wrap them up in plastic to protect them. I'd tear little bits off a plastic bag to wrap round the rocks. The boydem found this bag and matched the holes in the bag with the material wrapped round the shots found at Nathan's rental.

The boydem escorted me to Southampton boydem station, where they told me they were gonna do fingerprinting on the bag. I tried not to worry, thinking, They don't have nothing to pin on me. Eighteen hours after they put me in a cell, I was released on bail. No further action on the cannabis charge and said they'd get forensics on the plastic bag.

For the first time since I got involved in any kind of illegal activity, I thought I might end up going prison. Getting caught with Class-A drugs is streets apart from an undie nicking you for tiefing a tracksuit from Foot Locker. My mind conjured up images of sharing a rank cell with nutter girls, no fam or mandem to support me. A lot of the boys expect to go prison one day and mentally prepare themselves for it, and they got the comfort of affiliating with plenty of mandem inside of the clink. Not the girls. I never banked on prison. That weren't part of my plan. I fretted.

'Don't worry about a ting,' Leroy said, seeing how worried I looked. I had lumpy bags under my eyes from lack of sleep. 'They can't do CSI shit on no fucking plastic bag. They're just trying to intimidate you and make you confess.'

Leroy was right. A while passed and I got a letter saying the intent-to-supply charge had been dropped. But I was banned from entering Southampton city. I didn't see it as a big loss. I cursed Nathan and his foolishness. In the future, I told myself, I'd only work with people I trusted.

New location after that. Change it up. Keep it moving. We hunted out new endz, further and further away from London city, to places we'd heard were heaving with cats. Sometimes it'd be Bristol. Sometimes weird places I'd never even fucking heard of before. One time Leroy said he'd found some brand-new endz that were buzzing with cats.

'Nottingham,' he said.

'Where the fuck's that?'

'Look it up on de map' – grinning so's I could see the two golden teeth on his top row.

Them places are strange. No blacks or Asians or what-not, just lots of sorry-looking white people. We spent some time in these endz, but the problem is, although Nottingham or wherever ain't rodded, there's not an endless supply of cats like in London. Business dried up. We stopped going country and returned to the hood.

Some months later, I was walking through town centre and got talking to a couple of boys at a display table in the street. They handed out leaflets and free copies of Muslim books and quotes from the Koran. I ended up spending three hours talking to these boys and was so intrigued by the idea of Islam that I called Pasha immediately after and spoke about it. Our lives was fucked in the head. Nothing seemed to make much sense any more. People I knew and cared for were getting hurt. But Islam spoke to me in a different way; I liked how it wasn't just some private ting, but more like a big family, encouraging people to help those poorer off than them, and giving life some meaning. Although I was raking in some good p's from shotting, I felt not empty but lost. As if I lived in a room with no sense of left or right, up or down. Islam spoke about path and meaning and balance. It seemed to be the ting I was missing. Pasha warmed to the idea too.

The next day, we was strolling down another road, chatting about this and that, when we suddenly stumbled upon the local mosque.

'Rah, this is a sign,' I told Pasha.

'What for?' – Pasha quizzing me.

'To convert.'

The men at the stand the previous day had explained that in order to convert to Islam, we'd have to go to the mosque and recite *Shahada*. We entered and performed the recital that very day, although the imam of the mosque frowned at our short skirts and tight jackets and insisted on us wearing headscarves before he'd allow witnesses to confirm us.

Now we were official Muslim. Although we didn't link with no Muslim mandem at the mosque, as brothers and sisters pray separately, we did fall in with a few boys in the early days through meetings and Muslim community events. One of them was called Jamal, and he was one of the first proper Muslim boys I got to know. He took his Islam over serious. I seen no weed, cigarette smoke or liquor breach that man's lips. We weren't over close, but we was friends, and I got to know his girlfriend well, a girl by the name of Sakina who had been at the same school as me. Jamal tended to criticise me and Pasha for wearing tight little skirts that showed off our figures and said that we oughta be bustin' in hijabs. I weren't down with that, and neither were Pasha, but he had one convert in Sakina. With his designer stubble and light-black skin Jamal looked a bit like Ashley Cole. I wasn't to know it then, but later Jamal would turn on me – and show me where loyalties truly lay on the roads.

And these times, I knew true love for the first time.

His name? Rashid, the boy whose mandem shot Cheese.

SEVENTEEN

Gangsta's wife

I was chilling at a Muslim sister's house when I bumped into Rashid.

'I recognize you from somewhere,' Rashid said. He had a smart accent, clear and crisp, no trace of his home country of Morocco. He sat down on the armchair opposite me, resting his hands on its arms as if it was his throne. 'Name's Jasmyne, right?'

'Yeah, yeah. Jasmyne.' I'd had my fill of gangsta men, I thought. First Kendrick, then Wallace, Leon, Aishy . . . I was determined not to fall into a relationship with another road man. So I played along, pretended to be the girl he mistook me for. It seemed the easiest way out of a tricky situation.

'From Norwood?'

'Yeah.'

He stroked his curly, stubbly beard. 'You used to go out with Dabz.'

Much as I feared Rashid, I didn't want to admit I was Leon's ex-boyfriend, because Rashid had robbed Leon countless of times. Wallace too.

'Something like that' – me trying not to make eye contact with him. Despite his rep and my fears, I was attracted to him from the get-go. To his husky voice, his tidy attitude, his prickly sense of humour.

He frowned at something on his black Timberlands, brushed the golden eyelets. 'So what's the story, girl?'

'You know,' I said. 'This and that.'

'Cool, that's cool. Gotta keep it moving, you know.'

I made eye contact with him. I couldn't look away.

'Be seeing you,' he said.

Week later, I bumped into him at a party. A few girls were there I'd known since primary school. Rashid came over to where we was sitting. He walked like he talked, big long strides that carried him across the floor in five or six steps. He nodded at me.

'Aren't you gonna introduce me, Chyna?' this girl asked.

Rashid arched his bushy eyebrows. 'Wait a minute. You're not—'

'No,' I said, shooting this girl the evil eye. 'I ain't no Jasmyne. Don't even know who that is. Look, I lied to you.'

He looked hurt and I almost felt apologetic for lying to him. Thinking, How did that come about, that I'm getting all sympathetic for someone who robbed my ex?

'You've probably heard bad tings about me,' he said, staring at something past my shoulder.

I nodded.

'So why are you still talking to me, then?'

'Because you're showing me a different side,' I replied.

'Your mum warn you about boys like me?'

'Nah,' I said. 'I educated myself. Best way of finding out anything is to try it youself, innit?'

He smiled a smile that belonged on a Colgate advert. 'Ain't that true,' he said.

We chilled daily after that. I fell in love with him headlong. Rashid was a volatile mix of personalities, but the love we had for each other was uncontrollable. I knew he had done bad tings, but no matter how much I tried to think logical about our relationship, soon as my eyes met his, ants crawled up my spine. We had an intense love. Within a month Rashid had moved in with me at my one-bedroom shared accommodation. I had a massive bedroom in the house, enough space for both of us. We hooked up a widescreen TV, got the Sky connected, plugged in an Xbox for Rashid. Three Ikea wardrobes contained all our clothes. Our own little nest.

He was so laid-back around me that I questioned if the other side of his character was for real. Deep inside, I knew I shouldn't be hanging out with Rashid, that he spelled trouble for me and my friends, but the more I had them thoughts, the more I seen his sensitive side and the harder it became for me to believe the stories about Rashid on the endz. People would say Rashid did this or that, and the same night I'd meet up with him for a drink or to go to an expensive Thai restaurant and he'd open the door for me, take my coat, pull out my chair. Did this same boy duppy someone on the roads? I asked myself. Did Rashid, the boy who always picked up the tab and caressed my hands, roll with mandem who shot up Cheese in his leg?

Rashid had worked out this system where he separated his gang life from the rest of his personality. When we was together, he'd never brag about robbing this man or whatever. We behaved as if he just had some regular, boring job. He'd bring back the money to me, but none of his badness.

We had a nice domestic arrangement – with a few differences. One being the safe in the bedroom, a big, black metal job the size of a microwave and with a digital combination lock on the front. When Rashid came home of a night, he'd empty his pockets and ask me to count up the Queen's heads. Sometimes the p's came to seven or eight grand. Into the safe it went. Whenever Rashid linked with his mandem, there'd be bare guns on the kitchen counter, on the coffee table. All his bredrin packed tools from an early age. Whereas before, with Leon, I lived a Bonnie and Clyde existence, now I felt like I was a gangsta's wife. I was put up on a high pedestal and everyone knew me as Rashid's girlfriend. People treated me with bare respect.

I'd go out and never pay for a drink or an entry fee. On drum 'n' bass nights, the queue would sometimes stretch for 300 metres. Not for us. The bouncers would say hello to the boys, let us go straight to the front, complimentary Veuve Clicquot champagne from the owners waiting at our VIP table. The FLS mandem didn't normally touch alcohol or cigarettes, but they did like the odd glass of champagne. I'd wear a £15,000 chain on my neck, so big it felt as if I had a snake choking my airway, just to show off that I was Rashid's girl. I felt privileged.

These times I got hardcore into the raving scene. We used to go to clubs in East, North and South. We spent our weekends living it large in the high life in clubs like Plan B, Egg, Departure Lounge, Fridge, SE21, Yellow Bar and Mass, held in the basement of St Matthew's Church, opposite Windrush Square, where the first West Indian migrants lived. Mass was one of my favourites, playing a lot of funky house and stuff, tribal music too, with DJs like Super D, Dogtanyan, Safon B, Pioneer, all of them big, funky house DJs. Some people quaffed pills and MDMA. Others dabbled in a little bit of sniff. We didn't touch no gear but still had a good time, buzzing in the clubs and feeling the vibe. Everyone seemed happy and at peace, the music was beautiful, and we had mad love in our veins.

All of the mandem we went clubbing with carried guns. They rolled hardcore in the FLS. Sometimes for fun, they'd hit far endz in South and rob boys we knew. Someone like Wallace had been robbed countless of times by Rashid; although Wallace and his lot were big in their own little world, Rashid and the mandem were fearless and feared, violent and prone to casual violence. Certain of them boys in the gang were abandoned by their mums when they was eight, nine years old and forced to fend for themselves on the street from an early age, so they got into the gang lifestyle a lot more harder. They got into guns a lot more harder. They paraded up and down the endz I grew up in, the local mandem running for their fucking lives. They steamed shops. Busted guns in their low batties in the daytime, strolling right past the boydem station. They bowed to no one.

Every day was a rollercoaster ride with that crew. Once I was rolling with bare of the boys, me and Candice in her car, one of six cars in this group including a big Jeep, a Land Rover, two Volkswagens and a BMW. I knew four of the mandem carried guns – two niners and a couple of Lugers. The group of cars halted at this Yardie shop. On the outside it was a Caribbean food joint selling imported foods from Jamaica – spicy jerk curries, oxtail and stew, coconut sauce, ginger beer, hard-dough bread and Ting grapefruit drinks. But downstairs it sold a different type of food.

Drugs.

'Wait here,' the two boys in Candice's car said as they climbed out the back seats. Me and Candice stayed put and had no idea what was going on. Suddenly the other boys rushed out, fifteen of them bolting towards the shop, people screaming, the boys locking the door behind them. I swapped confused looks with Candice, thinking, They're steaming the joint.

I could hear shouting through the shopfront glass. And someone being thudded with something really fucking hard.

'What you doing?'

Boom, boom, boom.

'Shut up.'

Boom.

'Where's the ting? One person go with me. You stay over there.'

Boom.

'Got it?'

Boom.

'That's it, we're leaving.'

Boom.

The door opened and the boys came flying out, legging it to their motors so fast they were blurs. One of them had a big bag of something in one hand. The two boys riding with us dived into the back seats and yapped at us to drive. We had no choice. We breezed out. Once we'd put a mile between ourselves and the Yardie shop, the boys flipped. They hadn't robbed the Yardie man of food but some bags of dust the shopowner kept as dummies. He'd obviously been relieved of his packages before and had the dummies just in case anyone tried it on in the future.

Later that night, we were chilling on the corners, the mandem searching for the next ting to steal. We'd been out since nine o'clock, and at three in the morning, me and Candice was flagging and wanted to go home. But the boys were disappointed by the raid on the Yardie shop and needed to do something to get money. We cruised around the endz, listening to the boys in the back of Candice's car discussing robbery options.

'Telling yu, bruv, dat jewellery shop's the place where it's at.'

'Nigga, ain't yu seen dem shop windows? It's all dead quality.'

'Owners are Jewish, man . . .'

'If yu was talking about sum place in rich endz, then yeah, I feel it, but dere? Tch, yu got more chance robbing Queen's heads from yu own arse.'

As we hit a big hill, a long white van with two middle-aged black men seated in the front skidded to a halt after the BMW belonging to the mandem nearly crashed into it. Both the BMW and the van hit the brakes hard. It was nothing deliberate. Just two drivers not really concentrating on the road. No big deal.

As the van stopped, the boys in the BMW scurried out and launched into an argument with the van driver. Candice seen that the other cars had parked up and slowed down herself. I sensed that the boys were on a major hype, having gone empty-handed from the Yardie shop raid and any ting they could rob, they were gonna do it. I bounced out of Candice's car and warned the driver man. He and his friend chosen the wrong night to be drama-setters.

'Don't argue with these boys,' I said. 'They got guns, yeah?'

But the driver weren't for telling. He was a big black man, thinking he could have up his mouth and sort these yute out. 'Them going too fast on the roads,' he ranted. 'Nearly killed a man. I ain't standing for it.'

I went close to his face. 'Shut up or they're gonna—'

Before I'd even finished the sentence, a dozen boys attacked the van and gun-butted the driver's head off. Blood everywhere. The man's nose was mashed, cracked down the middle like a Brazil nut and twisted at the bottom. He kicked madly with his legs, scratched at one boy's face, the driver's friend got involved and got a fistful of knuckles, sending him flying, and the struggle went on for about thirty seconds when—

Crack!

A shot blown off four or five metres from where I stood. Soon as the shot got pulled, the boys scattered, ran back to their cars, me ducking down and wondering where the bullet went. I hurried into Candice's car and she hit the accelerator. The van men lay groaning and crying on the bloodied road.

We got fifty metres up the road and I looked at the van shrinking in the rear-view mirror. The two men, sacks on the ground.

'They must have fucked them men up proper,' I said. 'The van ain't moved yet.'

'Rearranged that man's face,' one of the boys in the back seat said. He showed me the barrel of the Luger. Dark, oily goo dripping off the black metal, like melted rubber. That gun was coloured.

'Are they dead?' Candice asked.

'What, dem old crusties? Nah, sister. They just needed a lesson, is all.'

That was a casual night for the boys. Don't matter where they are, who they're with, they'll do stuff spur of the moment, fuck people up, rob people, rocking with guns day in, day out, in their cars, whatnot. Trident was on their case permanently; they didn't give a fuck. They were scare-free about merking a man.

Was I scared of these mandem? Maybe if I'd gone straight from school to rolling with them. But in between I'd known shotters and robbers, deelas and gangstas. I'd slept in crackhouses and been questioned by the boydem. I was hungry for adventure, and treated life casually.

But I also had love for them. When I looked at each of the mandem, I didn't see violent boys who steamed shops and lashed out at anyone who so much as glanced at them in a funny way. I seen friends. Boys who cared for me and protected me.

Take Husayn – Rashid's best friend in the gang. They'd spent two years in prison together before; Husayn and Rashid shared the same block, lived next to each other in the same room and became really close.

Husayn was a good boy. Some of the mandem was Muslim in the same way white people call themselves Christian and never go church or give up liquor for Lent. Not Husayn. He knew his Koran backwards. Prayed five times a day. I never saw him getting hotted up unless he missed prayer.

He had a hard jive but under the surface there was a warmth to him. He could be sweet like Haribo. With his brown skin, the colour of woodchip, cornrow hair and styled thin moustache, from a distance Husayn resembled a tonked Taio Cruz.

My mouthiness also helped me settle in with the mandem. Whereas other girls might have been wide-eyed, looking to sleep with every boy, attracted to the fame of going out with the most notorious gangstas in London city, I'd cuss them, giving as good as I got. With the likes of Kazim and Husayn, we had major bust-ups before we became close. The arguments brought us together.

Husayn's baby mother called my phone, believing the number belonged to Pasha. She hung up. This happened during the spell when Pasha and Husayn were dating, and it pissed me off. I got on the line to Kazim and told him what happened.

'Listen, bruv. How you gonna let Husayn's baby mother phone Pasha and then she gets hold of the wrong number and calls me? You need to tell your bredrin to put that girl under control, you feel me?'

No other girl, or perhaps even man, would've dared to speak to the mandem like that.

'Rah, Chyna, you can't talk to us like that,' Kazim said.

'Do you know who the fuck I am? You know your man's my soldier, yeah?'

Meaning Kazim is older than Rashid. Meaning he has higher status. Trying to put my man, and me, in his place.

'I don't give a fuck who my man is,' I fumed. 'It's *me* you're talking to.'

Kazim had no comeback. He couldn't believe I'd said that to him.

Later that day, we all met up and Kazim sat down next to me. I thought he might give me an earful. He looked serious enough.

'No one's ever sworn at me like that,' he said, nodding. 'But you were right. I didn't show you the respect you deserved. Now I do.'

From that point on, Kazim and the others treated me and Pasha different from the casual girls they used to hang around. Them other girls got breeded up by half the mandem, boyed off and ended up lost. They spoke at them in rough voices, calling them blatant slaggish names to their faces, like 'Tits'. Kazim or Nasha, the boy who used to link with Breelyn and was also a member of the FLS, wouldn't think twice about telling a girl to store food in their house, but the mandem never asked me or Pasha to hide tings. Anyone wanted to stash some food in my place, one of them would say, 'Rah, can't do that. That's sister's house, innit?' I weren't viewed as no slag-bag; they seen I didn't care about nothing, that I'd answer back if I thought someone was lying or wrong and tell it to them straight.

Hanging around on level terms with the mandem, it made me feel invincible. I thought no one could touch me.

That feeling didn't last for ever.

One day, me and Rashid had one of our arguments over something tiny. I'm not the type of girl who's meek. When we argued, he'd spark up verbally and I'd take it to a physical level, hurling stuff at him, cushions and phones and china plates, yelling cusses and throwing his clothes out the window. My previous boyfriends had a habit of retaliating with their fists, but not Rashid. He'd calmly make for the door.

'When you're ready to talk instead of screaming, I'll come back,' he said, gently closing the door behind him. An hour later, he'd call me up.

'You cooled off now?'

'I'm still mad,' I'd reply, my voice scratchy from all the shouting. He'd come home, we'd kiss, and the tiff was history. Rashid had a handle on my temper tantrums. He understood me better than anyone. Maybe even myself.

This day, I shouted at Rashid about something stupid. The laundry, I think. When Rashid moved in, it was the first time I'd lived with a boy and all the little stuff got on my nerves. Even gangstas' wives moan about their man being lazy. I directed my annoyance, gave him both barrels, and like that, he was off. Left me to un-vex myself.

An hour or two, I thought, and he'll be on the phone, angling for peace.

Two hours came and went.

Two became four.

Four, six.

No sign of my man.

At eleven o'clock at night, my phone rang. I scrambled for it, mad pissed, thinking, I'm gonna give Rashid what for. He can't breeze out on his girl like this. Only when I clocked the display, instead of saying, RASHID, it was a local landline number: 0207 . . .

'Yeah,' I answered, pacing up and down the bedroom.

He sighed. 'I've been arrested, babe.'

The line crackled and hissed, but Rashid's tone was familiar as my own heartbeat.

'What – what for?' I blurted. I could feel my heart beating, thought it might explode any minute.

'Attempted murder,' he said.

'Aren't you gonna go court?'

That's what happens when you get charged. Court in the morning, bail, bosh, you're out until the trial begins. I thought, Even if it's only a few days or weeks, I'll see Rashid again. He'll be home. In my arms.

Rashid didn't answer.

'Ain't you going court tomorrow?' I asked frantically.

'I've been on the run, Chyna,' he said. 'I never told you. I thought it was for the best.'

Rashid confessed he was on licence. He'd been released from prison not long before I met him, locked up for twenty-eight months. While he was on licence for the rest of his sentence, the boydem wanted to question him in relation to an attempted murder case. All the time we were together, Rashid was on the run, bunked his probation meetings. Because of that, Rashid had been denied bail.

'I'm sorry.'

I crumbled. Cried hysterical, holding the phone away from my ear, tears raining off my cheeks and on to the carpet. I wasn't annoyed that Rashid hadn't been truthful with me. I figured that there was stuff in his past that he didn't want me to know about. You love someone, and then one day they tell you they're not going to be there any more, to listen to you and take you out to dinner or just watch TV with. I don't know what cancer feels like. I don't know what dying feels like. But losing Rashid was the worst feeling I've ever known.

Everything had been so happy with Rashid and I'd never had a boyfriend go prison before, didn't know how I was gonna manage to survive by myself. These times I didn't have no job: I'd taken a break from hustling because Rashid was bringing home all the p's.

Roxy and Pasha visited me, hugged me and told me not to worry, that I had to be strong for my man. We made some sandwiches and crisps to take to the boydem station, plus some money for prison expenses.

The pain had me cornered that night. It licked me bad, wrung every last tear out of my body and left me crushed in bed.

The next day, I got up extra early, splashed cold water on my face and told myself, Right. Time to get back on the roads.

EIGHTEEN

The street mentality

Pepper was a Yardie man and a big-time playa who never worked directly with shotters. I didn't really know him well. Had just seen him about the roads a couple of times. He never crossed my mind as someone I could do business with.

Out of the blue, Pepper called me up.

'Eveling, dawta,' he said, as if we was bestest best friends. I could hear dancehall reggae music in the background, Yellowman's voice echoing out, 'Them a mad over me.'

'Mi got two keys, good Jamaican toot,' he said. 'And me need a couple of di galdem to go deliver it off to dis man. Yu waan fi do it?'

'What's the catch?' With Yardie men, there's *always* a catch.

'Nuh catch,' he said. 'Jus give him da food and goes back to yu gates. Grand five hundred each.'

The deal sounded too good to be true. But still I wasn't sure.

'Mek up yu mind . . .'

'I'll do it,' I said. I needed the money, and if it was a simple trade-off, p's for coke, I didn't see what the problem could be. 'Tell me when and where.'

Pepper said he'd be in touch. He added that I'd need to find a second girl as I couldn't be allowed to go by myself. 'Fa security,' he explained. I said I understood, knowing instantly which girl could be relied on for sound back-up.

Pasha.

She was up for it too, having not had much success on the endz lately, what with everything being so rodded. Me and her both needed the p's big-time. When Rashid went into prison, I'd had to go on income support, £55 a week. I had a £100-a-week weed habit to feed! Either I got a job that just about covered my weed needs or I went for something that could double my money and sort me out for a while. Fifteen hundred each and I'd be bubblin'.

The next day, Pepper called to explain the deal. He'd give us a lift in his car, taxi us to a meeting point and drop us off, where we'd exchange the food for the p's with the deela man he was selling to. Then breeze out and hand over the phat coil to Pepper and pocket our sterling. Simple.

'Jus' one ting,' Pepper said. 'Don't let di man have more than a quick taste of di bulla. And don't be stepping out from di mandem with di toot. He has one quick sample, den dun.'

Pepper picked me up at ten o'clock in the morning in a black sapphire BMW 7 Series. Leather trim, metallic paint, the works. The motor shook with the heavy riddims of Ninjaman's 'Murder Dem' and the car had a sickly smell, fresh leather and chemical skunk mixing together. We said nothing the whole journey to Pasha's house.

I met Pasha in her room while Pepper waited outside in the Beemer.

'Ready to do this, fam?' she asked.

'Yeah, yeah,' I said, distracted. 'Listen, I been thinking. Two keys is a lot of food.' Pasha was tying up the laces on her Nike creps. 'I mean, we're talking *bare* grands.'

'What you saying, cuz?' – Pasha adjusting her hair.

'Here's the deal: I call up Kazim, get the mandem to come to the place and rob us.'

'So, we go to the car park in—'

'Burger King.'

'—and we get robbed.'

'By the mandem.'

'And then—'

'Sell it on,' I said.

Pasha bit her upper lip with her teeth. 'What if we get caught?'

'This Yardie man Pepper, he don't know who we're affiliated with. He ain't gonna suspect nothing, thinks we're just a couple of naive girls who need some quick notes. Why else do you think he's trusting us to do this delivery, instead of some boys he knows? Or even do it himself?'

Pasha kicked the heel of her left crep with the toes of her right. She wasn't sure.

'Look at it this way,' I said. 'For carrying out the delivery, we'll make a grand five hundred each. If we got the food and shifted it on to some deelas, minus the cut for the mandem, we'd be making a quarter of a mil.'

'Shit,' Pasha said, 'when you put it like that . . .' Her eyes narrowed. We'd been burned too many times before not to have tings play on our minds. I know, because I was thinking the same ting.

'Don't worry about Pepper,' I said. 'Man's ballin'. Quarter of a mil's big p's to us, but it ain't nothing to him. He's got his own fashion shops in Islington, got his own clubs, houses in Spain and Florida . . .' I lit a Mayfair. 'He's got fucking over money, cuz.'

This is where my street mentality came into play. I'm thinking, Rah, if we tief this drugs, this is me now. Me and Pasha can start up our own line, shot it by ourselves until Rashid gets released from prison and he can take over. Sorted.

'Nothing will come back to us. He won't never suspect a ting.'

'Fuck it,' she said. 'I'm sick of being broke. Let's do it.'

I rang Kazim and he arranged for him to come down with a baggamanz. Pepper honked his horn. Had to make it quick – he'd be wondering what was taking us long. I quickly sorted it out with the boys. Three of them would come and rob me and Pasha. We talked about the details, how they'd have to rough us up a little bit to make it look authentic. The one ting I didn't know was which Burger King Pepper was driving us to. I said I'd call them back soon as we arrived at the restaurant.

We clocked Pepper at the boot of his Beemer, ushering us over to have a look at the keys. Snug inside the boot, beside the spare wheel, was the package. It didn't look like much – two packets, each one the size of a Martina Cole book, white as a block of sea salt and smothered in cling film.

Pepper dropped us off at the Burger King, reminding us to only let the man have a small sample from the bag. I carried the two bricks into the restaurant, tucked inside a peach-coloured Furay tote slung over my shoulder. I ordered a Double Whopper meal, extra large, full-sugared Coke. Pasha went for an Ocean Catch bap, medium, Diet Coke. At eleven o'clock, the restaurant was more empty than not. We pulled up a pew at the window overlooking the car park. Every couple of minutes Pepper rang my phone, asking for an update.

'De mandem deh yet?'

'No, he ain't showed.'

'He soon come.'

I put a call into Kazim and told him the location of the Burger King. The plan was set.

I'd just polished off my burger when this Yardie boy entered and bolted over to us. Not a man, but a teenager.

'Yo, yu got de food? Gimme de food,' he said.

This boy can't have been a day over eighteen. He had

rough, rugged plaits that ain't been done for long, bustin' in navy-blue track trousers with a Nike top and white Nike trainers muddied smog-grey. I thought to myself, He didn't look like no major deela who'd be buying a quart of a mil worth of pure. Pasha glanced at me. Same ting crossed her mind.

'Mi said hand over de food,' the boy told us. A few customers looked over at the commotion.

The instructions that Pepper had given us was that the deela would be a man in his forties and driving a white van. He didn't say nothing about no fresh-faced Yardie boy decked out in tracksuit garmz and on foot.

'Nah, we ain't got nothing,' I said. The Furay bag was beside Pasha's chair. I spotted her slyly nudging the bag under the table with her foot.

'Yu tell a lie.'

'We ain't got shit,' I firmed.

'Yeah' – Pasha getting heated too – 'we don't know what the fuck you're talking about.'

The boy shot us a screw-face. 'Yu de two girldem meant to be linking up wit de food?'

His words rattled me. I kept my shock hidden and blagged it. How this boy had the inside track on the deal, I didn't know. It smelled dodgy to me. Someone was trying to rob us, and this definitely weren't one of Rashid's mandem.

'Fuck yu, den, wutless gals.' The boy stormed out of the Burger King and out of the car park.

'Oh shit,' Pasha said. She had the view of the window, me with my back to it.

'What is it?'

'Don't look now, but that boy's waiting outside the car park with two mandem.' The fresh-faced Yardie boy and his friend stood on the corner of the road. The boy spoke into a mobile. His friend smoked weed and eyefucked us. They looked on edge.

'Our boys are gonna be here any minute,' I said, my nerves tingling. 'Soon as they arrive, those Yardie yutes are history.'

'Tell them to put their foot down,' Pasha said, 'or the moment we step outside, them boys are gonna run us up.'

I nodded, distracted. Wondered over and over, how did these boys know we were supposed to be meeting for a deal? Then again, we were in fucking town centre of gangs. Word travels fast. Couple of young girls in town, with two keys of pure cocaine on them . . .

Once one person knows, everyone knows.

Pepper rang.

'De man's deh 'bouts, jus' round de corner,' Pepper said. Hanged up.

'Where's the mandem?' Pasha asked.

'Gonna get here soon as, cuz.'

Two minutes later, a white van checked in at the car park. Me and Pasha went outside to meet the driver. I gripped the

Furay bag tight. The Yardie boys had disappeared. I guessed maybe they were planning on jacking the van man after he left the Burger King with the food.

We went out, circling round to the rear of the van. The deela introduced himself as Quips. He prised open the doors to keep us out of sight. I offered him the teeny sample and gave him sight of the coke, letting him hold it and making sure we didn't leave him alone with the food, as Pepper instructed.

I was tense. Now Quips had arrived, I worried how fast we'd be forced to make the exchange, and the mandem's opportunity to rob him would be lost.

The deela rubbed the sample on his teeth to test its purity. No deela snorts the shit; you can't tell the quality of it that way. The best method for testing coke is to get a tiny little bit, put it on your index finger and rub it into your gums. You should feel a tingle on your tongue, like a buzz of electricity. A tingle means the product is pure and no artificial crap's been added to the mix.

'It's good, yeah?' I asked.

'All fruits ripe,' Quips replied, nodding. 'But I got naa coil on mi. De money be at mi flat.'

'And where's that?'

'Not far,' he replied, all evasive like. 'Just around the corner.'

'No,' I said, Pasha shaking her head, 'we ain't leaving here.' Quips had, by accident, tossed us a lifeline. I acted needled, said no way in the world would we accompany him to no flat. 'You'd better go get the p's, bring them to us.'

'It not be working like dat, shorty.'

'It *be*,' I replied. 'You've got your sample and you know the shit's good. If you don't want to do business, we'll fucking find someone else to sell to. Call it how you want it, but we ain't being messed around.'

My threat worked. The man acted tense and worried. He said he'd go to his flat and come back in twenty minutes. Enough of a time window, I hoped, for Rashid's mandem to 'rob' us.

The minutes tick-tocked. Kazim said they were stuck in traffic at Clapham Junction. Fuck me, I thought, we was up against the clock. I ordered another Coke. Pasha tapped her feet and nervously looked out over the car park.

'Where are you?' I asked Kalim in my thousandth call to him.

'Traffic, sis.'

'Get a move on, will you.'

That's my basic luck, I thought, to plan a fake robbery on a day London was haemorrhaging traffic.

Meantimes a black Volkswagen Golf nosed into the car park, resting at the exact same spot Quips's van had occupied. No one got out. I was immediately suspicious about this Golf and made a mental note to keep tabs on it. After half an hour, these two men climbed out of the motor and entered the Burger King. Older Yardies, about the same age as Quips, early forties.

One of them, rakishly skinny with a greying beard and a gold Jesus crucifix hanging from his neck, tilted his head at me. He planted a leather boot on the spare chair at our table.

'What's going on? Quips said you're supposed to go to his flat.'

I was nervous about Quips's friends. They were aggressive and had a look in their eyes said they'd kill for food if the price was right. I figured Quips wasn't good for the money but thought he might be able to steal the food off us by convincing us to go to his flat.

'Ain't happening,' I replied. 'He wants to do business, he comes to our office here, innit?'

The man grinned. He had a gap between his two front teeth you could pass a thumb through.

'We'll be waiting outside if you want to change your mind.'

They exited.

Our suspicions that Quips was planning to rob us was confirmed. Now we had two different sets of robbers waiting outside. The two men in the tinted Golf and the three Yardie boys on the street corner.

Still no sign of Kazim and the mandem.

One thirty in the afternoon and we'd been in Burger King for two and a half fucking hours. I picked at the ice cubes at the bottom of my Coke with the straw. Pasha chewed her fingernails. Time went slow, and we was scared shitless. We couldn't even leave if we wanted to. Pasha drummed her fingers on the table.

Eventually Pepper called me and asked the whereabouts of Quips. I told him he ain't showed since he made off to his flat.

'Fuck 'im. Mi come down now.'

'How long?'

This was all I needed. I couldn't delay Pepper – after all, it was his food.

'Soon,' was all Pepper said.

I phoned Kazim.

'Just hold on a bit longer,' he said. 'We're coming, don't worry, cuz.'

Five minutes later, a gold tinted Ford Focus sped into the car park at fifty per, tyres screeching and drowning out the shitty pop playing in the restaurant. The Focus bust a U-turn and coughed up a yute. He burst into the Burger King. From the get-go I knew them in the Focus were English bad boys, not Jamaicans. It was all about the way they drove. Yardie drivers boom reggae music out at cruising speed. English bad boys go for the tinted-windows look, erratic driving skills and American gangsta rap music. The yute was dressed in a dark hoodie and batties. No bright colours or gold. Defo not a Yardie man.

He didn't fuck about. Bounded straight to our table.

'Oi, gimme de ting.'

'What the fuck?'

'Dere's a bag here somewhere,' the man said. He weren't asking polite like. It was a straight-up robbery. I'm like, Rah, this *has* to be the mandem. Otherwise how would he know to go straight for the tote? But I'd never seen this boy before, and I hung out with the crew countless of times. And where was Kazim?

Before me or Pasha could respond, the boy swept up the bag and scudded out the door, scooting into the Focus as its engine roared. From speeding in to breezing out, the job had taken forty seconds. The Focus was gone, and our food with it.

'Who the fuck just robbed us?' Pasha asked, her mouth slack-jawed.

I reached out to Kazim. No answer. Voicemail. I left a message and told him to ring me back urgently. Five minutes later, the Golf abandoned the car park. I seen that the fresh-faced Yardie boy and his friend had fucked off. It was surface bait that we'd been robbed and there ain't no point spying on a couple of teenage girls minus their food.

My phone buzzed. I answered in a daze.

'How is it?' Pepper said.

'We got robbed,' I replied. I told him what happened, said we were fucking sorry.

'Nah, dat's cool,' Pepper said. 'Chill, dawta. Mi cool wid it.'

My mouth was so wide you could've popped an orange in there. I'm like, You've just lost a quarter of a mil and you're cool? No way. Don't matter how rich a man is, getting robbed is getting robbed.

'Quips di tief a tief mi food,' Pepper said. 'Mi see 'bout 'im.'

I joined Pasha outside for a cigarette.

'Pepper acted strange on the phone,' I said. 'He was chilled.'

Pasha nearly choked on her cigarette. '*Chilled*? After he just got robbed? Nah, man, that's proper dodge.'

'Some crazy shit going down' – flicking ash on to the tarmac. 'I can't figure out what, though. We're missing something here, cuz.'

The afternoon was bright and sharp and I'd under-dressed in a tight Muu Baa vintage-wash leather jacket. I smoked and looked out on to the street, innocent cars racing past. Half an hour ago, there'd been bare boys ready to merk me and Pasha for a big bit of food. I was shocked out of my daydream by my phone: Kazim.

'Did you rob me?'

'No,' Kazim said. 'What are you talking about? We haven't even got to you yet.'

I closed my eyes. Quarter of a million gone.

'Do you know what, I just got robbed for it.'

Kazim listened to our story. When I'd finished, he said, 'Tell me what the yute looked like. We know every single fucking yute in these endz. Wherever he is, we'll find him and get the food back. And tell me the model of the car. This ain't over.'

I gave him the description of the Focus.

Half an hour later, Kazim and the rest of the mandem located the Focus. Forced the yutes to open up the car boot and hand them the food. He called me with the news. I bounced up and down with joy. The food was ours. Phat £ signs danced in front of my eyes. I thanked Kazim, told him I owed him big-time and—

'Hang about, Chyna. You ain't gonna believe this' – Kazim cutting me short.

'What you talking about?'

'It's two bricks, cuz.'

I laughed. ''Course it is. I told you. Two keys.'

'Nah, nah,' he said. 'You ain't hearing me. It's two *bricks*.'

'What, like—'

'Bricks.'

As in mortar. As in the bricks you build houses with.

I felt giddy. I worked my way through a Mayfair in four heavy drags, trying to clear my head. The cigarette only made me extra dizzy.

Pepper had duped me and Pasha into conning this man Quips. He'd supplied us two real bricks, coated in flour and wrapped up again in cling film, with a small bag of real coke for us to use as a sample. Typical drug-deela tricks and cons. But I couldn't understand why Pepper, with all his p's, wanted to do one over Quips.

'He must've robbed his own link,' Pasha said. 'And then decided he'd con the next man down in the food chain. That way, he could sell his own food and get some extra money too. That's why he gave us a separate sample in a little bag and told us not to let the man cut the bricks for a sample.'

'Yeah, but shit, cuz. It's still hard to take. Imagine if Quips had opened the bricks. He'd have reckoned that we were trying to rip him off.'

There's nothing worse than being transaction virgins in the coke business. Because it's the most lucrative drug in the game and you can cut it up countless of times and mix it with glucose and other junk to re-sell it, you get bare people trying to rob each other daily. Me and Pasha had a lucky escape. We agreed that next time we'd do tings properly.

NINETEEN

West

With Rashid still behind bars and my coke hustle going down the pan, I had to rely on his mandem to look out for me. Within their circle I was treated as Rashid's wife. The rest of the boys had a duty to care for the wife while the husband was doing time in the clink. If it hadn't been for their support, tings would have been very swag for me.

They helped pay for essential bits like shopping. Nothing extravagant. These boys had to take care of their own families and bredrin too, so there wasn't much left in the pot for me. But they did what they could. Husayn was a big help. Remember, he'd spent time in prison with Rashid and was his best friend. Because of that closeness between the two men, he took extra care to sort me out with a bit of weed and some spare p's for clothes when I needed them. As well, he started dating Pasha, so the bond between us grew stronger.

Me and Husayn became over close these days. He became one of the only boys I've ever known that I could trust with my life and he asked for nothing in return except my friendship. We was cool like that; I'd link with Husayn in the mornings, swinging by at Pasha's place when she was getting ready to go off to work. You can't have that level of trust between your man and another girl normally. Most boys on the endz can't keep their zip up. But Husayn wasn't like that. He had bare respect for women and love for his sisters.

When Pasha was busy, Husayn licked jewellery from people and I'd pawn it for him: it was too risky for the same person what licked it to sell it in a pawnshop.

Five months after Rashid got sent down, I was broke. Husayn, Kazim and Nasha helped out, but I'd been living the life of a gangsta's wife; I found it a struggle adjusting to a budget. The money they supplied me with covered the bare essentials, but I had weed habits and clothes needs that were above the support they provided me with. Basic bottom line, I needed serious p's. And there was only one way I could get my hands on them.

I decided to go back into shotting.

All my old connects were in prison, leaving only one person I could speak to about sourcing some food: Husayn. We hooked up at Pasha's flat and smoked. I had my gear; he had the sess. After a few pulls, I told him I was down with banking extra p's, trying to be subtle about my intent.

'You shouldn't get no job,' Husayn said. 'That ain't proper for a Muslim man's wife. You know this. Women shouldn't work, and anyways, you're looked after by your brothers and sisters, right?'

'Yeah, but tings is tight.'

'They don't pay a lot of sterling in Tesco's, Chyna.'

'I didn't mean working in a shop.'

'You mean doing what I do?'

'Shotting? Yeah.'

He fixed his eyes on me. 'Have you shotted before?' Before I could answer, he shook his head. 'No, no, forget it. Even if you have, the game's changed these days, Chyna. We got guns and goons on every corner, heat on every endz . . .' He paused, lost in his thoughts, like I wasn't in the room. 'Do you know how many people have gone down lately?'

'Bare, man,' I replied. 'But I really need the money and I've got experience. I know how the game works.'

Husayn stroked his goatee. 'If Rashid finds out, he'll go mental.'

'He won't, I promise. I can keep a secret.'

'Trust me, if you don't tell him, someone else will. Look, I gotta be somewhere.'

'Give me the opportunity and you won't regret it,' I said.

'I'll think on it.'

The ting with me is, I'm a strong-headed person. If I have it in my head to do something, I'll do it and screw anyone else's opinion. I loved Rashid, and I didn't like to upset him, but I told myself, What he don't know won't hurt him. Shotting was my skill. Other people got work experience in factories or offices, whatever. Mine was on the roads. Over the next few weeks I pestered Husayn daily, ringing him up and texting him. I worked hard to persuade him. A month of this, I forced the issue.

'There's a bag of boys can consign me, if you don't help me out.'

'Yeah?' Husayn figured I was bluffing.

'This boy in Cardiff,' I said. 'But it means having to go there and shot out of this crackhouse in town centre, bare boys and crackheads around me, sleeping on the floor. I'm gonna have to stay there for three or four days.'

'No. You're not doing that.' He breathed heavily down the phone and was quiet for a minute. 'All right, come to my place. I'll show you the ropes and we can get you shotting on the best endz in town.'

'And where's that?'

'West,' he said.

My first time in West was an eye-opener. I thought that the Hill and country were goldmines for shotting. When Husayn mentioned the West End, I thought, Nah, can't be. Millions of tourists, CCTV and bare boydem. How could there be cats in these roads?

I was wrong.

We headed out at ten o'clock at night, to the first of three spots that Husayn shotted from. Each spot, or corner, was a five-minute walk from the other two, and we changed up every forty minutes so we didn't look suspicious to the boydem who drove up and down the winding, littered roads in their red BMWs, automatic guns on their laps. The area we were based around had a rep as prostitute central, bare gay bars and street walkers, as well as brothels in unmarked buildings. Sometimes the crackheads acted as go-betweens. If a suit man's looking for a brothel, the crackhead will take them to a building and get some p's or a small bit of crack for bringing the customer to the doors of a whorehouse. He might also source some crack for the prossy – a lot of the sex girls only accepted payment in drugs, not cash money.

West was frantic. We had cats out 24/7 for food. At least in South the cats go to sleep. They might want a bit of something in the morning, say around seven o'clock till ten, but they go to sleep at night, and they're mainly poor white people, chavvy style on benefits and spend their days tiefing stuff. They look shit, raggedy, wearing sucked-in faces, greasy hair and dirty tracksuits. On account of them being so fucking poor, they pay for £20 of food in loose change they've begged for or stolen.

West cats are always up, bang on it from morning to midnight and every hour in between. And whereas I'd be shotting brown to a single block of itchy cats on the Hill, now I dealt sniff to businessmen too. Lawyers and bankers queuing up for the big clubs and looking for a little ting to go in with. They'll get the prostitutes to come up to you, rather than risk being seen by the boydem buying drugs, ordering two rocks for the club and three pebbles of brown for the comedown.

I got to know one prostitute really well. Her name was Maggie, and she was a middle-class woman with a posh accent who'd take men out, get them drugs from me and

Husayn. On a normal night, Maggie would come up to me fifteen times, bustin' money from the party people, me giving her the sniff, her going back to the man. Back and forth, back and forth.

The crackheads in West mostly lived nearby. Nearly every cat we dealt with lived in a hostel of some kind; I think most people living in them places must be on something. We'd get all sorts of cats in West: Indian businessmen on a business trip to London and letting their hair down; Iraqis who took pure heroin in their own country and became addicted to the artificial shit in England; transvestites looking for a hit after sucking some married man's dick in a back alley for £50.

That first night, me and Husayn clocked on at ten and busted our last shot at four o'clock the following morning. We kept the main stash in Husayn's car, or Pasha's if she was shotting too, inserted behind the fan unit on the dashboard, or hidden at the back of the removable hi-fi unit. We'd take nine or ten pebbles each, dash them in our mouths and take a bottle of water too, in case we need to swallow the pebbles quick. The drill was, drink it, swallow it, shit it out later.

Husayn could see that I knew my stuff, because putting the pebbles in my mouth was natural to me. At first, pebbles are uncomfortable and they swim around. It's not so bad, but you're just very aware of them. Like I said, I'd worked out how to place them under my tongue; I'd deposit ten or twelve in my mouth, easy as slipping change in my pocket. The cat comes up to you, wants one or two pebbles, you spit them out, off you go.

I had no fear of shotting. Cats, boydem, other shotters, none of it worried me, because by this time I'd decided that I wasn't going to take life seriously.

You get up.

You live that day like it's your last.

You don't care about what happens in the future, because as far as you're concerned, you don't got one.

I might have loads of money one day and nothing the next. But tomorrow's tomorrow, so why get in a fix about it today? You deal with the hand each day throws you, and if you live from one day to the next, power to you, sister.

If you ain't got no future, then you can't be scared.

In those first weeks in West I turned over £2,000 a night. Each pebble costs £20 and on some nights I'd be banging out fifty pebbles in under three minutes. Other nights, trade was slower, but never too sluggish to the point where it wasn't worth our whiles. Of that £2,000, £1,500 went back to Husayn, the rest into my pocket. We was on it four or five nights a week, so I'd be making like £2,500 profit a week and I didn't have to get up no early hour in the weekday, commute on a fucking Tube to work, take shit from bosses I didn't respect. I kept the notes in a cellar next to my room on the ground floor of the shared accommodation block I lived in. Tucked them inside the thick cardboard box from a bottle of Moët Grand Vintage Rashid had given me for my birthday.

Monday to Thursday, it was all about the shotting. Comes Friday, me and Pasha went out raving.

Thursday evening, I'd wake up at around eight o'clock and with Pasha we'd head to the Mint Bar in Streatham for a loosener where they did two-for-ones on cocktails. We each got a Russian Spring punch made of Sputnik Vodka, crème de cassis, fresh raspberries and topped off with champagne, served tall on the rocks. A couple of drinks there and we'd leave, head to West for a bit of shotting, work until four or five o'clock in the morning, go back to Pasha's house for a snooze.

On the Friday, we'd head to the Departure Lounge in East, near to Tower Hill Tube, or if we was feeling like more of an adventure, then we'd swing by Mermaid's in Woolwich. Me and Pasha rolling up with like twenty-five man, VIP treatment, bouncers kowtowing to the mandem like they was kings. We'd hit an after-party at three o'clock in the morning, everyone on the hype and doing lots of Es.

Sometimes on the raves we'd spike boys' drinks and get the mandem to rob them.

One night at a club in West, Pasha and me were buzzin' on Es. We'd been dancing for hours, our bodies swaying to the riddim of StoneBridge's 'You Don't Know', until our leg muscles stiffened and we dropped ourselves at the table. Husayn ordered a bottle of Dom Pérignon Vintage 2000 and a couple of bottles of water to keep us cool because the club was stuffy, the air thick with the sweat of three hundred people feeling the vibe. Hot sweat dripped down the back of my neck. As we chugged ice-cold water, I noticed Pasha scoping out a boy seated at a table opposite ours.

'Who you looking at?' I shouted above the fast beat.

Pasha said something. I couldn't hear her voice. She leaned into my ear and said, 'That boy's chain. I want it.'

The boy was dressed nice in dark Armani jeans, an Obey T-shirt with a Palestinian woman's face on the front, and a D&G leather jacket on top. He was twenty metres away. I spotted the Rolex watch on his right wrist, his arm resting on the top of the sofa. The boy seemed to be alone, sipping at a Coke mixer while his friends partied on the dance floor.

The chain Pasha had her eye on was an epic, twenty-five-carat ting with a map of the world hanging from the end of the chain. Plain as day the boy was ballin' money. Ten empty bottles of Cristal stood on his table, lined up like bowling pins, each bottle costing a grand. He weren't entertaining a cheap night on basic vodka.

'That chain's worth *p's*, bruv.'

'You can't just go over there and nick it.'

Pasha motioned to Husayn. 'I got an idea,' she said.

Husayn breezed over, putting his arms around me and Pasha and giving her a peck on the cheek. Pasha explained to him that she had designs on the boy's grimy chain.

'I'll buy you one,' Husayn said.

'I don't want one bought,' Pasha replied. 'I want *that* one.'

Husayn's arched eyebrows peaked. He shook his head and smiled playfully. 'Tell you what. If you really, really want that chain, I'll hold him up and relieve him of the ting. But this ain't South. I'm not gonna go over to some boy and tief something from around his neck. You gonna have to earn it.'

The best way to get hold of the chain, we figured, was to stick the boy up in a dark street away from the club, far from the boydem and eyewitnesses. Husayn went back to the mandem and returned five minutes later with a little something in his hands, a single brownish capsule. MDMA is basically the crushed powder used for making ecstasy tablets. It looks like wet sand. Husayn planted the capsule, containing 4 milligrammes of MDMA, in Pasha's hand.

'Honeytrap the boy.'

We approached the victim. He eyeballed us, big smile on his face, like he'd just won the lottery. Who wouldn't? He was on the receiving end of nuff attention from two chirpsing girls. Pasha danced with him and I asked if he wanted another drink.

'Yeah, yeah,' the boy said. 'Vodka and Coke. The Reyka stuff, not no ordinary shit.'

While Pasha showed him her essence, I ordered the boy's drink from the bar. Took my scheming self to a secluded corner and tipped in the contents of the MDMA capsule. I had to be nailed-on sure the drink knocked the boy for six, so I slipped a bit of sniff into the mix. Pasha and the boy had stopped dancing and returned to the table, Pasha leaning into him, dishing him compliments.

The boy never suspected us of spiking his drink. He was caught up in the attention and the fact that girls were all over him, whispering in his ears, buying him drinks. He downed the spiked drink over quick. A few minutes later, he was hyped, ordering up a couple of bottles of Dom Pérignon pink and I started to worry that maybe the spiking weren't strong enough. The boy left to go toilet. Pasha frowned and adjusted her Oasis lace corset.

'Why ain't it working?'

'Maybe he needs more,' I said.

'Nah,' she replied. 'That MDMA's enough to put the boy out for England.'

Five minutes later, the boy returned from the toilet. He was fucking out of it, staggering like a street tramp and bumping into people. He collapsed at our table. Slumped in his seat, I saw his Obey T-shirt was drenched in sweat, as if he'd been standing under a shower. His pupils dilated.

'Idunfelsahgu,' he slurred.

'What?' I asked, leaning in.

He took a deep breath and repeated, 'I don't . . . feel . . . so good.'

'It's the music, mate. Why don't we go back to yours?' Pasha said.

'Safe' – the boy flashing a self-satisfied grin, eyeballs rolling this way and that, as if they were loose in his sockets.

We was all set to leave. I texted Husayn, let him know the score. The boy collected a bag from the cloakroom and we made for the door.

'Tax-eeee,' the boy said, the word dribbling out of his mouth. 'We need . . . taxi.'

'We'll get one round the corner.'

The club being on a bait main street, we led the boy up on a side road. This was where the plan might blow up. I hoped he wouldn't realize we were going into a darkened street, far from the cabs, but he seemed proper mashed and had to prop his arms against me and Pasha to stay vertical. I thought, Ain't no way he's gonna smell trouble. Shit, the boy hardly knew what day of the week it was.

'I like your garmz,' I said, trying to put him at ease.

'Got myself a Benz, girls.' He reached for something in his pocket, pulled nothing out. 'You two are fly . . .'

Twenty metres from the corner, I clocked Husayn's Beemer on a side street, engine purring.

'What's your job, then?'

'I'm a professional footballer.'

I studied his face. 'I don't recognize you. Play for Arsenal?'

'Nah,' he said.

The instant we hit the corner, Husayn and the mandem shot out of the BMW and assaulted the boy. He was too fucked to put up a fight. Ten seconds later, they'd pulled the chain off his neck and rushed back into the car and driven off, me and Pasha in tow.

'Let me see the chain,' Pasha said inside the car.

Husayn, in the front passenger seat, chucked it back.

'Happy now?'

'Crap,' Pasha said. She looked sad.

'What is it?'

'You snapped the link, bruv.'

Other occasions we'd flirt with boys in the clubs, ones we knew were big-time deelas or looked like they had a lot of p's, but instead of spiking their drinks, we'd get into their car after the club and our mandem would bolt out of a side road, blocking the car's path. They'd nick the man's wallet, his credit cards, get his pin number, take his mobile and his laptop and, if it was a deela, any food and sterling he had on his person too. Sometimes these men would go out with big bags of food or money in their boot. Our mandem would drive off, leaving us to fake it and go mad on the man, accusing him of putting us in danger. That way, he'd never suspect we was in on the con.

The rave scene got mad. We almost always went to an after-party when the club ended for the night. The after-party would go on from four or five o'clock in the morning to midday. Once a friend of the mandem invited us to an after-party she was hosting. The music was over loud, we were buzzing, spliffs stoked, and at six o'clock in the morning, as we were getting into the flow, we heard a loud rap on the door.

'Police, open up!'

We were shaken out of our bubblin'. We panicked. Six of our mandem packed niners and raced through the flat, desperately searching for somewhere to hide their tings before the boydem discovered them. More angry knocks on the door. Finally the mandem burst into the kitchen and pulled out a rack of chicken wings cooking on a baking tray in the oven. They dumped their niners between the wings just as the front door cracked open and the boydem barged inside.

They scoured the house for drugs. Failing to find anything incriminating, they gave the girl hostess the familiar lecture: keep the volume down, respect your neighbours, rah, rah, rah. They left. The mandem fetched their niners from the oven. The guns were spread between strips of chicken burned crispy black. A boy lifted it off the tray, forgetting that the ting had spent ten minutes in 200-degree heat. The grip scorched his hand. He juggled the ting like a hot coal. Dropped it. The gun clattered against the kitchen lino at an angle.

Bang!

The party silenced. We weren't sure if the boydem had driven off yet. They might still be outside. Someone scanned out the window. Coast seemed clear. We all breathed a sigh of relief and laughed about the gunshot. I turned to my right and smelled burned plastic. A smoking bullet hole in the kitchen wall stared back at me. I joined in the laughing, thinking, Rah, that's the second time a bullet's narrowly missed me. I shouldn't have found this funny. But life weren't serious. To me, it was just one big game.

Six months of shotting and raving left me in need of a break. Husayn suggested me and Pasha head up to Cardiff for a big weekender.

We ended up in Cardiff for three weeks. My friend had a beautiful five-bedroom in a village beyond the city. She had a garden the size of a London park, with purple flowers and bumblebees. Coming from South, where my next-door neighbour was under my foot, to a place where my next-door neighbour was down the road, that was a good feeling. I spent hours watching the squirrels and foxes in the gardens, catching the bird tweets and drinking in the fresh air. For those three weeks I forgot about West and South, cats and pebbles.

TWENTY

Breaking da rules

When I returned to London city, Husayn had secured a room in a cat-infested hostel in West. Instead of having to hike all the way up from South daily, we shotted in shifts. Me, Candice and Husayn took it in turns to work the corners, sleeping in the room between hours. Husayn did the early shift, from six o'clock in the morning until eleven, followed by a two-hour break, Candice one o'clock till six, another break, and then I'd be on it from eight till three. Three to six in the morning, the streets was dead so we didn't work. The night shift suited me, because in the evenings I was up. Daytimes I could sleep.

Under the shift rota, my earnings soared. I made £3,500 daily, with £1,500 into my pocket. In a hard graft Monday to Thursday routine I'd be raking in £6,000. Some I spent on garmz and raving. Rest went into the Moët stash.

I was making gangsta p's and bubblin' at the weekends, but life was beginning to get to me. Sometimes I'd break down and cry in a club toilet. Other times I'd cry myself to sleep in the hostel, wiping my tears on the dirty pillow while Candice shotted down below. The man I loved, Rashid, was behind bars, and all the weed and liquor in the world couldn't smooth over the hole in my life. I remember this feeling of heaviness, as if my bones had melted down into my feet.

At least I had the opportunity to speak to my man every day. Rashid had acquired a mobile phone in prison. They're supposed to be banned in the clink, but most of the boys I knew who did time had themselves a mobile inside. Long as you got the sterling and affiliation, you can get a phone. Anything you want in prison is ten times more expensive than on the outside world: a shitty old Nokia will set you back like £200. I had to pay for some little 8310 that I bought for £50 to be smuggled into the clink. The way it worked was, I handed the Nokia to some girl, as well as 200 notes – sort of like paying FedEx to pick up something from your home. This girl was friends with someone who worked in the prison canteen, and that person handed tings over to Rashid during mealtimes. The canteen person didn't import for everyone inside, just Rashid and his people, because they used to run up the prison. No one obtained a phone, no one hustled without Rashid or his people's say-so.

If you were shotting food inside prison, you had to pay Rashid protection money. That way, you were guaranteed not to get robbed by no one. If Rashid said someone wasn't to be robbed, that man could walk up and down the block with £20 notes clipped to his shirt and nobody would so much as lay a finger on him.

The p's Rashid made mostly came back to me in postal

orders. With each letter, Rashid seemed closer to coming home. I'd speak to him on the phone and tell him how much I loved him and missed him and couldn't wait for him to hold me in his arms again. A million wasps stung my heart when each call ended, and I'd try to look on the bright side. Think positive. Another day ticked off.

Each weekend I went clothes shopping and I'd snap up some threads for my man too. When he came out those gates, I wanted him to have a brand-new wardrobe of quality suits and jeans and shirts. I tiefed him a Cartier watch from a boy in a West nightclub. The boy was so piss-drunk he'd passed out at the table. Comatose. I got a fetish for watches and I clocked the black strap with the silver links, immediately recognizing it as a Cartier brand.

The boy wasn't alone. A friend sat next to him, sipping Coke from a tumbler glass. He wasn't drunk at all. I needed some back-up here, so I asked Kazim if I was good to nick it. He had the status where every man recognized him and knew of his business, and if Kazim said something was cool, no one was about to argue with him.

'Bore tru, Chyna,' he said. Meaning go through with it.

While his friends raved on the dance floor, I unclipped this five-grand watch from his wrist. His friend's eyes moved from the watch to me, to the watch. He shook his head slowly.

'Don't do that.'

'Kazim said it was cool.'

The piss-drunk boy's friend stared across the club to Kazim, who raised his champagne glass and winked at him.

'I ain't seen nothing,' the friend said, turning away.

I slipped the Cartier into my handbag. Piss-drunk boy never knew a ting.

I added more p's to the Moët stack. These days I'd saved away £8,500. I had to put away as much as possible, knowing that when Rashid came out of prison, he'd need to have some money to start his own line, maybe buy a car and enjoy himself a little bit with the mandem.

My stack took a hit, however, when Candice got hooked on the sniff.

Sniff's a dangerous drug. I smoked weed, but I never, ever touched no sniff except to sample it. Samples was a tiny bit on my teeth; none of that crap ever went up my snout. I'd seen people get fucked up from sniff before.

To begin with, me and Pasha was the only girls shotting in West. Soon Candice hooked up with us, as well as a friend of Candice's, name of Sophie. She happened to be a friend of Pasha's but never been in no gang. Sophie's what I call a street girl: she had a gang mentality, criminal skills, but no proper affiliation and thought loyalty was something to do with a Nectar card. I didn't trust her. Still, I enjoyed welcoming Candice back to my fam, and because Pasha knew Sophie, I figured she was probably safe, even if I didn't rate her. Then the two of them came out clubbing with us, and I saw that tings were wrong.

Every half-hour in this club, Candice and Sophie disappeared into the toilets for bare minutes. They'd come back out tittering and rubbing their noses.

They're on the sniff, I thought.

The number-one rule of any shotter is this: don't blow your own package. It's tempting for some people, especially when it comes to weed and coke, because they're not seen as evil drugs like brown, more like social accessories, and some deelas think to themselves, Rah, just a teeny bit off the top. Boom, next ting they know, they've smoked or snorted half of fucking Jamaica and they can't afford to pay back their supplier. That's what happened to Candice. As she shotted the sniff, she'd also shoved it up her hooter.

I reckon it was Sophie what got Candice into trouble. Sophie comes from a sniff family. They got coke heritage. Soon as we met her, we'd go to her house to take drugs because her mum didn't give a fuck. Long as we sorted her out with a £20 stone of sniff, she'd let us in to smoke weed, do Es, whatever. I'd be sitting in the living room with Pasha, smoking draw and watching Sophie and her mum bustin' rails together on the coffee table. If you met Sophie and her mum in the street, you wouldn't guess they were mother and daughter. Her mum behaved more like a friend of the family. She was this big woman, very loud, ghetto, white trash, the type who's only ever dated black men and has five kids and don't give a fuck what mischief the daughters are up to as long as she's got her sniff.

Sophie's coke habit became a dependency. She was like her mum, hooked on the shit. Me and Pasha confronted her about it one day while her mum was out.

'I can't help it,' Sophie said. 'I'm a hoover.'

To be fair, her family history worked against her. Apart from her mum, Sophie's nan, aged seventy-two, dabbled in a bit of sniff. Her nan's sister would go into the bathroom while we was cotching and do lines. Doing hard drugs was wired into that girl's DNA.

Husayn consigned me, Pasha and Candice at the same time, once a week, meaning we was jointly responsible for paying back what we owed him and taking our cut off the top. This arrangement worked fine as long as there's a level of trust between the shotters.

A few weeks later, Candice and Sophie had to pick up the next food consignment from Husayn. They should have called me and Pasha right afterwards. We didn't hear nothing. Tried ringing their phone. Switched off. Clear as cut diamonds what's gone on here, I told myself. Candice and Sophie have made off with the food, leaving me and Pasha to pick up the tab. It didn't matter that Husayn was our good friend. The drugs scene is like a sea. Me and Pasha were the little fish, Husayn was a bigger fish, and above him was the really big fish. Above them the sharks. Husayn had his own boss to answer to. That's how it works.

I was dreaded. Managed to consign some extra food from another connect, sold it on, paid the money back to

Husayn. Used the next consignment to pay the other man back. Had to shift p's around like laundered money. My Moët stack was sliced in half. All told, we was five months in paying off Candice and Sophie's big bit of food.

Their conniving also polluted my status. I worked hard on the endz to get a platinum rep. If a deela knows that they can give some drugs to you and they'll get their p's back and on time, 100 per cent, they're more likely to increase the amount they're willing to consign you. I was consigned more than the boys because I proved myself trustworthy. Owing a lot of money to certain people made me look bad, and the word on the roads was that I'd done the sniff for myself.

If anyone wanted to know the truth, they only had to clock Candice in the street. The big, tall aggressive girl I'd known, the one who'd filled out a size 12 in a nice way, had shrivelled to a gaunt size 6 who looked more like a size 0, eyes glazed over, spots under her nose. That was the last time I saw her, before she stole my food. These times everyone in the hood knew they were sniffing and gossiped about how they'd turned to tiefing tings to support their habit. Them girls was what's known in the trade as coke-broke.

The problem with sniff, and why I don't touch it, is that the shit itself ain't addictive. It's the crap it's mixed with that turns people into fiends. I'd seen for myself what the deelas put in the mix: glucose, talcum powder, sugar, baby-milk powder, caffeine. Anything to make it addictive. The pure stuff? Makes your nose bleed. That's what I used to get from my deela. But street stuff is cut up countless of times.

Six months passed since I'd last seen Candice. I got a phone call from a boy I knew. He'd spotted Candice shotting in fresh endz. Word on the street was Candice had been doing solid trade. Healthy profits meant there had to be a stash somewhere.

Perfect, I thought. Take the piss out of me, I take the piss out of you.

I planned out my con. The following day, I phoned up Sophie out of the blue, pretending that I'd forgotten about her and Candice stealing the flake.

'Cuz, 's'up? Ain't heard from you for longs, darling.'

'Uh, yeah, safe . . .' I could picture Sophie's skeleton face, her white-trash lips puckering at the phone, puzzling why I was reaching out to her.

'Shot me a draw, will you?'

'You . . . want me . . . to shot you a draw?' That crunching sound was Sophie's coke-fried brain trying to work out how a shotter as wired as me could ever be short of weed.

'My deela ain't got none and the other mandem are busy.' Before she could quiz me, I went on, 'I want two eighths,' which is two £20 weed draws.

'Um, yeah, OK,' she said.

'Great. Come to my house and I'll sort you out some p's.'

I knew Sophie would be desperate for money. All sniff fiends are. Same as the crackheads.

Soon as I killed the call, I was on the phone to my link. My cousin, Rashid's brother Taban, some of the younger boys from the mandem, they was all in on the con. They hidden inside my home.

When everyone was in place, a cranked Ford Fiesta rocked up to my front door. Out popped Sophie, looking full-on anorexic. A boy climbed out too. Despite her addiction, Sophie weren't 100 per cent out of it and had brought a mandem rolling as her bodyguard, in case I did a number on her.

But one bodyguard weren't gonna save her.

I opened the door and ushered Sophie and the boy into the living room. Closed the front door and snatched the car keys out of her hand.

'What the fuck?'

As the boy moved into my face, Taban and the youngers leaped out from behind the sofa and door, bundling him to the ground. Sophie made a play for the front door. I beat her to it, slammed her to the ground and boxed her up.

'We're kidnapping you,' I said.

She was hysterical. 'What for?'

'Don't gimme that, bitch. You know the reason.'

We stopped short of torturing Sophie and settled on dishing out hard boxes and slaps to rough her up. I seen she wore a Rolex watch belonging to Husayn on her wrist, and a gold ring on her middle finger, also his. Spitting mad that she busted in possessions of my bredrin, I ripped the Rolex and the ring off.

'That's my friend's stuff.'

'What the fuck! Husayn gave it to me, Chyna.'

'He didn't mean for you to take it down Cash Convertors, though, did he? And let's face it, that's what you're gonna do with it sooner or later.'

After four hours of being slapped about, Sophie gave up the location of her stash. Said the food was secreted at her mum's place.

'You're kidding. You're leaving sniff in your mum's place and she ain't touched it?'

Sophie eyefucked me. Her blue eyes faded like old denim.

'Well, we'd best go there now before she snorts it all.'

From Sophie's mum's house we landed ourselves a big bag of food, plus a couple of grand in p's. I split the packages with the mandem who'd come down to help me kidnap Sophie. Breezed out of her endz. I knew that she'd be on the phone to Candice, telling her what had happened. I didn't care.

Determined to have the last word, Candice and Sophie contacted the wardens at the prison Rashid was locked away in and snitched that he had a mobile phone. The day after I'd kidnapped Sophie, his cell got raided and he was sent down to another block with less freedoms. Sophie and Candice denied it, but to me, that ain't no coincidence.

I sometimes see Candice out and about. We talk, but I can't be close with her like back in the day. Not after she'd betrayed my trust.

After that episode, Candice opened her eyes to how bad she'd been hooked on the sniff. She cut that shit out, and you have to give her respect for that. When we see each other now, it's like, 'Safe,' and that's as far as it goes. Candice knows I dissed her and can't have people think she was a fool.

PART FIVE

THE GAME

'Karma's a fucking bitch'

– Chyna

TWENTY-ONE

Serious 'p's

I hooked up with Paige. We went to my endz and had a brandy and Coke, put on some old-skool Wiley, 'Sorry Sorry Pardon What?', and chatted about the old times, how tings had moved on, how we'd all been changed by the streets. She told me she'd started dating some boy by the name of Darnel and they'd been getting on over well until he went down for a stretch in prison. Bank robbery.

Darnel got sent to the clink because him and a link of his had followed a man into a bank branch. They had worked out a plan to target people who ran small businesses, thinking that those people walked in and out of banks every day with big bags of p's.

How it worked was that Darnel would follow the man into the bank while his link, Daequan, would stand guard outside. On this day, they did a robbery special. Waited outside for the businessman to make a phat withdrawal. Darnel followed him and punched his head in until the man was unconscious.

Both Darnel and Daequan eventually got arrested, and even though they knew they were going to do a stretch, they were still shocked when the judge read out their sentences. Daequan got four years, while the judge handed Darnel eight because he tiefed and punched the fuck out of the man in that first robbery. Using his body as a violent weapon, they said.

A few days later, after Darnel was sent into the clink, I was chilling with Paige when my Nokia buzzed. I thought it might be one of the mandem or girldem calling, picked it up and seen that it weren't no call, but a video clip. From a number I didn't recognize.

I pressed play. A dark, fuzzy image displayed. Some boy, nineteen or twenty years old, was tied to a chair in a room cramped by darkness. His hands were behind his back. A white sheet had been stuffed into his mouth and tied round his jaw. The video was waste quality. There were bruises over his face as another boy gave him a proper licking; he was tall and had a thickset build on him, muscles like Vin Diesel. The gagged boy shitted himself. The captor boxed him in the face, giving him big bangs. He turned to the camera.

I recognized him from the get-go.

Darnel.

'Fucking wasteman,' Darnel said on the video.

Tied-up boy screamed himself hoarse through his gag.

'Him fucked,' another boy said off-screen.

For a moment I was all zoned out.

'You all right, bruv?' This from Paige. I snapped out of my shock and stared at her.

'Cuz,' I said. 'Shit. It's your man Darnel.'

'Don't be messing, cuz,' Paige said, grinning as if she

thought I was fibbing. She nodded at my Nokia. 'Give it here.'

My hands was shaking as I passed the phone to her. I felt sick.

She watched the clip dead silent, chaining it on the cigarettes, playing the clip again and again. Finished each cigarette in a couple of drags. Finally she handed the Nokia back.

'Rah, this some madness, fam,' she said.

'Do you know the boy Darnel's fucking up?'

'He don't look like no one' – shaking her head.

I already knew how Darnel had got the video clip to my phone. He'd got one of his mandem to film him knocking this boy senseless and sent it to me. I couldn't figure out why, though. What the fuck did he need to show me the clip for?

My phone vibrated again. A call this time. Same number that had sent the video clip.

'Do you know a boy called Wax?'

The name rang a sort of dim bell in my head. He was a friend of a friend of a friend.

'Yeah. I mean, not really, no, but I've heard of him.'

'Got his number?'

'Hang on,' I said, and ran through my address book. I had, like, bare numbers on my mobile. Literally thousands of people.

'Yeah,' I said, clocking the entry for Wax.

'I want you to send this clip to him.'

'OK . . .'

'Do it now, Chyna, and send a message asking him to call me.'

I sent the clip to Wax, just as Darnel had said.

Ten minutes later, Darnel called me back.

'Put Paige on the line,' he said.

I handed my mobile to Paige.

They talked. The call didn't last long. Paige said three words the whole time. 'Safe . . . Safe . . . Safe.' When she was done, she asked me to two-twos her another cigarette. Half-hour without a smoke for Paige is torture.

'Shit, I'm out, bruv.'

'Rah, let's buy some more, then. I need to clear my fucking head.'

As we reached the local Nisa, Paige told me about the call.

'That boy you sent the clip to, he's the bredrin of the boy Darnel is torturing,' she said. 'They had a chat on the phone. The bredrin's got to give up a shitload of drugs and money . . .' She paused. 'Otherwise Darnel's not gonna let the boy go.'

'Which people do you mean?'

'It's the Coolie Boys, cuz.'

The Coolie Boys had a big-time connect and operated on a different level to the mandem. They were bad people. Violent thugs who robbed themselves as much as they robbed other people. They didn't give a fuck about the bling and the cars and the lifestyle. All the Coolie Boys were interested in was p's. Loyalty and fam, respect – those words meant nothing to the Boys. And they had a rep for torture. Basically, you didn't rob these men unless you were serious and didn't give a fuck what trouble came your way.

'There's more,' Paige said. 'Darnel, he needs this stash.' She took in a heavy draw of breath. She looked pale. 'He *needs* it, fam.' Paige explained that Darnel had some trouble with another mandem and he owed them big-time. Even though he was stuck in the slammer, if he didn't settle his debt to this other mandem, they were gonna box up his family, spray his house with MAC-10s, maybe even shank him in the clink.

'What are we gonna do?' I said.

'Well, ain't no two ways about it. We got to get the money and the drugs.'

A Yardie man at the counter haggled the owner for one cigarette. Paid his 20 pence for a single Marlboro Red. Paige dashed her coins on the counter for the Mayfairs and we breezed out.

'So we just gotta collect the money and the food?' I asked.

'And then deal it and give the money to the man's people what's on his back. We can keep a bit for ourselves, Darnel told me. Long as he can pay off his debt, he don't care what we do with the rest.' She lit a smoke.

'Where do we need to go?'

'North,' Paige said.

Although the boys were on the roads in South, the heat around those endz meant the bigger playas took the time to move their stashes out of the endz to somewhere the boydem wouldn't think to search.

Me and Paige climbed into her white Fiat Punto. I drove.

'So we'll pick up this money.'

'Just like a drive-thru, Chyna.'

'And what about the drugs?'

'The boy said to me it's kept someplace else in North, but he can't get hold of the girl who's sitting on it. This is what we'll do: pick up the p's and then split to the safehouse and collect the food. They ain't gonna do nothing to us. Darnel's got their bredrin banged up. If they touch us, Darnel's gonna fuck him good and proper.'

She stared out of the window, twisting a strand of hair round her finger.

'Shit, who am I fooling?' she added. 'It's not us I'm worried about. Darnel . . .'

'Let's do what your man says,' I replied. 'That's the best way of helping him, bruv. No point stressing over what might happen. We can save him.'

We shuttled through drab Elephant and Castle, past the rotten-fruit stalls and the ancient Chinese all-you-can-eat, the bombed-out shopping centre and the tower blocks built from zigzagged concrete.

The roads North were jammed with traffic. We rolled

through streets lined with Turkish and Polish food stalls, depressing laundrettes and shitty pubs with Irish flags draped over the windows and old men standing outside, drinking cider and smoking cheapest roll-ups.

'How long has Darnel got to pay the mandem?'

'A week,' Paige said, biting a manicured finger.

'And we gotta turn over the food in that time?'

She nodded slowly, curling up her lips. We both knew how hard it would be to turn round any big quantity of drugs in such a short span of time. I thought about other ways we could offload it that quick, get Darnel the p's he needed to get the mandem off his back.

We parked up nearby to the McDonald's where the boy had told us to meet and crossed the road to the restaurant. The sun had done a runner and rainclouds the colour of coshes dominated the sky. It pissed down.

'The boy told you to wait outside or in?' I said, shielding my hair from the wet with my hoodie top. I was wearing thin summer shoes and didn't fancy getting soaked.

'Out,' Paige said.

'Fuck it, mate. I'm going in.'

'But, Chyna—'

'You coming?'

'Yeah,' she said.

I was starving, having smoked my way through a couple spliffs earlier. We breezed up to the counter and gave our orders to the pizza-faced boy.

'Chicken nuggets and a Diet Coke,' Paige said.

'Give me a double cheeseburger, large fries, Coke, chicken nuggets,' I said.

Paige shot me a jealous look. I'm so skinny I could eat for England. Paige is the opposite. All she had to do is *look* at a burger and the pounds stack on.

We sat down at a table by the window and watched the rain whoosh down on everybody in the streets. I thought North endz looked soulless, sooted and grey, like living in a lead box. But North people probably looked at the endz where me and Paige came from and thought they looked crap too.

I was so hungry I ate my food in a couple of bites.

The doors swung open and this boy walked in, sat down next to us. There was a brown paper bag in his right hand, like the McDonald's one without a logo. He placed the paper bag on the table next to the food tray. The paper bag was proper bulked, as if a couple of bricks had been stuffed inside it. The boy eyeballed Paige, then turned on me. He had fish eyes.

The boy shot up, breezed out. Never said a word.

We left a minute later and didn't dare check the bag until we were in the car and driving away, sure that no one was tailing us.

'How much?' I asked.

Paige dug a hand into the bag and pulled out the most fattest wad of £20 notes I had ever seen.

'Fucking five grand five hundred,' Paige said.

Darnel needed a lot more than that. He was in debt to the tune of ten grand. But it was a start. We drove to a nearby post office and snapped up a few postal orders. When you're in prison, you're not allowed to receive paper money, but you can get postal orders. What you do is you buy a postal order and then get it made out to 'the Governor'. You write the name of the prisoner on the back, 'Darnel Williams', and his prison number. The maximum you can send in a single postal order is £500. Once we'd popped that in the post, we stashed the rest.

It was night-time when we got returned to our endz and linked with our mandem. Paige got the green light to collect the food from the safehouse, but I felt wiped and had to be up early the next day for a meeting with my Muslim sisters. I asked Paige if we could go the following afternoon.

'Can't, bruv. The boy said I need to go and pick it up tonight. Don't worry, I'll take Stocks with me. He'll box anyone who tries it on.' Stocks was Wallace's friend from his crew, the one obsessed with comic books who'd shot outside Sharise's house. He'd been off the scene for a while, doing this and that. Now he was back around the roads, and having someone with experience and a familiar face would be good for Paige.

'Take care of youself,' I said.

At ten o'clock at night, Paige dialled me. She woke me up.

'Come over to my house,' she said. Something in her voice told me she was excited.

I rocked up to her house at ten thirty. She lived fifteen minutes' walk away, or five minutes by bus.

Paige paced up and down in her bedroom. I reckoned she'd wear a hole through the floorboards. I'm not the sort of girl who fucks about. A lot of my fam thought I was a bit boyish like that. I just come out with what's on my mind. I could see something playing on Paige's mind.

'Something wrong, cuz?'

Paige bit her nails and stopped walking. 'I went to the safehouse, right?'

I sat on the chair next to her bed. 'Yeah, and what happened?'

'I go to the address.' Paige toyed with her chops. 'It's this place in the middle of fucking nowhere and I don't know no one on these roads, so me and Stocks are uptight. We waits for long. Finally the door opens and this girl comes out, really fucking big. Like *fat* fat. She's holding this Tesco bag. Anyways, she's walked right over and chucked it through the window.'

'What's so weird about that?'

Paige held her eyes level with mine. 'I don't think she knew how much food she was giving me.'

Seeing I was confused, Paige reached under her bed and slid out an Aldo shoebox. She lifted off the lid. Inside I clocked the Tesco bag. The bag's stuffed, I thought as I looked at it. Bare of weed. But weed is weed. If pure sniff is gold dust, weed is like mud. Anyone can get hold of a bit of draw. I used to sell it at the bus-stop waiting to go school – £3 for three joints or ten for £5, special offer.

Then Paige opened the bag.

Inside was the most biggest lump of brown I had ever seen. This bag was the size of a Rubicon mango-juice carton, one of those litre ones you get in the supermarkets. It was a browny-yellow colour, like dirty, wet sand.

I'd shotted enough brown and rated the contents of the Tesco bag at £50,000 total, maybe more. Rah, I thought, we can do a lot more than just settle Darnel's problems with this. We can flip it and make bare grands for ourselves too. After all, Darnel told us that we could keep whatever was on top of his debts. It'll be the easiest money we'll ever make, I told myself. My heart jumped around inside.

'We've got to be careful,' I said. 'People are gonna try to get this food off us.'

'This is gonna change our lives,' Paige said, ignoring me. 'We can buy a bigger bit of food, get bare lines going, buy consignments direct from the connects. No more flipping pebbles to fucking cats.'

'True that,' I said. 'But we've already got one problem.'

'What's that?'

'Your boy Stocks.'

Stocks going with Paige to make the collect meant that a third pair of eyes had seen the drugs, other than me and

Paige. And Stocks was no fool. He had a brain on him and knew exactly how much that bag would have been worth. No doubt, taking Stocks with her had been a fatal mistake. If only I'd tagged along, none of the shit that followed would ever have gone down.

The roads were alive with word that we had a big bag of food on our hands.

Paige rolled up to my house in her Punto. I hopped in.

'Cuz, we gotta talk.'

We hit Pizza Hut for a bite to eat.

'What's up?' I asked.

'Do you know who rang me today? Some boy called E.'

'Who?'

'That's how you *know*!' she said, our way of saying, 'Exactly.' 'He rang me at eight o'clock in the morning, telling me to get out of bed. I'm like, "Who's this?" and this boy is like, "My name's E," and I'm like, "I don't know no E." I'm paying no attention, right. It's over early for any stupidness.'

I nodded between mouthfuls of cheesy-bite crust.

'He says, "I'm outside your house."'

I stopped chewing.

'I'm freaking out. What the fuck business has he got with me? I tells him again, "I don't know no boy called E." I go to my bedroom window and look out the front, but there's no one there. So I don't think nothing of it.'

'That ain't right, bruv.'

She nodded. 'Funny ting is, right, in the last three or four hours I've got like a hundred missed calls from three numbers and I don't recognize any of them. Don't you think that's weird?'

As we talked, Paige's Samsung flared up again.

'It's Darnel.'

I nipped to the toilet. When I returned, Paige was giving her phone the screw-face and flicking through the missed calls.

'Darnel says if we're not comfortable holding on to the drugs to give it to his boy Warren. Let him take care of the sale.'

'What did you tell him?'

'I said, nah, we're safe. What have we got to worry about? Some boy called E who don't even find the right address for the person he's talking to? We've both of us faced worse.'

We left the shopping centre and headed back to Roxy's Punto.

'Need a ride?'

'I'm all right,' I said. 'I'm gonna go see Sakina.'

'Stay safe.'

I went across town to see Sakina, a Muslim girl I met properly through our get-togethers at the mosque. We'd gone school together but never really talked. Islam had brought us together as friends. Jamal, Sakina's boyfriend and the boy I'd met when me and Pasha originally converted to Islam, was also there. We went up to her bedroom, closed the door and – bang – we got on the draw straight away, no messing about.

'I heard you got hold of some brown,' he almost whispered, like he was afraid someone was listening in.

'I don't know about that.'

'Warren told me.'

Fuck, I thought. These endz got an addiction to gossip. I played it cool, didn't bat an eyelid. 'Don't know nothing about it,' I said. 'It ain't mine.'

'It's Paige's, right?'

'What, suddenly I'm that girl's shadow? Really and truly, I got no clue, Jamal.' I took a pull on the joint.

'Be that as it may,' Jamal said, fanning the smoke away from his face, 'you know where the food is. And you can get us a sample, can't you? If the stuff's good, I'm down for a consignment.'

The joint snuffed out.

I thought about Jamal's offer. Jamal, like a lot of the boys he associated with, was able to be both a practising Muslim and a drug deela, no problem. Jamal was affiliated to Rashid and his bredrin, and I had a good ting going on with Sakina too.

I thought to myself, Rah, moving all that brown in small packets on the roads is gonna take long. If we could sell it to other deelas rather than to the cats on the Hill, we'd be able to pay off the money to the mandem pressing Darnel. By selling it on to Jamal and others like him, we'd also be rid of the brown quick as, and not have to worry about the boydem finding it in a house search.

But I also knew no offer on the endz comes without strings. I didn't want to commit to nothing, especially without having Paige's ear first.

'Let me speak to her and see what I can do,' I said.

'Just get me a sample,' he said. 'Then we'll talk money.'

'Safe.'

I called Paige. Like me, she was up for getting Jamal a sample. Like me, she wanted to be done with the food. Like me, she didn't see no reason not to trust Jamal.

I told him the good news and he beamed a smile that showed off the two gold teeth he had on the front row. Half an hour later, Paige showed up. She burst into Sakina's room with the sample and Jamal's eyes near enough popped out of his head.

A sample of draw might be a joint, because the bag of weed you're selling on is big and the total value ain't extra riches. Brown is different. A sample of brown is small. It has to be, because the gear you're shotting is in grammes anyway and you don't want to waste packets of it on deelas who might not even buy nothing off you, end of. Normally a sample of brown is 0.2 grammes. No more than a little piece of dust.

What Paige was holding in her hands was not no speck of dust.

There was a plastic shopping bag wrapped up into a ball. She opened it up on Sakina's bed and revealed this wedge of brown the size of an ackee. Soon as Jamal clocked the size of the taster, he no doubt figured that the total amount of food we had was big. Jamal had asked for a sample and Paige had given him a flipping *rock*.

'How much food have you got, all told?' he asked.

In hindsight, taking along a supersize sample was the worst mistake we could have done. It put certain of ideas into Jamal's head. Or maybe the mentality was already there, but the possibilities suddenly occurred to him.

Jamal was a robber. That's how he did.

He weren't no shitty street robber neither. I found out later that there was another side to Jamal. He specialized in robbing drug deelas, like Omar in *The Wire*, going around the endz armed with a MAC-10 and looking for shotters. He didn't bother with the small-time deelas. He was only interested in them shotters who had big bits of food and p's.

The most tiniest voice inside me said, If he thinks you're naive or weak, he might . . . No. I cut the thought out. He would *never* do that. Jamal knew my status.

'How much food?' he asked again.

'Not that much,' I replied.

'I wasn't born yesterday,' Jamal said. 'Or the day before.'

'We're not trying to fool you,' Paige said.

'In all my days, I never seen no one give a sample that

big. That there is no sample. That there is bloody half of Pakistan.' He eyeballed Paige. 'Where's the rest of it?'

'With a friend.'

'Yeah? Which friend?'

'Just someone I know.'

'From the roads?'

'From out of town,' Paige said. Her lies were ropey. Jamal's eyes burned a hole through Paige. He stood there and stared at her for longs. None of us dared say anything. Jamal breezed out a few minutes later, but his words kept us on edge.

When it hit half twelve at night, my Nokia sparked up. Warren, Darnel's bredrin, the one who had offered to take the food off our hands. Warren had a rep as a boy who didn't mess about. He was straight and on the square, and I knew then that for him to be reaching out to me, someone outside his bredrin . . . well, something had to be badly wrong.

'Where's the drugs?' he said. Warren didn't do hellos.

'Why are you ringing my phone? Call Paige. It ain't got nothing to do with me.' My first instinct was to play dumb. Boys had a bad habit of thinking they were more street-wise than us girls, making it easy to manipulate them.

Paige stared at me, mouthing, 'Who is it?'

'Come on, girl. Talk to me. You and Paige are good friends.'

'Look, Warren, Darnel's not my boyfriend. He didn't sort

out the food for me, do you get me? You need to call Paige. I'm just a friend. I ain't about this, period.'

'Give me the phone,' Paige mouthed.

I shook my head. I'm a big girl. I can handle this.

'I'm serious. This ain't no game, Chyna.' He breathed heavily down the phone. 'A lot of people know you've got a big stash of food. You need to tell me where the drugs is. Otherwise someone else is gonna rob you for it.'

'I told you already, it ain't with me.'

'Fuck it. OK. Just drop it round to mine,' Warren said. Like he hadn't listened to a word coming out of my mouth. It sounds strange, seeing as how Darnel and Warren were tight and all, but I didn't trust him to hang on to the food. Neither did Paige. We just had this instinct that he was too enthusiastic about wanting to get hold of the drugs.

Although I'd been shotting for many days, this was different to selling bags of weed at school or brown to the cats on the Hill. I'm not selling drugs to someone on the roads these times. The positions had changed. Now it's *our* drugs, and there were people out to get *us*. I was seeing the game as the big-man deelas seen it. We were a legit target.

People make out drug deelas to be arrogant, but truly, they're paranoid and live in constant fear that someone close is gonna rob them. I know, because that's how I felt.

'The only food I got,' I said to Warren, 'is in my freezer.'

'Chyna, I'm not dicking around. This ain't no little bit of

drugs we're talking about here.' Although Warren didn't know how much we had, I figured he'd heard word on the street about the size of our so-called 'sample'. 'When you're holding on to that kind of quantity, people will do bad tings to get a bit of the action, you feel me?'

'Rah, now you're scaring me,' I laughed. 'Jokes, man. What kind of tings?'

'Kick in your front door. Run up your mum's house. Hold your mum hostage. Stick niners in her face until you fess up. Your blood sisters too. *Anything*.'

Paige pointed at the phone. 'Give it to me.' I gave it. She didn't mess about.

'Are you intimidating my girl?'

I heard Warren shouting down the phone.

'Shut it, Warren. Look, we'll bring the food round to yours, yeah? Good. Where are you? The estate? Wait for us there. I don't know. We'll reach you. Yeah, wait. Laters.'

'We gonna do this?' I asked as Paige passed me my Nokia.

'It's not worth it,' she replied. 'Every boy's ringing yours and mine phones. Do you think they're gonna go away?'

'But can we trust Warren to sell it on for Darnel?'

'He's Darnel's boy, bruv,' Paige said, trying to convince herself as much as me. 'His flippin' soldier. He'll do it, no doubt, otherwise why would Darnel be telling us to give it to him? And anyway, it'd take us long to shot that much food. We're bound to get shiffed before we can move it on.'

'She's right,' Sakina said. 'The heat on you is gonna get worse.'

We said goodbye to Sakina. Walked out to the Punto.

'I think I got a plan,' I finally said.

'Yeah?'

'I'll tell you on the way.'

We reached Paige's to pick up the brown. One thirty in the morning by the time we rolled up, her mum and sisters tucked up in bed.

'So what's the plan?'

'Here's what I'm thinking,' I said. 'There's no point you giving *all* of the food to Warren. I mean, it's not like he knows exactly how much we have. Darnel's gonna get his debt paid off by Warren, and that boy's gonna keep the rest to his own good self. For real. But that ain't right. I mean, fam . . .' I turned my voice low as she put her key in the front door. 'We had to do all the legwork here.'

'True dat' – Paige nodding. She could see where I was going. Like me, she had a solid street mentality. Hatched plans like hens did eggs, that girl.

'So . . . we might as well make what we can out of it,' I said.

'What, you mean keeps a little bit for ourselves . . . ?'

'And shot it, why not? Face it, soon as these boys take the food off our hands, we ain't seeing a thin penny. I'm up for making some money, compensate us for the stress factor, you feel? Plus it's back-up in case Warren don't follow through for Darnel.'

Paige heaved the Aldo shoebox out from underneath her bed and disappeared into the kitchen. She returned with a teacup, a plastic food container and a cheap plastic bag. Dipping the teacup into the brown, she scooped out a full cup and tipped it into the plastic bag. I stood and watched. The teacup had barely made a dent in the package. Our one little cup looked pathetic.

'Do you think that's enough?'

'We should take some more,' I said. 'It's not as if we can come back and get second portions. Whatever we take, that's whatever we're left with.'

Paige spooned four more cups into the plastic bag. Then she sealed the bag inside the container box. Put the container inside a pink Nike backpack. Shoved the backpack under her bed.

Even though we'd taken a good amount of drugs, there was still a massive bag of food left in the Aldo box. Paige smoothed over the package, patting down the hole to make sure no one could see that we'd lifted the balance. We hid the container in Paige's wardrobe and took the main consignment downstairs.

We didn't fancy driving to the estate. We had so much of drugs on us that if the boydem pulled us over, we were looking at charges and court appearances and probably prison. In these predicaments, your local unlicensed cab is a lifesaver. Paige rang for a driver and we got ourselves an Afghan cabbie. If any boydem cars tried tailing us, worst-case scenario we could dump the box on the floor and tell the boydem, 'This is a cab, mate. One of them dodgy ones. Fucked if I know how the food got there.' The driver would protest, but there would be two of us versus one of him, his cab weren't legal, and probably neither was he.

The estate was a series of breeze-block buildings in a part of South that's in need of a makeover. Hoodie boys watched their dogs chew up old car tyres in the park, the only shops are local off-licences, and the phone boxes had their glass knocked in. Half the windows on the blocks were dirty grey, like someone had washed them with old soap-water. The other half boarded up with old *Metro* newspapers or black bin bags.

'Shit,' Paige said. The battery on her Samsung was dead.

'I'll call him.' The cab raced out of the roads before our feet had even touched the ground. For some reason, taxi drivers don't hang around our endz.

I buzzed Warren. Three rings. Four rings. Five.

A group of five or six boys were walking towards us. They were big boys, early twenties, and one of them was riding a Schwinn chopper bike.

Six rings. Seven. Come on. Me thinking, Answer the fucking phone, Warren.

Crunk music boomed out somewhere in the distance, bass jarring the endz. From the other direction I seen a couple of younger boys, fifteen or sixteen, with a brown

Staffordshire bull terrier. Dog yanking at the chain so hard I thought it might snap.

Eight rings.

Voicemail.

'Fuck.'

'What's going on?'

'Warren's not answering.'

Paige darted her eyes, like left to right. 'We can't hang about here.'

'I know it,' I said.

The block Warren said he lived in was dark as a sewer and the streetlights were punched out. We weren't familiar with the mandem in these roads, had no associates we could call on. Really and truly, we were on our own. I was over conscious of the fact that we had a big bag of B on us. When you're handling drugs, your fear level goes through the roof.

Then it struck me.

'We don't have to wait on Warren,' I said.

'Are you buzzin', mate? We've come all this way. We ain't gonna call no cab man and go back home with the food.'

'Not that. Look at the bins.'

A separate hut was rooted next to each block, where all the bin bags had to be taken and dumped inside of these massive metal dumpster bins. I wanted a closer look. The big red doors to the hut weren't padlocked, only secured with a rusty bolt that could be tugged loose. I made my way over to the hut round to the side of Warren's building, out of sight of the boys and slid the bolt back on the door. Had to really pull on it before it finally gave way. I opened the door and a wave of nastiness hit me like a cloud. The hut stank of shitty nappies, rotten fish and mouldy curry, stuffed to the brim with bright-blue cornershop bags and knotted-up Tesco bags. Flies darted about my face.

'Give me the box,' I said to Paige. I took the Aldo shoe-box and shoved it underneath the dumpster. It was dry underneath and as good a hiding place as any; this smelly bin hut would be the last place any boys would think to look.

'Hurry up,' Paige said.

I crawled out of the hut and carefully slid the bolt back along, making sure it didn't make no loud banging noise.

As we scarpered round to the front of the building, one of them boys shouted out to me, 'Yo, sister!'

'Let's get out of here,' I said.

'Ey, sis! Come here!'

We broke into a run, sprinted all the way to the Hill. From there we grabbed a night bus back to our endz. On the way, I called Warren. No answer, so I left a voicemail saying, Rah, this is where the food is, collect it when you can. Job done. I got off the bus, as it went past my house first, and told Paige I'd speak to her tomorrow. She looked shattered. Reckon I did too. It had been a long night.

I didn't realize that it was going to be an even longer day.

TWENTY-TWO

For real

Eight thirty in the morning and I woke up to urgent knock-knocking on the front door. I squirmed out of bed, sploshed freezing water on my face and lit up a spliff. Answered the front door. Paige was in my face, looking worse for wear and proper breathless.

'Did you hear back from Warren?'

I checked my Nokia. 'Nothing.'

'Give him a call.'

I tried. No answer. Voicemail.

'Maybe he's out of credit.'

I was dressed in a cashmere dressing gown with a black-and-white kimono print on it. Strolling back into the bedroom, I closed the door and opened the window. Paige took a long pull on the spliff.

'Your phone's ringing,' she said. These times I had Wiley's 'Wearing My Rolex' announcing incoming. I answered.

'*As-Salamu Alayki*,' the voice said.

'*Wa-Alayka as-Salam*,' I instinctively replied, returning the Islamic greeting.

Jamal.

'Where are you?' Jamal said.

'Cotching at my house.'

'Come outside for five minutes, Chyna. I want to talk to you.'

'You're at my house?' Thinking, He's only a few minutes behind Paige. 'Rah, give me ten minutes to get presented.'

Jamal being a Muslim, me being affiliated to people who knew his people, I had no reason to fear him. Maybe I didn't trust him the whole distance, but that was only because I don't tend to trust no one I ain't known for longs. But on the outside, Jamal seemed like a nice guy. He'd always call me 'sis', because in Islam everyone's a brother or sister. Faith and trust were really important for Jamal. He tried to stick to Ramadan, didn't drink or pop Es, did his prayer five times a day. A good Muslim, basically. You might be wondering, Rah, Jamal's a tief and a liar, how can he be a good person too? He loved his family and he treated his girl Sakina right. What can I say? Two sides to every coin. I knew bare boys like that going all the way back to Kendrick, and none of them ever scared me.

Next to my house was a car park. Usually it was filled with old bangers. On that morning a black Ford Mondeo was parked up and standing out next to all the old motors.

The Mondeo belonged to Jamal.

I stepped outside just as Jamal was getting out of his rims. I clocked more dark shapes inside the Mondeo. Jamal wasn't alone.

'Yo, sis, checks you *out*,' Jamal said, clapping his hands as he clocked me and Paige. 'Both of my bredrin looking

very choong, and not an inappropriate skirt in sight.'
Nodding his head, like he approved.

We kitted ourselves out head to toe with the garmz we
snapped up the day before with a few notes from the paper
bag of money, wearing brand-new Rocawear jackets. We
sported brand-new Nike Vandal kicks. Tight jeans.

'But tell me' – rubbing his chin – 'where d'you get the p's
for all these threads?'

'What, this? Ah, tiefed it, brother.'

'Where's the drugs, sis?' Jamal asked in a casual, soft
voice, the way a boy might ask for the box to his favourite
DVD.

'I ain't got no drugs,' I said.

'Tell me the truth, Chyna.' Jamal didn't raise his voice or
look like he was raging, but I picked up a little bit of edge to
his lilt. Like he was trying to say, 'Don't make me angry,
now.'

I told him again and again, I didn't have the drugs. I
couldn't stop thinking about Darnel. Had this image in my
head of some boy shanking Darnel in the prison, him lying
in a pool of blood, guards looking the other way. Me and
Paige couldn't let down Darnel like that.

'OK,' Jamal said, swinging the car keys on his finger.
'Tell me on Wallahi.'

Wallahi is a ting where you swear something on God.
Like, if I was to say, 'Wallahi, I'm broke,' it means 'I swear to
God that I'm broke.' If you swear on Wallahi, it's basically

like in English when someone asks you to swear on someone else's life. Jamal wanted me to cross my heart and hope
to die that I didn't have the drugs. Trying to put me in a shitty
position. As a Muslim, I didn't want to lie. Then again, I
didn't have the food, so I wouldn't be lying.

'Wallahi, I ain't got the drugs,' I said.

Jamal couldn't argue with me. Not on Wallahi. I kept
saying it over and over again. I thought if they heard me say
it a hundred times, no flipping way they could say I was
lying.

'Wallahi, I ain't got the drugs,' I said again.

'All right, sis.'

Now, on my endz there are two entrances to my road.
One entrance for cars. The other was more of an alleyway
that snaked up and around the back of the street. From
our position by the Mondeo, we could see this alleyway
face-on.

I seen this boy pounding it on foot down the back alley
right towards us. His hands were behind his back. I thought
he might be hiding a ting. As he neared us, he pulled one of
his hands out. Nothing – but my heart did a somersault
anyway. I couldn't show I was scared, how badly my hands
and feet were shaking. Everyone had always taught me,
don't show them what's going on inside because if people
smell weakness, they pounce on it.

This boy pointed at me and Paige, shouting, 'Get them in
the car!'

'Are you for real, Jamal? Me and Roxy got nothing. If we had it, we'd have given it you already.'

''Course, Chyna,' Jamal said. He looked over my head when he spoke. As if I weren't there.

'What's going on?' I asked.

'Nothing, sis.'

'It don't look like nothing.'

Jamal was a tall boy with big shoulders, and when people first seen him, they thought he looked mean. He had narrow eyes, black as coat buttons, eyebrows drawn in a permanent cross, and he never smiled. To Jamal, everything was deadly serious.

'D'you think I'd ever let anything happen to you?' Jamal asked. Before I could come back, he went on, 'You're family, Chyna. No one would ever lay a finger on you, not while I'm around. We're just going to go for a ride, that's all.'

'Swear on Wallahi?'

'Wallahi, you're safe.'

We had no choice but to get in the car. If we argued and refused, they would've dragged us inside. No doubt. If we ran away, well . . . it'd look like we got something to hide.

So we climbed in the back, the two of us, with Jamal up front. He chucked the keys to the driver. A third boy squeezed into the back seat, on the right side, squashing Paige in the centre and me on the left side of the car. One look at this boy freaked me out. He had bare gold teeth in his mouth, a tonked boy with hands that could crumble stones. A camouflage cap was pulled low over his eyes, hoodie tucked underneath it. Shadows stroked every part of his face except his lower lip.

We drove around the streets aimlessly, Jamal and the driver all sweetness to me and Paige. Eventually the driver turned back into my road. Up ahead I saw the boy who had ordered us into the car. He was with another three boys getting into a silver Ford Focus, and as our Mondeo passed, he fired up the engine. The Focus tailed us. Fuck, this ain't good at all, I thought.

'If you're up to something, just tell me,' I said to Jamal.

'Nah, sis, it ain't nothing like that.'

I played along with their little game. Inside I was trembling, but when you've been in the gangsta lifestyle long as me, you learn to control yourself. You front it, keeping the terror inside your belly. 'We're just going for a ride, right?'

'Yeah,' Jamal said. 'But let me ask you . . . if you ain't got the food, who does?'

'Don't know.'

'Come on, don't fool me, Chyna.'

Jamal was basically asking me to snitch on Darnel and Paige. If I mention him, I thought, Darnel's friend Warren is a target. And if they get the food, Darnel's finished. But if I kept my mouth zipped, I countered, both me and Paige were fucked. I weighed it up in my mind.

'Warren's got the brown,' Paige suddenly blurted. 'We gave it him last night.'

We were caught in a proper bad set-up, and Paige had made the right call. Darnel wanted the money for his debt, true; but he wouldn't want us to get killed over it and we still had a bit of time on our side to rustle up some p's for him – get some product on consignment, maybe.

Jamal took out his mobile and punched in Warren's number. Before he dialled, I knew there'd be no answer. Warren worked a nine-to-five and wouldn't be able to reach his phone until he finished up for the day. Jamal tried him three, four times. Nothing.

We stopped at a Tesco petrol station, Jamal trying the sweet approach again.

'You want anything to drink?'

'Fanta,' I said. 'And get me some crisps as well – I'm starving.'

Jamal brought back my drink bottle but no crisps. We sat in a parking space beside the shop, watching the traffic breezing by.

'You said Warren's got the food, yeah?'

'Yeah, dat's true,' Paige said.

'Where?'

'What do you mean?'

'Where d'you give him the food?'

'The estate,' Paige said. It didn't matter if we told Jamal now, I figured. Paige read my mind. We'd left a voicemail with Warren the previous night and just assumed he'd received it and collected the stash. If he hadn't, that was his tough shit, not ours. And anyways, we had no choice. We knew what would happen if we didn't play it straight with the mandem. They didn't fuck about. If they said they was gonna do something to you, they did it. Them boys carried guns on the regs, shot men on the regs, boxed people up on the regs.

'You what?'

'We had to leave it somewhere and that was the only place going. Warren weren't answering his phone—'

'Leave it. Let's hit the estate.'

These times we'd been in the back seat for two and a half hours and tings was getting proper stressful with Jamal and his mandem.

We pulled up outside the estate. The Focus halted about ten metres behind us. A kid's bike leaned against this lamppost, painted purple all over, frame, handlebars, spokes.

I made to get out of the car, but Jamal flicked the door-locking latch. 'Let the other boys go,' he said. 'We can watch from here.'

The Focus boys dashed to the bin hut.

My Nokia shook. I'd switched it to silent when Jamal first ordered us into the Mondeo. Now I dug it out of my jeans pocket, carefully looking at the boy next to Paige. His eyes were glued to the window, same as Jamal and the driver. I chanced it and answered, sliding the mobile halfway up the sleeve of my Rocawear jacket to keep it hidden. Pressed my hand close against my cheek.

'Yeah,' I barely whispered.

'Where are you, sis? Is Jamal there with you?' Sakina was hysterical.

'Uh . . .' I couldn't risk saying too much: the mandem would definitely hear me.

'Cough if he is,' she said.

I coughed.

'Shit. You've got to get out of there now,' she said. 'He's going to rob you, Chyna.'

I tried not to panic. Sakina knew what Jamal was like. What he was and wasn't capable of. Suddenly the dread I'd felt in my belly rose up to my throat and I found it hard to breathe. It was like I'd been hiding from the fear, trying to make it go away. I'd hoped that the Muslim ting between me and Jamal would stop him from trying to rob us. But when there's a big play for food to be had, I guess loyalty's no long ting.

'You need to breeze, cuz.'

'I can't,' I said, quiet as possible.

I heard a *whirr* as Jamal rolled down the window, shouting something to his mandem.

'Where are you? I'll come and get you myself.'

'The estate.'

'Just wait for me. I'm gonna be there soon as.'

I leaned over, scoped out the window to see what the fuss was about. I seen the boys swung open the door to the bin hut. First boy inside dived into the nasty bin. There was that much rubbish in the dumpster that a load of it spilled out, Chinese takeout boxes and empty plastic bottles of Tesco Kick scattering on the floor. The other boys tagged behind him and rushed the hut. Couple of minutes later, they came back out and walked over to the Mondeo.

'Fucking nothing there,' the boy who dived into shit told Jamal. His bad smell carried through the window: rotten fish and piss.

Jamal clicked his tongue. He looked at me through the rear-view mirror. His eyes were dead, like black holes.

'We know they're not in the place you said they'd be, so I'm gonna ask you nicely, one last time, sis. And this time you'd better be straight with me. Wallahi or no Wallahi.'

'Warren must have taken it.'

'Sure, cuz. Sure.'

The other boys hopped back into the Focus.

'Can I borrow a fag?' I asked the driver.

'Fuck off.'

The mood turned.

It was quiet for I don't know how long.

'You need to tell me where the drugs are,' Jamal said, his voice deep as a bass note. 'If you don't' – he turned round – 'I'm gonna box you in your face.'

I was terrified. I had a lot of front, but Jamal's words cut right through it. He wasn't joking; he was dead serious. My whole body was tense. A lump of green gum tumbled out of Paige's open mouth and fell on to her lap. I looked out of the window. Mummies pushchairing their babies. Kids riding bicycles. Normal people doing normal tings. It seemed like they were on another planet. I wanted to cry.

The mandem applied more heat on Paige. After all, it was her connect and her people that had delivered the food to her in the first place.

Jamal hassled her again and again. We'd been in the Mondeo for four hours and his patience was beginning to thin. The driver finished another cigarette. Jamal told him to roll up the window and drive back towards my home. I secretly hoped that they'd given up on the food.

We reached the end of the road and banged a right down a steep hill with massive estates banked on our left and right, half hidden behind thick oak trees. The driver nosed the Mondeo up the entrance to the estate on the left and bucked towards a tall block about thirty storeys high. It seemed to touch the clouds. He killed the engine.

'Last chance, my sisters,' Jamal said. He sighed, closed his eyes, as if he was praying. 'If you don't tell me the truth, this is what happens. We ride the lift all the way to the top floor and go up to the rooftop. I'm gonna take one of you – I'm not saying which one – and hold you by the leg and dangle you over the side of the roof until the other tells me where the brown is. If you don't tell . . . maybe one of my boys loses his grip.'

'You're fooling,' I said, laughing jaggedly. 'This is jokes, right?'

'No, Chyna.' He opened his eyes. 'This is for real.'

Paige was hypnotized by the block of flats. I pictured myself hanging from the rooftop, the boy releasing his fingers, my body dropping through the air. I looked away. Told myself, Jamal's just trying to intimidate you. He'd never let the mandem do that to you. Then another voice piped up, Since when did Jamal fool around about anything?

'That ain't the end of it. We're gonna do a proper number on you, do you get me? When we're done dangling you over the edge, we're gonna box the shit out of you and shoot you in your fucking kneecaps. My soldier got the niner right there' – gesturing to the silent boy. 'This can go on and on and on, if that's how you want to play it.'

My hand instinctively reached for Paige's and gripped tight. I tried to control my breathing, but my body was mad with fear. I thought – I believed, Jamal was gonna put me in a wheelchair for the rest of my days. I bit my lower lip to stop myself crying. Don't show him, Chyna. Don't show him . . .

'It doesn't have to be like this,' Jamal said. 'You can end it right now by telling us where the food is.'

The standoff dragged. At five o'clock, we'd been in the car for over eight hours. They went on with bare threats until Warren answered his phone, fucking finally, and told Jamal he'd come down directly from work to meet us. Soon as I heard that, my heart stopped pumping like a pigeon on a hype. Now all Warren had to do was give up the food to Jamal and we were safe.

At five thirty, Warren rocked up with a couple of his mandem for protection. He came over to the car and nodded at Jamal. Completely blanked me and Paige.

''S'up?' Warren said. 'Look, I don't know why you called my phone all these times, 'cos I ain't got nothing.'

I turned feverish hot. '*What?*'

'I don't know where this food you're talking about is. Them two never gave me no bag of brown. Make of that what you will, blud.'

I flipped. I went sick. I fumbled with the door lock and tried to break out. Gave up and tried to launch myself through the gap between the front seats, waving my fists at Warren and telling him I was going to lick him like he'd never been licked before. Tears rolled down my face. I couldn't believe Warren would do that – screw us both, especially the girlfriend of one of his friends. I felt as if we were totally lost now.

Jamal calmly grabbed my fists in his thuggish hands and threw me back on to the seat as if I weighed of air, Warren playing it cool and looking at me like I was mental.

'He's lying, Jamal. Let me out. I'll teach him—'

'I believe him,' Jamal said, and bang went my hopes of this shit ending. 'Warren ain't got no food. If he was hiding it from me, would he seriously come all this way down here to tell me that?' He shook his head. 'Man would have to be mental.'

Warren split, leaving us at Jamal's mercy. I was deadout,

couldn't move a muscle. Jamal would do stuff to us, I was sure. We were gonna get hurt.

I asked him straight, 'Are you kidnapping us?'

No answer.

I asked again.

'It's not like that,' Jamal said. 'We're brothers and sisters.'

But I seen what was going down. The only reason Jamal hadn't boxed the crap out of us – yet – was because the mandem saw us as sisters. *And how long do you think that's gonna last?* That voice creeping up inside me again.

The threats tumbled out of Jamal's mouth.

Shooting us up.

Hanging us over the sides of bridges.

Beating us senseless.

By now there was about fifteen mandem around us. Extra cars rolled up with more boys. More mandem meant more trouble, because each boy expected his cut of the food. Fifteen cuts rather than the three originally between Jamal, his driver and the other boy. Fifteen boys wanting to get their hands on the food.

The sun was setting. The sky bled red, like it was on its period.

'Fuck this,' Jamal said, staring out of the window. 'Let's go for a ride.'

'Where to?' I asked.

'Helmand.'

No. Please, no.

Helmand is a council estate in South. I don't even know what the real name of the estate is. Not like there's a sign outside or anything. Everyone just calls it Helmand, because there's fuck-all CCTV cameras, and bare entrances and walkways through the estate for people to run away from the boydem. When someone says they're taking you to Helmand, it's code. Means they're going to beat the crap out of you. Or worse. Whatever they were gonna do to you, it was gonna get done.

We argued. We raised hell. Shouted and screamed and had tears streaming from our eyes, begging them not to do this. Jamal and the driver kept telling us to shut the fuck up.

The boy next to us, Gold Teeth, opened his mouth for the first time. 'If you lot are lying,' he said, voice thick as cement, 'I'm gonna shoot you in de kneecaps.'

A few minutes later, the driver arrowed the Mondeo into Helmand.

It was ten o'clock at night, and that voice at the back of my skull said, This is it, Chyna. It ends here.

I found myself looking out the rear window as we squeezed through the tight roads of the Helmand estate, thinking maybe this was the last time I'd ever see the outside world. No one in the gangsta lifestyle expects to live very long. But I'm only twenty. It feels too young. I want to do stuff with my life.

You hear all the street talk about this and that boy getting shot or tortured, and you never think it will happen to you. I'm too smart to end up like that, you kid yourself. I saw that I'd been lying to myself for long. And now it was too late to do anything about it. I cried on the inside and the out. I cried not because I was afraid but because I'd fucked up, and I was about to pay for it with my life.

Thirteen hours in this car. I couldn't take no more. A gun was tucked into Gold Teeth's jeans. The butt of the gun was visible. Black pistol grip. I must've been so overcome with panic, I thought, that I'd failed to notice it before.

I've seen enough tools in my time to know what type they are, and this one was definitely a niner. Why would they bring a gun along if they just wanted to threaten me and Paige?

I knew the answer, but chose to ignore it.

So that's it. He'll kneecap you first. Then you say you still don't got the food. After a while, you'll bleed to death or he'll pop one in the back of your head and dump your body somewhere, like you're a dog.

All this time my Nokia buzzed nonstop, Sakina trying to reach me. By the time she'd hit the estate, we was already entering Helmand. I slyly texted Sakina to let her know where I was. One-word message: B-dad.

Just as I pressed send on the message, Gold Teeth snatched my Nokia.

I went ballistic. My phone was the last connection I had to the outside world. Confiscating it from me felt like they were saying, You don't need this any more. Not where you're going.

'Rah, give me my phone.'

'You'll get it back later.'

'Suck your mum later, blud. That's mine.'

'Do you wanna keep your kneecaps?' he said.

'What fucking right you got to—'

Something barked, interrupting me. I angled my head and saw two black boys walking towards the car, each holding a dog on a lead. English mastiffs the size of bears. They had wide, raging eyes and chewed-up ears.

I took one look at them and nearly fainted. I have a big fear of dogs. When I was a kid, a friend's dog went and bit me on my ankle. A big half-Staffie, half-Rottweiler breed that dug its teeth deep into my shin. I had to go to hospital to get stitched up. Since that day my most biggest fear is dogs and I won't go near them.

The boys unhooked the dogs from their leashes. They hungrily tore up to the car windows. This big dog had its paws on the glass, drool hanging from its razor-sharp teeth. Jamal lowered the window a few inches. I smelled the dog breath in the gap. It jammed a paw through the gap, trying to scratch at my face. I backed up against Paige. I was terrified.

'This can play how you want it,' Jamal said, having to shout above the dog yaps.

'Make them fucking go away, Jamal.'

Jamal hit the door-locking latch. I heard the *click* as the safety unlocked. 'In a few seconds I'm gonna get out the front. So's my boys.'

Whirr. The window lowered a little bit more.

'We'll leave you two girls in here with the dogs. They'll chew you to bits.' The dogs growled. 'Fucking *bits*, Chyna.'

I looked to Paige. To Gold Teeth. To the mastiffs.

Got to be a way out of this, I thought.

Not this time. This is how the story ends. Chyna, shotter and brawler, mouthiest girl in South and dated some of the baddest boys in the endz. Survived crackhouses and shoot- ings and escaped the boydem.

Turned into dog food.

'What's it to be?'

Jamal grabbed a hold of his door handle. Gold Teeth and the driver likewise. They'd have to spring out over quick from the Mondeo, because the second those dogs spotted an opening, they were gonna bite whatever was in front of them.

'Fuck this,' Jamal said. 'You've had bare chances.'

'No, no!'

As he moved to open his door, I lunged forward and threw my arms either side of the seat in front of me, clamp- ing them tight round Jamal's neck. My arms had no muscle on them and Jamal was a tonked man, but I dug my fingers into my wrists and clung on with every bit of strength I had. In the rear-view mirror, Jamal's eyes bulged.

All I am thinking is, If we're gonna get chewed up, so's Jamal.

Jamal's thick fingers had a grip on my arms. He was over powerful. Slowly he began prising my hands apart, loosening the tightness round his neck. I screamed and shouted at him.

'You wanna get bited too, yeah? Come on, then, stay with us, Jamal, see who the dogs wanna have a chew on first,' I belted.

'All right,' Paige piped up. 'We'll give you the drugs.'

It was like someone hitting the pause button. Jamal stopped struggling. The dogs gave up their barking and snarled.

'For real?' Jamal said.

'Would I play you?' Paige replied.

'Prove it to me.' My arms dropped from Jamal's neck like limp rope, all pairs of eyes in the Mondeo on Paige. Driver, Jamal, Gold Teeth, dogs. 'You lied about it last time. Why should I believe you now?'

'It's round my house,' Paige said. 'Drive us there. I'll get it for you. Then leave us the fuck alone.'

Everything clicked.

My mind went back to the cups of brown we nicked out of the main stash. That was our way out. No doubt the boys would be pissed when they saw the weight of food we had – the four cups we took worked out to about £8,000 or £10,000 and, split fifteen ways, it weren't exactly big-time p's – but at least we'd get the mandem off our backs for the moment. I fought to get my breath back. The dogs were dragged away from the Mondeo and the driver rolled the car out of Helmand.

My Nokia, I thought. Gold Teeth still had it in his fat hands. I reached beyond Paige to get it back and seen him playing with buttons and frowning at the screen.

'What you doing? Don't go through my stuff.' I leaned over to see what he was up to.

Gold Teeth watched the video clip of Darnel licking the boy in prison. If he moved a muscle, I didn't see it. He stayed silent and did a good impression of them statue people you gets in West.

His lips moved. 'That's my cousin.' He deep-breathed, his big shoulder muscles blowing up.

'What again?' I played dumb, trying to think up an excuse.

'The boy your man's licking,' he said, now looking at Paige. 'That's my cousin Mugs.' I'm thinking, This was the day of all days for shit luck. It got worse. 'Mugs had money too. Where's that?'

'We don't have it,' I said.

Gold Teeth handed me back my phone, the clip deleted.

'I'm gonna speak to Mugs. If you lie, we be on your case. *Believe.*'

Half-hour later, we were on the way back to Paige's house. She called her little sister. We didn't want to involve her in this situation, but we saw no other way of getting the drugs without Paige's mum finding out and going mental.

Her sister answered. Paige told her to fetch the Nike backpack from under her bed. Jamal's eyes sparked like Christmas lights as Paige talked. He knew he was so close to getting his hands on the food he could almost touch it. All the boys were jumpy. The driver put his foot down.

'You see them recycling bins out front?' Paige told her sister. 'Leave it in there. And make sure Mum don't hear you or nothing.'

Fast-forward ten minutes. The boys in the Focus departed to Paige's house. We trailed them a bit and Jamal told the driver to stop on the way back through the estate.

The Focus pulled up. A boy in the front seat scuttled with the Nike backpack towards the Mondeo. Jamal broke out, snatched the bag and dumped it on the hood. He tore the backpack open, ripping the lining and out fell the plastic box. I couldn't tell whether he was happy with the brown, disappointed there weren't more there or what. He had this face that was impossible to read. He shook the backpack.

'You're a good Muslim girl, Chyna,' he said. 'It's not for you to be selling drugs. We're taking this away from you for your own good. Remember what the Koran says: "The harm of drugs is much greater than their benefit." We'll dispose of this junk.'

He stared at Paige. 'And shame on you for getting Chyna involved in this. None of this needed to happen if you'd been straight with us from the start. We're brothers and sisters. You should know not to lie to us.'

Air came out of my mouth where words was supposed to be. After all they'd threatened us with, they went back to the sugar and sweetness, as if everything from the last twelve hours had been a bad trip. Twenty-four hours ago, I'd believed what Jamal said about us being tight. Now I had myself some second thoughts.

'Give these girls a lift back to Paige's house,' Jamal said.

It was near enough one in the morning when we was dropped off. Lights out, street dead except for the sound of rubbish rustling in the wind. The five different bins out the front of the house had been turned upside down and emptied. Nasty banana skins, empty Coke bottles, old magazines, crisp packets. Like her front had been used as a skip.

'Fuck this, bruv,' Paige said. 'Look at this mess.'

'We'll clean it up tomorrow. Shit, I'm wiped,' I said. 'Imagine if we didn't take some of the food away earlier. They'd have killed us.'

Paige said nothing but lit a cigarette.

'Mad,' she finally said. And then, blowing out smoke and grinning, 'Do you want to know a secret?'

'Tell me, bruv.'

'Before you came round, I took another little scoop out of the brown. Just in case of emergencies, like.'

'How much?'

'Five or six grands' worth, easy.'

I managed – well, no smile. I'd been too violated and shattered and scared for that. But something like a smile. 'So that means Darnel—'

'Between this and the p's, he'll have enough to get the mandem off his case,' Paige said. 'Just let's not tell Warren about this, yeah?'

We'd had a close escape. Neither me nor Paige talked about it as I pulled up to sleep on her sofa, but we both had the same thought running through our heads. Sooner or later, we'll either end up dead or in prison.

I wondered, almost as if I was thinking about a stranger, what would happen to me.

TWENTY-THREE

Nothing lasts forever

Eighteen months after he was sent down, Rashid was released from prison. We had a big barbecue and party for him, all the mandem came along, eight girls of mine too. Some of my N2L girls had gone straight: Nangs, Tantrum, Split and Bigs. It was good to see my fam again and catch up with the chatter.

'I ain't see you for longs, b,' Tantrum said. 'Still on the roads?'

'For real,' Nang replied for me. 'Don't you know that Chyna was born on the road?'

Split started cracking, so Nang amped it up, joking, 'Chyna lives on the road. She goes to sleep on the road. She eats on the road. She goes to school on the road . . .'

'Hush your gums, blud,' I said.

I reckoned they were just jealous of the p's I was raking in. Split looked more confident and less nervous about herself. She'd grown up a bit since the timid girl who sweated it at the sight of a gun. And as for Bigs, well, she was still the big momma of the fam and still looked at us that way.

All the time Rashid was inside prison I hadn't visited him – he didn't want me to see him in the clink and for the second half of his sentence he was moved to Liverpool because the authorities said he was gang-affiliated in every London-city prison.

The first couple of hours back together felt strange. Rashid had lost weight and dropped from a thirty-four-inch waist to a thirty. He'd picked up a bit of a Scouse accent, talking about how he was 'made up' to be free and asking Kazim to 'giz us a ciggie'. The whole day seemed dreamlike. The sun set, Rashid felt tired, and people dispersed. When it was just the two of us, Rashid held me tight and looked me in the eyes and smiled.

'Thinking about you kept me strong,' he said, cupping my hands in his. 'You know how much I missed you.'

'Me too,' I replied. 'I'm just glad you're back with me.'

We lay on the sofa, in each other's arms, quiet and happy, happy, happy.

'Oh,' I said. 'I got a little surprise for you.'

'Yeah?'

'Well, more like fifty surprises . . .' I took him by the hand and led him through to the bedroom. Opened up the wardrobe. His smile crept further and further up his cheeks as he set eyes on the brand-new designer garmz. Shirts, jackets, jeans, sweaters, creps, tees. I gifted him the Cartier watch. He was lost for words. The smile quickly crawled back towards the corners of his mouth. Rashid scratched his head.

'Where d'you get all the money for this?'

I told Rashid to sit tight and everything would be clear. Off I went, unlocking the cellar door and bringing the Moët box up with me to the bedroom. He opened the cardboard flaps at the top and peered inside, hesitant. Rashid dipped a hand into the box and pulled out a band of £20 notes. Out came a second one. Then a third, a fourth, a fifth. It was like an extra-lucky dip.

Rashid looked at me for long. He ran his eyes over my face, not sad, but not happy neither, like his expression was stuck in neutral.

Finally he said, 'You've been shotting.'

'Yeah.' I thought, No point hiding the truth. He'd have found out sooner or later from the mandem or one of the girls.

'Who helped you?' Rashid tightened his jaw. 'Don't hide nothing from me now, Chyna.'

'Husayn,' I said. Rashid rubbed his forehead. 'But it ain't his fault. I told him if he didn't help me, I'd go shotting country.'

Rashid quietly stepped round me and left the bedroom, new garmz tossed on the bed and floor. He'd get over it, knew what I was like. If I wanted to do something, I'd do it. Nobody could stop me. I hadn't listened to a single person since the day my mum kicked me out. If I wasn't doing what my mum told me, why would I listen to what anyone else said? The one lesson life had taught me was, you want something, you got to get it yourself. Ain't no one else gonna help you.

'I forgive Husayn,' Rashid said later, 'but you shouldn't

have done this. I sent you p's. The mandem was there for you. And you out there on the roads, shotting to the cats, that's like burnin' me.'

'I did this for you. You're ballin' in p's now.'

Rashid snorted, 'P's that my wife grafted.'

'Why the fuck are you talking Scouse all of a sudden?'

Rashid gave me his silent back.

'I wanted you to have some money to come home to, do you see it?'

Rashid did, I think. Eventually he stopped arguing with me and said, 'You're gonna have to cut that all out.'

Fair enough, I thought. I'd done my bit. If Rashid wanted to take over, I was happy with that.

One Friday, we was prepping to go to a club in North. One of Husayn's friends, boy by the name of Eagle, arrived at the club earlier than us and ended up in a bother down there with some boys who were being rude to his girlfriend. When Eagle run off his mouth at these boys, they tried to bottle him. Eagle rung Husayn.

'Rah, come down the club. I got a problem. And, brother, bring the ting.'

'Ting' meaning 'gun'.

'Safe. I come soon.'

Husayn had history. He'd shot people before. Taking a gun to a club didn't hold no fear for him. He was also incredibly loyal. A Muslim brother asking him to come down and resolve a beef – there was no question Husayn would help him out.

Husayn said to me, 'You planned on going that club tonight?'

'Yeah.'

'Change your plans, sis.'

'What?'

'Don't go up there. I'm on my way to the club now, but I ain't going to rave, do you get me?'

'What's going on, Husayn?'

He was tight-lipped. 'I don't want to see you there. If you're there, it's gonna cause an argument between me and you. You can't be at the club. End of.'

Anyone else told me not to go to such-and-such a club, I'd tell them to go stick it, but me and Husayn was tight. He introduced me to his friends as his sister. When you're that close to somebody, you understand when they're fooling around and when they ain't. That night, Husayn was serious.

'Fine,' I said. 'We'll go someplace else.'

'Pasha too.'

'Bruv, if I ain't rolling to the club, Pasha ain't gonna hit the joint neither.'

We hit the bar, sank a couple of Grey Goose vodka mixers, and then a group of us hit a massive club in North endz in search of some house and club riddims. The club was made, with a beautiful garden and a big balcony terrace, bare rooms and a grimy vibe. Me and Pasha was piss-drunk on vodka, brandy and champagne. We'd been there for longs when Husayn called me and asked where we were. I told him.

'Don't leave. We'll come and find you.'

'Safe.'

I clocked Husayn moving past the throb of clubbers. He skulked, like his creps was made out of lead. His skin, normally like polished bronze, was drained flat, as if he'd been bleached. When I smiled and said hello to him, Husayn looked at me from fifty miles away.

'What's wrong?'

'Nothing,' he said.

'You look sad.' His eyes had lost their shininess. 'We're brother and sister,' I said. 'You can talk to me.'

He closed his eyes and let out a deep sigh. I felt his warm breath on my face. Husayn put an arm round me and led me away from the group, to a spot where the music wasn't so loud and the lights was dim. Deadmau5's 'Ghosts N Stuff' rocked the club, the bass over heavy. The whole club shaking. I sipped my double brandy and Red Bull. Husayn fixed his eyes on a spot on the floor, his face anti-hyped.

'Tell me,' I said.

'Forget it.' He looked around, scratching his elbow. 'I can't stay here. It's not safe.'

'OK, we can go.'

The group of us left the club, Husayn acting funny. I

pressed him, asking what was up. His face looked like a zombie. But he batted away my questions, said he wasn't feeling too good.

'It's nothing, Chyna. Leave it, all right?'

The next day, I seen a report on the news: a man shot in the club Husayn was at. He took two bullets in the chest and died on the spot. I asked myself, Did Husayn have anything to do with this? I confronted him. He denied it. I said he had to promise me. Shooting up a man over some beef involving Eagle was jokes, and if he got sent down, Pasha would have to experience what I went through while Rashid was inside. Husayn wrung his hands and said nothing.

'I didn't do nothing,' he said.

'Promise?'

'I don't do promises, Chyna,' he said, looking me direct in the eye.

The boydem felt differently. Months later, Candice got a knock on her door one morning. Husayn had used her car to drive up to the club on the night of the shooting and CCTV cameras had captured an image of the licence plate. Candice was shiffed.

Sophie got shiffed.

Husayn got shiffed.

Boydem knocked on my door, told me to go and take part in an ID parade up North endz. The boydem released me without charges and put out a £20,000 reward for information about the killer. I pestered Husayn about the shooting, but every time he clammed up and said he didn't know nothing about it. He was my bredrin and I wanted to believe him.

No one ever got caught for that boy's murder.

The following week, Husayn got arrested for shotting in West. As the boydem moved to him, Husayn swallowed his pebbles. The boydem took him down to the station to wait for him to shit the drugs out. That didn't work. That boy held his bowels for Britain. The boydem switched to Plan B. Raided his house to search for drugs and found three bullets for a western-style Magnum gun. He got two years for possession of them bullets alone. That might sound harsh, but the law says it's one year per bullet, so he got off a year light. With good behaviour, he'd be out after a twelve-month stretch. It could have been worse. The Magnum was with someone else. If the boydem had found that, he'd have been looking at an eight-year stretch in the clink.

Husayn going down was the start of the FLS mandem getting caught up with the boydem. Not long after, Kazim got arrested for murder. A fight broke out between the black English boys and the Yardie men in a rave club. Shots was fired and five FLS boys got arrested. Kazim was the main suspect, although he didn't do nothing. He spent best part of a year in jail waiting for the trial. The jury returned a not-guilty verdict.

But everything crashed. Pasha had broken up with Husayn right before he was imprisoned after she discovered him cheating on her with his baby mother. I took the raving scene a little bit easy, partly because my boyfriend had been released and I wanted to spend time with just me and him, playing catch-up on the time we missed, but also because the number of guns at the rave nights made it over dangerous. For six months I kept my head down. Rashid was out shotting and robbing, but he rolled low-key. If something looked too big or too good be true, he walked away from it.

Tings got chiefed up. Rashid's younger brother, Dalmar, an extra-hyped version of Rashid who didn't give a fuck, got shot over some kind of beef. The bullet entered his chest and exited an inch away from his heart. Left him fighting for his life. The stress ate away at Rashid. He had to support his brother as well as hunt down the boys who shot him for revenge. Everyone in the endz knew that Rashid was out to get back the boy what shot Dalmar. On the roads people were talking shit – 'Rashid's gonna do what he's gonna do', 'That boy's gonna get got.'

Rashid distanced himself from me at these times – his main concern was to keep me out of the beef and I had to respect his wishes. Rashid's a hard person to get to, you see, and if I was somehow seen as part of the revenge attack, that'd make me a target for kidnap. I knew why he had to do it, and him going underground was for my safety.

TWENTY-FOUR

The guns and the hype

While this heat was on, one of my friends died. His name was Tyson. He had gotten into a fight with a boy he'd had a feud with for long. As soon as I saw this boy come into the club, I knew there'd be trouble because whenever my friend and this boy bucked up, something always happened. I'm talking ongoing feud.

I said to Tyson, 'Stick tight to me. That boy won't start nothing if he sees you rolling with a girl.' For an hour or two, tings was cool and I thought, Rah, maybe this boy ain't gonna move to Tyson tonight. Then at some point Tyson went off and this boy set on him like a hungry dog. A big scuffle broke out. The bouncers chucked them out and locked the door, so they couldn't bring their fighting back inside.

But that also meant I couldn't leave and help my friend.

Me and a couple of boys and girls shouted at the bouncers to unlock the doors so we could separate our friend from the other boy. They opened. I prayed that the boydem hadn't arrived and arrested Tyson. Boydem was nowhere. Tyson was buzzin'. He's OK, I thought. Thank fuck for that.

'Ty, what's that on your shirt?'

Tyson lowered his eyes. His white shirt had roses on it. I neared and seen that the rose patches were blood spots.

'You got blood on your head too,' I said, my voice shivering at the oily stuff leaking from his hair, riding his nose and streaking his lips. He put a hand to the top of his head.

'It's sticky,' Tyson said, frowning at the blood in the palm of his hand.

He blinked. By now he was soaked in blood. On his neck, his chest, his arms. His white shirt was dyed red. He slumped against the wall and slid down to the pavement. Closed his eyes. Opened them. Closed them again. Like that, he passed out.

I shouted out to nobody, 'Is Ty shanked? Whose blood is that? The other boy's?'

Nobody answered back.

So much blood. I couldn't see where it was coming from. The ambulance showed, blood pouring from Tyson like his body was a colander. I was covered in it too. I had this terrible, sickly feeling. This ain't gonna be OK. My friend ain't walking away from this; the world don't work that way.

Only one person could travel in the ambulance. The rest of us drove.

By the time we arrived at the hospital A&E, twenty minutes later, Tyson was dead.

He'd been stabbed nine times. In his face, arms and stomach. One of the knife wounds fractured his ribcage. The combined stab traumas caused massive internal bleeding. That's what killed him. The year before, his brother had died. His family felt the loss hard. Some people don't realize, when a boy or girl gets merked, there's a mum somewhere in the background, crying and asking God why her son or daughter is lying cold in a hospital morgue.

The boy who shanked Tyson was arrested and got fifteen years. All over some endless beef that neither boy could probably remember what started it all. Life on the endz became darker day by day, as bare people I knew were getting shanked and shot at. I worried about Rashid. I worried about Husayn. I worried about Pasha and Roxy and Styles. Every one of my girls. The roads seemed more violent than when I'd been a teenager naively shotting weed.

Rashid and the mandem knew the direction their lives was headed. 'I'll be surprised if I make twenty-five, you know,' he'd always say to me. Then he'd give out a weak laugh.

Husayn got released from prison that spring.

Eight months of shotting, beefs and revenge attacks followed. Hardly any of these shankings and shootings made the news; people getting merked was a regs ting for our roads, and when it's black and Asian people involved, the media don't really cares. With each new day I thought about getting out of the gangsta lifestyle. I mentioned this to Roxy one day when we was cotching in her crib.

'I got relatives in youth work,' I said. 'Maybe they could help me quit.'

'But where would you go, Chyna? What would you do

for p's? You gonna walk into H&M and give them your CV, all typed up. "Thirteen to fifteen: tiefing. Sixting to nineteen: shotting to crackheads"? You ain't got no GCSEs, same as me.'

'Styles's got a hair salon,' I said. 'She's out of it.'

'True dat,' Roxy nodding her agreement. 'I can't cut hair, though. My skills are shotting.'

Roxy necked a big swig of brandy. Me likewise. We was drinking heavier these times, smoking bare weed.

'Face it,' Roxy said. 'Life's hard for us, blud. Them people on TV talking about being in a recession? Bredrin in our endz been in one our whole fucking *lives*.'

'I know that.' I remembered Tyson's dried blood caked on my arms. How I had to scrub it off, watching this stream of peach-coloured water disappear down the plughole, the last of Tyson. 'I just don't want to end up a gangsta's widow.'

'Rashid's a big boy. He can look out for himself. And he's got his mandem.' She punched me playfully on the shoulder, trying to cheer me up. 'You, me, Pasha . . . all us fam. We've got to stick tight.'

'I ain't meaning to leave my girls behind. It's the guns and the hype.' I took a long pull on the draw. 'I'm scared.'

Me and Husayn fell out soon after his release from the clink. He chose to spend time with Candice and Sophie, even though I told him how they'd done a number on me. Husayn protested that he weren't friends with them, claimed it was just a business ting, but I took it as disrespect that he was giving them two girls the time of day.

Our spat lasted two months, until he texted me out of the blue on a bright Saturday afternoon in September.

We shld go out for drinks and get things back on track. Youre my sister and i love you.

I texted Husayn back: Yh sounds great. When yer ready phone me C XX.

He was my good, good friend.

TWENTY-FIVE

Sisters and brothers

Several months after the shooting took place in North, me and Pasha planned to hit a club in East. There was a big party taking place at the club for a DJ's birthday and all the mandem would be going. In the end I couldn't make it, but Husayn went with two girls that I didn't really know.

This club was brimming with mandem from all over East, every gang in them endz bustin' their guns. South people didn't go out of their way to be seen at this club, and if you were going to be fronting, a Southside boy needed to be with his crew, his tings, and he needed to be certified.

He don't go to this kind of rave with a couple of girls.

This particular morning, my Nokia shook me out of my dreams while it was still dark on the roads. I checked the phone. Fifty missed calls. Bredrin reaching out to me at, like, five o'clock in the morning. I rubbed the sleep out of my eyes and thought, What are my people calling me so early for? And Pasha too. Husayn's baby mother. Straight up I knew it was gonna be bad news. The worst news in life, I've come to realize, is delivered down the end of the phone. That's my experience.

At six o'clock, Pasha phoned me.

Wearily, I answered. I heard her weeping down the phone. Delirious screaming and wailing.

'What's wrong, cuz?'

She cried and cried, and took these deep breaths, fighting to get the words out.

'Husayn's . . . He's . . . dead . . .'

My first reaction was, 'No, he's not. I spoken to him last week. How is he dead?'

It's not that I didn't believe Pasha. More that she might be exaggerating the facts. I thought, Perhaps he'd been shot or shanked. That might sound like a big deal to some people, but the times I known Husayn he got shot twice and been involved in countless of gunfights. And sometimes tings got misreported. You'd hear people say, 'Husayn got shot over this or that,' but in reality, he's the one what did the shooting.

'Nah, he can't be dead.'

'Chyna, phone his girlfriend. She'll tell you.'

I still didn't seriously think Husayn had been killed. I went to the shop and bought a loaf of bread and carton of eggs for breakfast, a pack of twenty Mayfair and a box of Rubicon passion-fruit juice. That's how much I figured Pasha had got it wrong. When I returned to the flat, I called Husayn's girlfriend, his baby mother.

'Hello,' I said. 'Where's Husayn?' My tone was light-hearted. I cradled the phone and fried my eggs sunny side up.

'Chyna.' She paused for so longs I checked the signal to see if it'd broken up. I pressed the phone close to my ear. The egg whites bubbled.

She said, 'Husayn's dead.'

That pause did it for me. Somehow it made me realize, She's speaking the truth.

'What do you mean, he's *dead*?'

'He's gone, Chyna. Husayn's gone.'

My mind started spinning.

'He's gone,' she kept saying over and over, as if the more times she said it, the more I'd believe it was real. 'He's gone. He's gone . . .'

'Where is he?'

'In the hospital,' she said. 'He's awake—'

'*Awake?* I knew it, he ain't dead!'

'—but we're gonna switch off the machine.'

Turned out that Husayn wasn't dead, but he wasn't really awake neither. A machine helped him to breathe. Without it, he'd die.

'Tell them to keep on the machine,' I protested. 'You've got to—'

'No, Chyna, he's gone.'

'I'm coming down there. And don't dare let them turn that fucking machine off.'

Hands shivering, eggs burning in the frying pan, I phoned back Pasha.

'Put your shoes on. I'm coming to get you.'

We took a cab. All the while a little bit of me refused to believe that Husayn was gone, that if they kept the machine on, he'd soon wake up and be his old self. We arrived at the hospital. Bare people eyeballing me and Pasha as we rushed down countless of corridors. The deeper we went into the hospital, the heavier my legs felt. I thought I might fall over at any moment.

The room they put Husayn in was cold and white. That's all I remember of it. A cold that pricked my skin like needles. The ceiling, floors, walls, tables, bed, all sprayed white, like we were in a mist cloud. The moment I saw Husayn on that bed, I experienced a horrid, dark sensation, like nothing I'd ever known in my life.

He'd been shot in the head at close range. Husayn's head was gone. Disintegrated.

Husayn didn't have eyes, or a nose, or lips. His eyes just weren't *there*. Like someone had sucked them out with a suction pump. Whenever I think of Husayn now, that's the image I have in my head. He was such a good-looking boy, and now he had holes where his eyes were supposed to be.

'Can he hear me?' I asked the doctor.

'Partly,' she said.

So I talked to Husayn and felt sick, knowing he couldn't say nothing back to me. I tried to talk as much as I could without crying. Mostly, I did both.

Husayn's family were by his bedside, crying and hugging each other. His mum looked vacant, like there was nobody home. Husayn really loved his mum. He treated her right, she never went without. Over looked after his children too.

You look at this almost-dead body and know that's how these boys live their lives. They can go at any time, any place. Ain't none of them banking on growing old and retiring graceful. The mandem used to laugh about it, but there's nothing jokes about seeing someone in the state Husayn was in. No glamour or status to be got from having a bullet mess up your face.

When the nurses came in, I shouted at them, 'Why can't you fix him? He's alive. Just wake him up. Just . . .' I grew exhausted. I slumped back into the chair and sat and cried with Husayn's family.

I couldn't help thinking of the bad tings Husayn had done in the past, and maybe it was karma that he'd been shot. But thinking that made me even sadder. People do good tings and people do bad tings. All I knew was, this boy was my good, good friend and I wanted him to open his eyes more than anything in the world.

The doctor came in to switch off the machine.

'Goodbye, brother,' I said.

He had no eyes, Husayn, but tears flowed out of those black holes and down his cheeks at the sound of his mum's voice.

I watched my best friend die.

He was twenty-three years old.

I stayed at the hospital until they took his body out. Me

and Pasha caught a bus and cried the whole journey. When we got home, we drank. And drank, and drank, and drank some more, until I couldn't feel my lips or my legs. Until my brain was paralyzed and I couldn't think not one thought. We worked our way through two bottles of brandy and six bottles of red wine. When we'd finished our supplies, we went to the cornershop up the road and bought a big bottle of Bell's. We drank. We smoked. We mourned.

The next day, I linked with a few of Husayn's old friends and told them the news. Some were sad, others stunned. One or two nodded, like they'd been expecting it. For them boys on the streets, no one's death comes as a major surprise.

Three of my friends who was tight with Husayn were in prison. I booked visits. The first boy I seen puked on the spot. He came into the visitors' area. Pulled up a pew. I took a deep breath, said, 'Husayn's dead.' The boy yakked the very next second. Vomit splashed down his chin and on to the desk. A smell of rank acid filled my nose.

'You should have phoned and told us,' the guard said, while someone mopped up the puke from the table. But I didn't want no guard breaking the news to my friend. They told me to leave. I wanted to hug my friend so badly, to comfort him and tell him everything was gonna be all right.

Another boy in prison took it badly. Day after I told him, he got put on blocks for starting a major fight.

I guess the moral of the story is, karma's a fucking bitch.

In the weeks and months following Husayn's death, I was zoned out. Had no energy, no desire to do nothing. Husayn's death had shocked me to my core and finally convinced me to try and go clean. For a while I wasn't shotting or anything like that. The whole of my life was swallowed up in grieving and trying to sort shit out in my head.

The hardest ting about quitting the gang lifestyle is cutting yourself off from your support network. All my friends and fam was into gangs and shotting. That was my entire world. I wanted to do something else with my life, but I didn't know where to turn. I was still Rashid's girlfriend and grown acquainted to a life of quick p's.

After Husayn's death, I suffered a nervous breakdown. I didn't eat, couldn't focus. People said they'd be talking to me and my face would be zonked. Eyes tranced by a spot on the wall. I didn't understand life. How it began, how it ended, how it seemed random and fruitless. His funeral broke me. For two months I locked myself away in my room, drinking by myself each day. At Husayn's funeral, I knocked back liquor first ting in the morning so all those horrible feelings wouldn't hit me so hard. I just wanted to feel numb. I polished off a bottle of Hennessy at the wake.

If someone had offered me a new life there and then, somewhere else, I would've taken it. There weren't no rules to the world I was in. As everyone went to prison, I gradually found myself separated from that lifestyle. Kazim came out of prison. Went straight back in for attempted murder. Rashid stood trial. He and the mandem went to do a robbery on an estate and the CCTV camera picked up one of the boys carrying a gun. Rashid got lucky because he stayed in the car and never touched the weapon.

I was in the mindset where I thought, You know what, truly, I got to do something positive with my life. But even though I had this good intention, it was hard for me to leave everything behind. I was still involved in the street life, hanging around the wrong people. And the money was quick. That's the most addictive ting. You make your p's a lot faster on the street than you do taking people's orders at McDonald's or driving a bus.

The last time I got arrested I was in a stolen car and the boydem found brown in my house. I had to go on trial but got let off. I was relieved to be let off.

Rashid had trouble earning money – with most of his mandem in the clink, his connects dried up. No connects means no food means no profit. The gangsta lifestyle lost its sheen.

Me and Rashid split up after our relationship became over volatile. I went from dashing plates at him to grabbing big kitchen knives and threatening to shank him. Rashid never hit me, but he'd manhandle me, gripping my arms, shaking me. We was both temperamental and in the end I thought, Rah, I'd not had no independence, barely been a day single since the age of fifteen. I needed some breathing space. Me and him, we was like two parts of a bomb. Mix them together and boom! We were better off apart, we decided, and better friends than lovers.

I don't speak to Rashid any more. No idea what he's doing with himself. I just pray he takes care of himself and makes the right decisions in life. And sees not just his twenty-fifth birthday, but his thirty-fifth and forty-fifth too.

There's a saying we got on the roads: ain't nothing guaranteed. You might make a mil one month and nothing for two years. The roads were good to me for two years straight, but in the third year, it all balanced out. Karma. I was handed a suspended twelve-month sentence and told by the judge that if I got caught with so much as a spliff, I'd go direct prison. No more chances.

Bottling up the feelings about Husayn's death drove me mad. I realized maybe the best ting to do was talk about how I felt. I went along to youth workshops organized by my uncle. I seen people up on stage giving testimonials and I thought, Rah, this could be the way to express how I felt. I could help someone trapped in the gangsta lifestyle, and also help myself. Make sense of my life.

'Why don't you give it a shot?' my uncle said. 'Got to turn over a new leaf someday, Chyna. You can't be the girl in the hood for ever.'

For the first time in long, I listened to someone else's advice.

I delivered my first testimony in front of an audience of three hundred students, barely making it to the end before I broke down and wept. The audience was quiet, boys' and girls' faces peeling tears, sad and pitiful. Afterwards, there was a lightness in my legs. It seemed as if a big weight had been lifted from my shoulders. Just to talk about it suddenly made tings seem a little bit better. My message to the kids was, either you're gonna end up in prison or you'll end up dead. You can have the mentality of 'Rah, I'm invincible on the streets', but that type of thinking gets you nowhere – real fast. My ex-boyfriend Rashid had been shot five times, chucked inside of the clink, and countless of his friends have died. People sprayed up his friend's house with MAC-10s. How G is that?

No one in that lifestyle lasts for ever.

I had to cut a lot of people out. Some of those people, they're still doing the same ting I was doing at fifteen, sixteen. Shotting the same corners, dealing to the same cats. Making p's and spending it just as quick, they ain't got fuck all to show for it at the end of the day. Blowing their p's on raving and threads. Rashid used to rain two grand in a club. You're living fast, so the money goes fast.

Once I banned raving and shotting, stopped hanging around certain people, some haters talked behind my back. Said shit about me. Criticized me for bottling it. They never said nothing to my face, and every time I heard someone being negative about my choice, their words just made me stronger. It helped that Roxy, too, had decided to quit the roads. We supported each other's struggle to go straight.

If I'd been a boy, it would be different. They're sucked into a system where they go prison, come out, can't get a job and have to earn p's the only way they know how: through crime. Us girls, we'd get chatting to other girls, make new friends and form new groups. With the boys, they're with the friends they have for life. They roll with the same crews. Get into the same hypes. Back into prison again. They go to a job interview, the company does a CRB check, finds out they got done for this and that, and no way are they gonna get the position. People in the news and politicians talk about being tough with crime, but what are these boys meant to do? Ain't no way out for them. And they refuse to go on benefits, because to them, there's no bigger shame.

For the yutes, tings is gonna be even tougher because they're getting much more hardcore into the gang lifestyle from a very early age. Yutes now steam shops and pack niners at fourteen, some even younger. They ain't afraid of nothing. Even go out robbing security vans. In my endz, the vans have to be tailed by a boydem escort. The little yutes know there's gonna be thirty, forty grand in the box, so they'll rush the van and tief it. Something like 50 per cent of the vans gets raided round where I live.

As more yutes move in gangs, more shootings happen. They're young and do silly tings, ain't got good mentality levels. They're too immature to say, 'Yo, this is how we're gonna do it.' They end up shooting first and thinking later.

It's a cycle in our endz. People be like, 'Why don't you

just stop and get a legit nine-to-five?' But it ain't that easy when you got no one around to support you. One of my friends' mums is a prostitute and a brownhead. My friend was going out at seven years old, tiefing milk to feed to her four baby siblings. Cow's milk, not even baby milk, because her mum was out on the roads dawn till dusk selling her body and smoking brown. She had to be a mum aged *seven*. What fucking chance did she have? Other friends of mine shotted from young because that's what their brothers and sisters did, and they ain't got no one to tell them different.

The government says family is important. No doubt. But what if you don't have a mummy and daddy at home, putting food on the table? What then? Me, I had a choice of going on benefits and scrounging or getting a job that didn't cover half my rent. If I wanted to study at college, I couldn't claim no benefits. Another door closed in my face.

We did what we had to do to survive, and because opportunities was denied us. All around us we saw people robbing and fighting and moving drugs. We had no other reference points for living our life. Some boy at a posh school, he sees his friends playing golf with their dads or whatever. At our school, all we ever heard other people doing was licking it.

My people robbed, licked, shotted and rolled with me. A few of them stole from me and acted snakishly, but they also gave me shoulders to cry on, friends to laugh with, people to support me when tings was rough. They were my sisters and my brothers. We stuck together because the rest of the country left us behind.

My fam.

The girls moved on to other tings. Smiles recently had a baby. She may not be bredrin any more, to me anyways, but we're back on speaking terms now. I see Smiles as an associate, not a fam. Styles is still about. Bigs and Nang got legit nine-to-fivers after the gang. Fierce is about. Pasha's gone straight. She's still my girl. Roxy too.

For me, a bond that's broken – it never existed. We've been through nuff tings together in the fam, and if any of my girls needed me, I'd be there for them, no questions asked. Take Split: she was by far the quietest one out of all of us, but no way could I pass her in the street and not go up to her, give her a hug, check her and ask when we were gonna meet up next with the rest of the bredrin. Any of my fam, I might not ping them from day to day, but I'll see them on the regs. They're my old-skool girls. We share good memories, ones I'll never forget.

In that way, we turned the fam into something positive. A ting that brought us together and gave us friendships for life, and a way of checking for each other in a world that can be crueller than kind. It also helped heal some of the damage to our blood families. I get on well with my mum these days. I'd say she's more of a good friend than a mother figure, but that's how we both like it. We're close again. I guess I had to go on that journey before I could reach a point where I was mature enough to be level with my mum. All the same, I'm happy we're on good terms.

The mandem didn't fare so good. Most of them are about prison. Coming in, going out. For some boys, the prison gate is more like a revolving door, and ain't no escaping it. It drives them crazy, and it gets me thinking, Rah, prison ain't the answer. Word had it Straps was talking to the birds in prison. He's out now, and having difficulty adjusting to life on the streets. They've all made mistakes, but I hope they get another chance at life.

As for the other girls, either they breed or they turn wash-up and start smoking hardcore drugs, going from Charlie to crack to get the extra buzz. They smoke it. Then they pipe it. Then they do brown. They end up losing their kids to the drugs or the social services, and the cycle starts all over again.

With them, it's 'Hi' and 'Bye' in the street. Sometimes, you know, you got to leave certain people behind.

Keep it moving.